Lecture Notes in Computer Science 16183

Founding Editors

Gerhard Goos
Juris Hartmanis

Editorial Board Members

Elisa Bertino, *Purdue University, West Lafayette, IN, USA*
Wen Gao, *Peking University, Beijing, China*
Bernhard Steffen, *TU Dortmund University, Dortmund, Germany*
Moti Yung, *Columbia University, New York, NY, USA*

The series Lecture Notes in Computer Science (LNCS), including its subseries Lecture Notes in Artificial Intelligence (LNAI) and Lecture Notes in Bioinformatics (LNBI), has established itself as a medium for the publication of new developments in computer science and information technology research, teaching, and education.

LNCS enjoys close cooperation with the computer science R & D community, the series counts many renowned academics among its volume editors and paper authors, and collaborates with prestigious societies. Its mission is to serve this international community by providing an invaluable service, mainly focused on the publication of conference and workshop proceedings and postproceedings. LNCS commenced publication in 1973.

Preface

The 2025 edition of the Annual Privacy Forum (APF 2025) was co-organized by Goethe University Frankfurt, Karlstad University, RSAC, and Plattform Privatheit, supported by the European Union Agency for Cybersecurity (ENISA), the European Data Protection Supervisor (EDPS), and the European Cybersecurity Competence Centre (ECCC). The conference was hosted in Frankfurt am Main, Germany, in October 2025.

APF has established itself as a key interdisciplinary event that brings together stakeholders from policy-makers, academia, civil society, and industry to explore the evolving landscape of privacy and data protection. In its 13th edition it continued its tradition of enabling informed dialogue and collaboration.

The accepted papers of the 2025 edition featured three topical areas:

1. Supporting Laypeople and Users: Design Approaches, User Perceptions, and Problems
2. Emerging Risks from Upcoming Technologies, Misunderstandings, and Regulatory Derogation
3. Professional Methods & Tools for Analysis and Decision Making

In response to the call for papers, APF 2025 received 27 submissions. One submission was desk-rejected. The remaining submissions underwent a single-blind peer-review process by members of the international Program Committee (PC) and additional reviewers involved by some of the PC members. One submission was rejected after two clear reviews asking for this. The other submissions received at least three reviews, several of them four and more. The average number of reviews per submissions was 3.78. Based on the quality of contributions, relevance to the Forum themes, and academic rigor, nine papers were selected (33.33% acceptance rate) for inclusion in this volume.

We extend our sincere gratitude to the members of the Program Committee for their critical and constructive evaluations, and the authors, whose research drives the dialogue forward and whose interest in the forum is the main driver for its organization.

October 2025

Narges Arastouei
Meiko Jensen
Kai Rannenberg

Narges Arastouei · Meiko Jensen ·
Kai Rannenberg
Editors

Privacy Technologies and Policy

13th Annual Privacy Forum, APF 2025
Frankfurt am Main, Germany, October 22–23, 2025
Proceedings

Editors
Narges Arastouei
Goethe University Frankfurt
Frankfurt, Germany

Meiko Jensen
Karlstad University
Karlstad, Sweden

Kai Rannenberg
Goethe University Frankfurt
Frankfurt, Germany

ISSN 0302-9743　　　　　　　ISSN 1611-3349 (electronic)
Lecture Notes in Computer Science
ISBN 978-3-032-07573-4　　　ISBN 978-3-032-07574-1 (eBook)
https://doi.org/10.1007/978-3-032-07574-1

© The Editor(s) (if applicable) and The Author(s) 2026. This book is an open access publication.

Open Access This book is licensed under the terms of the Creative Commons Attribution-NonCommercial-NoDerivatives 4.0 International License (http://creativecommons.org/licenses/by-nc-nd/4.0/), which permits any noncommercial use, sharing, distribution and reproduction in any medium or format, as long as you give appropriate credit to the original author(s) and the source, provide a link to the Creative Commons license and indicate if you modified the licensed material. You do not have permission under this license to share adapted material derived from this book or parts of it.
The images or other third party material in this book are included in the book's Creative Commons license, unless indicated otherwise in a credit line to the material. If material is not included in the book's Creative Commons license and your intended use is not permitted by statutory regulation or exceeds the permitted use, you will need to obtain permission directly from the copyright holder.
This work is subject to copyright. All commercial rights are reserved by the author(s), whether the whole or part of the material is concerned, specifically the rights of translation, reprinting, reuse of illustrations, recitation, broadcasting, reproduction on microfilms or in any other physical way, and transmission or information storage and retrieval, electronic adaptation, computer software, or by similar or dissimilar methodology now known or hereafter developed. Regarding these commercial rights a non-exclusive license has been granted to the publisher.
The use of general descriptive names, registered names, trademarks, service marks, etc. in this publication does not imply, even in the absence of a specific statement, that such names are exempt from the relevant protective laws and regulations and therefore free for general use.
The publisher, the authors and the editors are safe to assume that the advice and information in this book are believed to be true and accurate at the date of publication. Neither the publisher nor the authors or the editors give a warranty, expressed or implied, with respect to the material contained herein or for any errors or omissions that may have been made. The publisher remains neutral with regard to jurisdictional claims in published maps and institutional affiliations.

This Springer imprint is published by the registered company Springer Nature Switzerland AG
The registered company address is: Gewerbestrasse 11, 6330 Cham, Switzerland

If disposing of this product, please recycle the paper.

Organization

Program Committee Chairs

Narges Arastouei — Goethe University Frankfurt, Germany
Meiko Jensen — Karlstad University, Sweden
Kai Rannenberg — Goethe University Frankfurt, Germany

Program Committee

Narges Arastouei — Goethe University Frankfurt, Germany
Isabel Barberá — Rhite, The Netherlands
Athena Bourka — ENISA, Greece
Robert Cronk — Foryte Web Services, Inc., USA
Giuseppe D'Acquisto — Garante per la protezione dei dati personali, Italy
Matteo Dell'Amico — University of Genoa, Italy
Vasiliki Diamantopoulou — University of the Aegean, Greece
Prokopios Drogkaris — ENISA, Greece
Ana Ferreira — University of Porto, Portugal
Simone Fischer-Hübner — Karlstad University, Sweden
Michael Friedewald — Fraunhofer ISI, Germany
Christian Geminn — Kassel University, Germany
Olga Gkotsopoulou — Vrije Universiteit Brussel, Belgium
Elias Grünewald — Charité - Universitätsmedizin Berlin, Germany
Nils Gruschka — University of Oslo, Norway
Agnieszka Gryszczyńska — Cardinal Stefan Wyszynski University in Warsaw (UKSW), Poland
Marit Hansen — Unabhängiges Landeszentrum für Datenschutz Schleswig-Holstein, Germany
Jaap-Henk Hoepman — Radboud University, The Netherlands
Marko Hölbl — Univerza v Mariboru, Slovenia
Kristina Irion — University of Amsterdam, The Netherlands
Meiko Jensen — Karlstad University, Sweden
Christos Kalloniatis — University of the Aegean, Greece
Irene Kamara — Tilburg University, The Netherlands
Liina Kamm — Cybernetica AS, Estonia
Murat Karaboga — Fraunhofer ISI, Germany

Sokratis Katsikas	Norwegian University of Science and Technology, Norway
Cedric Lauradoux	Inria, France
Konstantinos Limniotis	Hellenic Data Protection Authority, Greece
Teresa Martínez Sánchez	Spanish Data Protection Authority, Spain
Victor Morel	Chalmers University of Technology, Sweden
Frank Pallas	Paris Lodron University of Salzburg, Austria
Harshvardhan J. Pandit	Dublin City University, Ireland
Sebastian Pape	Social Engineering Academy GmbH, Germany
Daniela Pöhn	Universität der Bundeswehr München, Germany
Kai Rannenberg	Goethe University Frankfurt, Germany
Delphine Reinhardt	University of Göttingen, Germany
Ina Schiering	Ostfalia University of Applied Sciences, Germany
Stefan Schiffner	Berufliche Hochschule Hamburg BHH University of Applied Sciences, Germany
Erich Schweighofer	University of Vienna, Austria
Jan Tolsdorf	George Washington University, USA
Dimitri Van Landuyt	KU Leuven, Belgium
Isabel Wagner	University of Basel, Switzerland
Christian Zimmermann	Robert Bosch GmbH, Germany

Additional Reviewers

Nima Akbari	University of Basel, Switzerland
Ivan Baheux-Blin	Inria, France
Alisa Pankova	Cybernetica AS, Estonia
Shiva Parsarad	University of Basel, Switzerland
Valentyna Pavliv	University of Basel, Switzerland

Organisers

This work was co-funded by the German Federal Ministry of Research, Technology and Aerospace (BMFTR) under contract number 16KIS1372K (Plattform Privatheit).

With funding from the:

Supporters

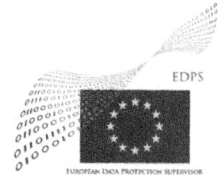

Contents

Supporting Laypeople and Users: Design Approaches, User Perceptions, and Problems

"I Will Never Pay for This": Perceptions of Fairness and Factors Affecting Behaviour on 'pay-or-Ok' Models 3
  Victor Morel, Farzaneh Karegar, and Cristiana Santos

"Abort the Login": Understanding Phishing Susceptibility Through Warning Design in the Context of 2FA 29
  Agnieszka Kitkowska, Jorina Freya Gerken, Zhaoying Wang, and Bruce Ferwerda

Expert Strategies to Assist Laypeople in Making Decisions and Adopting Privacy-Enhancing Technologies 49
  Shirin Shams, Sebastian Jakob Schillinger, and Delphine Reinhardt

Emerging Risks from Upcoming Technologies, Misunderstandings, and Regulatory Derogation

Interfacing Human Brains: What Could Go Wrong?: Research Paper 77
  Marta Beltrán

Anonymity-Washing 102
  Szilvia Lestyán, William Letrone, Ludovica Robustelli, and Gergely Biczók

Simple Now, Complex Later: The Questionable Efficacy of Diluting GDPR Article 30(5) 127
  Harshvardhan J. Pandit

Professional Methods & Tools for Analysis and Decision Making

Turning to Online Forums for Legal Information: A Case Study of GDPR's Legitimate Interests 153
  Lin Kyi, Cristiana Santos, Sushil Ammanaghatta Shivakumar, Franziska Roesner, and Asia Biega

Illuminating the DPIA Blackbox – A Survey of Data Protection Impact Assessment Practices in Organisations 178
  Malte Hansen, Greta Runge, Nils Gruschka, and Meiko Jensen

Information Inference Diagrams: Complementing Privacy and Security
Analyses Beyond Data Flows 202
  Sebastian Rehms, Stefan Köpsell, Verena Klös, and Florian Tschorsch

Author Index 221

Supporting Laypeople and Users: Design Approaches, User Perceptions, and Problems

"I Will Never Pay for This"
Perceptions of Fairness and Factors Affecting Behaviour on 'pay-or-Ok' Models

Victor Morel[1](✉)[iD], Farzaneh Karegar[2][iD], and Cristiana Santos[3][iD]

[1] Chalmers University of Technology and University of Gothenburg,
Gothenburg, Sweden
morelv@chalmers.se
[2] Karlstad University, Karlstad, Sweden
farzaneh.karegar@kau.se
[3] Utrecht University, Utrecht, The Netherlands
c.teixeirasantos@uu.nl

Abstract. The rise of cookie paywalls ('pay-or-ok' models) has prompted growing debates around the right to privacy and data protection, monetisation, and the legitimacy of user consent. Despite their increasing use across sectors, limited research has explored how users perceive these models or what shapes their decisions to either consent to tracking or pay. To address this gap, we conducted four focus groups (with $n = 14$ participants) to examine users' perceptions of cookie paywalls, their judgments of fairness, and the conditions under which they might consider paying, alongside a legal analysis within the EU data protection legal framework. Participants primarily viewed cookie paywalls as profit-driven, with fairness perceptions varying depending on factors such as the presence of a third option beyond consent or payment, transparency of data practices, and the authenticity or exclusivity of the paid content. Participants voiced expectations for greater transparency, meaningful control over data collection, and less coercive alternatives, such as contextual advertising or "reject all" buttons. Although some conditions, including trusted providers, exclusive content, and reasonable pricing, could make participants consider paying, most expressed reluctance or unwillingness to do so. Crucially, our findings raise concerns about economic exclusion, where privacy and data protection might end up becoming a privilege rather than fundamental rights. Consent given under financial pressure may not meet the standard of being freely given, as required by the GDPR. To address these concerns, we recommend user-centred approaches that enhance transparency, reduce coercion, ensure the value of paid content, and explore inclusive alternatives. These measures are essential for supporting fairness, meaningful choice, and user autonomy in consent-driven digital environments.

Keywords: Cookie paywalls · 'Pay-or-ok' models · Consent · Fairness · User expectations · Data protection · GDPR · advertising

1 Introduction

The shift from free digital content to paid models has triggered significant debate, particularly concerning the 'pay-or-ok' model (also known as *cookie paywalls*)[1]. 'Pay-or-ok' models, as conceptualised by the European Data Protection Board (EDPB) [11] can be defined as models where a data controller offers data subjects a choice between at least two options in order to gain access to an online service that the controller provides. The data subject can either 1) consent to the processing of their personal data by tracking technologies for a specified purpose, generally, or for behavioural advertising purposes; or 2) decide to pay a fee and gain access to the online service without their personal data being processed for behavioural advertising purposes. Meta's 'pay-or-ok' model implemented in 2023, giving users the choice between consenting to the use of Facebook and Instagram with targeted ads or paying a monthly subscription for an ad-free service [9], was recently considered unlawful under the Digital Markets Act (DMA). It was determined that those users who do not consent must have access to a less personalised but equivalent alternative [13]. 'Pay-or-ok' used to be but are no longer confined to news websites (still amounting to 21.4% of websites); they have expanded across a broad range of categories, including business (7.7%), technology (7.3%), and are increasingly appearing in areas closer to our everyday lives, such as entertainment (4.6%), health and medicine (2.7%), leisure and recreation websites (3.6%) [45].

Moreover, the use of this model is becoming prevalent in the EU. Although this model is mostly present in Germany, which hosts 633 of the 805 websites detected by Stenwreth et al. [45], other EU countries such as France (38 detected websites), Spain (33), Italy (29), and Austria (26) were also reported to host such models [45].

A growing body of research has examined consent banners, particularly focusing on their prevalence and compliance [6,10,18,19,30,31,41,47], user's perceptions [10,16,22,24,27,37,48], and their relation to deceptive designs (also called dark patterns) [3,17,26,28,30,37,40,44]. In contrast, 'pay-or-ok' models have received comparatively less attention. Existing studies have primarily addressed their prevalence [33,34,39] and lawfulness [4,9,11,20,33,34]. To the best of our knowledge, only one study reported that 99% of users consent to targeted ads [35]. However, no prior research has explored the decision-making processes users engage in when faced with these binary choices of 'pay-or-ok', nor the underlying factors influencing their decisions.

Considering this gap, this paper investigates users' perceptions and expectations of cookie paywalls, and explores whether certain factors might ultimately encourage them to pay – as the payment decision could enhance the protection of their personal data and right to privacy, demonstrate the validity of consent, and could financially benefit publishers [35]. We defined two research questions (RQs) to guide our research:

---

[1] In this paper, the terms 'pay-or-ok' and cookie paywalls are used interchangeably.

- **RQ1** How do users perceive the objectives behind cookie paywalls, the choices they present, and what they expect from them?
- **RQ2** What factors influence users' decisions to either pay or consent when faced with a cookie paywall, and how do these factors impact their decision-making process?

To address our RQs, we conducted a series of four online focus groups with a total of $n=14$ participants to explore the mental models of users towards cookie paywalls, through a contextualization supported by scenarios and mockups.

Our research reported in this paper makes the following contributions to the literature:

- We provide **the first in-depth qualitative study of users' perceptions of cookie paywalls**, offering rich insights into how users understand their purpose, including perceived motivations such as monetisation, legal compliance, or data protection and privacy.
- We reveal how **users' perceptions of fairness are highly conditional on exogenous and hypothetical scenarios** – they deemed cookie paywalls fair if transparent, with authentic content, and considering they could exit that website – but often leading to conflicting but deeply reasoned judgments.
- We identify **key decision-making factors** potentially influencing whether users choose to pay, consent, or exit the websites exposing them to cookie paywalls, including exclusive content, pricing, and trust in providers; although ultimately, no killer feature would lead users to pay.
- We contribute **user-centred and policy recommendations**, including calls for greater transparency, the inclusion of meaningful alternatives (e.g., contextual ads and a "reject all" option), and mechanisms to ensure content authenticity, while raising critical questions about the ethics and lawfulness of consent in economically constrained contexts, and ultimately, about the legitimacy of this model.

By exploring these dimensions, our study offers practical, legal insights for platform designers, regulators, and policymakers seeking to align digital consent mechanisms with user expectations, legal requirements, and fairness in practice.

2 Methodology

We addressed our research questions through four online, 90-minute focus groups run on Zoom between November 2024 and January 2025, plus one pilot session. Focus groups are a widely used method in Human-Computer Interactions relying on qualitative analysis with few participants [25]. They can provide deeper insights than quantitative methods (such as surveys), while being less labour-intensive than individual interviews. They also present "a broad range of viewpoints and insights", and "can help overcome many of the shortcomings of interviews" such as having non-talkative interviewees [25]. For the main focus groups,

14 adults (FG1 = 5, FG2 = 4, FG3 = 3, FG4 = 2^2) were recruited on Prolific—an online platform for academic research that offers reliable, pre-screened participants and advanced demographic filters—under the following criteria: English fluency, residence in the EU/EEA or Switzerland, and a working microphone; no prior privacy expertise was required. We did not collect participants' exact countries of residence, in line with the principle of data minimisation, as this information was not necessary for our analysis. Instead, we used Prolific's screening filters to ensure that all participants were located in the EU/EEA or Switzerland. This approach made it possible to recruit a more diverse sample in terms of both region and age compared to on-campus recruitment, which would have been slower and less diverse. Our setup for Prolific filters also yielded a gender-balanced sample (7 women, 7 men). After consent, participants completed the demographic questionnaire listed in Appendix A.1.

Our sample size was modest, and we do not claim to have achieved *full theoretical saturation*, the point where no new themes or insights emerge from additional data collection. However, given our focused research aim and consistent inclusion criteria, we approached *code saturation*. The rich 90-minute discussions and iterative team-based analysis provided meaningful exploratory insights.

Table 1 presents an overview of demographic information. Most participants were young (10/14 were 18-34 years), well-educated (11 held ≥ bachelor's degrees), and came from varied fields, e.g. economics, marketing, early-childhood care, and computer science. Nine were (self-)employed, three were job-seeking, and one was a student; half reported earning < € 1335 per month after tax and 43% earned € 1335-2225 (one non-response).[3] Note that the annual median net income is € 21588 in the EU.[4] We cannot provide more details on their economic situations (e.g., the country, cross-checking with age, etc.) due to anonymity reasons and to follow the data minimisation principle. While all felt confident using computers, self-reported cookie-banner understanding was lower: one participant managed banners effortlessly, seven encountered minor issues, five needed occasional clarification, and one struggled frequently.

Sessions followed Krueger's guidance [21]. Zoom audio was recorded locally and transcribed with Amberscript; transcripts were analysed thematically following Braun & Clarke's method [7] (details of our procedure are in Appendix A.2). **Ethical considerations:** The study was approved by Karlstad University's ethical advisor (HS 2024/1242) and Chalmers University's Data Protection Officer. Data were handled in compliance with the GDPR. Participants used pseudonyms and disabled cameras during recording. All attendees, including the pilot group, were compensated. Prolific participants were compensated at €10 (£8.67) per hour (€15 / £13.00 for 90 min), following Prolific's recommended rate.

---

[2] One focus group had only two participants because three registered participants did not show up or notify us in advance, making it impossible to reschedule. Despite the small size, the session still produced valuable insights through active discussion.

[3] Currencies have been converted to euros in the paper for consistency.

[4] https://ec.europa.eu/eurostat/databrowser/view/ilc_di03/default/table?lang=en.

Table 1. Demographic overview of focus group participants (F: Female, M: Male, HS: High School)

FG	Age Range	Gender	Degree
1	18–24: 2, 25–34: 1, 35–44: 1	F: 1, M: 3	BSc: 2, HS: 2
2	25–34: 3, 18–24: 1, 35–44: 1	F: 2, M: 3	MSc: 1, BS: 3, HS: 1
3	25–34: 2, 65+: 1	F: 2, M: 1	MSc: 2, BSc: 1
4	35–44: 1, 25–34: 1	F: 2	MSc: 1, BSc: 1
Total	18–24: 3, 25–34: 7, 35–44: 3, 65+: 1	M: 7, F: 7	MSc: 4, BSc: 7, HS: 3

2.1 Course of the Focus Group

Each session followed a four-steps script: (1) an introductory segment that re-explained the focus-group format, confirmed oral consent, and set ground rules; (2) a short briefing on cookie banners and cookie paywalls; (3) an open discussion to gauge participants' general perceptions and expectations of cookie paywalls; and (4) scenario-based discussions using mock-ups. Participants were thanked and compensated immediately after the session.

Presentation of the context and general discussion. We began by reminding participants that cookie banners are legally mandated (e.g., GDPR) and distinguishing personalised from contextual advertising. Next, we defined *cookie paywalls*, showed real-world screenshots, and situated them within the broader 'pay-or-ok' model, contrasting Meta's tracking-permissive subscription (the pay option only states that personal data will not be used for ads) with a true cookie paywall that lets users avoid all tracking. Participants then described (i) their usual reactions to ordinary banners, (ii) any experience with cookie paywalls (did they pay, accept all cookies, or leave?), and (iii) their views on the *purpose* and *fairness* of paywalls compared with regular banners. The discussion was open-ended, but prepared prompts kept it on track when needed.

Scenarios and mockups. To probe what shapes willingness to pay, we showed six Contentpass-style – a leading Subscription Management Platform (SMP) – mock-ups and asked participants to act as though they had just landed on the page, choosing to either pay, accept tracking, or leave, and to justify that choice. Mockups for all scenarios are presented in Figs. 1a to 1c in Appendix A.

Scenario 1 – Tracking & ad-free vs. ad-free only. Baseline design (SEK 30/€ 2.67 per month). At the first step, we compared a full tracking- & ad-free option with an ad-free-only option.

Scenario 2 – One-click payment. Same price/features as the baseline, but payment was framed as a single, equally effortless click. We highlighted that in both options (baseline and one-click), technicalities and trust issues were not critical (i.e., payment was safe and working).

Scenario 3 – Exclusive content. Paying also unlocked unique material; participants were encouraged to think of what "exclusive" content would tempt them.

Scenario 4 – Cheap price. The fee dropped to SEK 5/€ 0.45 per month, plus a non-discounted yearly fee (SEK 60 SEK/€ 5.35), so they could weigh different price points.[5]

Scenario 5 – Transparency on third-party sharing. Banner explicitly stated data would be sold to "300 + vendors", whereas the pay option promised full privacy. Participants were asked to picture a site they already trust, so trust itself would not dominate responses.

Scenario 6 – Various website types. Four imagined sites, recipes, sports news, health advice, and e-commerce tested whether data sensitivity or personal interest changes willingness to pay.

For each scenario, we captured the decision and the stated reasoning, providing rich material for the subsequent thematic analysis (see Appendix A.2).

3 Results: User Perceptions and Decision-Making of Cookie Paywalls

Our thematic analysis identified four themes (**TX**: **T1** to **T4**), with three addressing RQ1 (reported in Sects. 3.1-3.3), and one addressing RQ2 (reported in Sect. 3.4). An abridged version of the codebook (only presenting the most important codes discussed in this section) can be found in Table 2, while the comprehensive codebook can be found in Table 3 in the Appendix. Codes are labelled as **TX.X** (e.g., **T1.2** represents the second code under the first theme). Some codes emerged from discussions within specific subsets of focus groups, indicated in the format **TX.X [FGX]** (e.g., **T1.2 [FG1, FG2]**, where FG stands for Focus Group), while others were present across all focus groups, in which case the focus group reference was omitted.

We report verbatim comments from participants (PX), comments have been edited for clarity without altering their meaning.

3.1 Perceptions of Cookie Paywalls Objectives

The first theme related to RQ1 is our participants' *perceptions of cookie paywalls' objectives (T1)*. This theme shows participants' perception of service providers' objectives for presenting users with cookie paywalls. The most commonly perceived objective of cookie paywalls was **monetary purposes for the websites - make money either way (T1.1)**. The majority of participants across all focus groups (13 out of 14) believed that, whether users choose to pay or accept cookies, the website ultimately benefits financially. As P9 (FG2) explained: *their goal is always the same. It's to make money. It's to*

---
[5] We actively encouraged participants to picture what 'their' cheap price was.

Table 2. Abridged version of the codebook resulting from our thematic analysis.

Themes	Codes
T1 Users' perceptions of cookie paywalls' objective	**T1.1** Monetary purpose for the websites - make money either way
	T1.2 To maintain users' privacy
	T1.3 To comply with regulations
T2 Perception of fairness of cookie paywalls	**T2.1** Fair as users are not forced to take any options
	T2.2 Fair as nothing comes for free
	T2.3 Fair if transparent
	T2.4 Fair if authentic and original content
	T2.5 Unfair because forced to make a choice (can't reject)
	T2.6 Unfair as privacy should not be a privilege
T3 Expectations of cookie paywalls design	**T3.1** A third option - Reject all
	T3.2 Better ex-ante transparency and control of data practices
	T3.3 Additional choice to have contextualized ads only
	T3.4 Cookie paywalls should not exist
T4 Factors affecting behaviour/decisions on cookie paywalls	**T4.1** Access to exclusive content/service (regularly)
	T4.2 Not paying regardless of the situation
	T4.3 Cheap/fair subscription price
	T4.4 Not bothered/influenced by ads
	T4.5 Get rid of (blocking) ads
	T4.6 Feeling of pervasive tracking and data sharing
	T4.7 Perceived manipulation of content/design
	T4.8 Trust in the service provider

make profit [...]. So either they take your data and use it to make their advertising or databases more accurate and more efficient, or they get some money from you [...], a direct monetary compensation. P4 (FG1) also believed that consumers should not be concerned with how service providers generate revenue and saw cookie paywalls as *just additional money on top*.

Nonetheless, participants had differing opinions on whether accepting cookies or paying would be more beneficial for service providers. For instance, while P11 (FG3) believed that accepting cookies is more beneficial for them: *they make more of that [...] they can create a pattern [...] They can see what you're interested in [...] by accepting the cookies, you give them way more like valuable information because they kind of see they can profile you*, P1 (FG1) had a contrasting view, stating *the pay option is a way for the websites to generate a higher average revenue per user because I think they make more money if you pay. But I also know that they know that most people are not going to pay. So they just put the accept all [...] we are going to get targeted ads and they might make commissions.*

To comply with regulations (T1.2 [FG1, FG3]) was another objective mentioned by three participants; this topic came up less often than monetary purposes. P4 (FG1) believed that *they need to give another option besides accepting the cookies legally speaking. And this may be a way to skirt that responsibility or give another option.* P11 (FG3) phrased it as *the illusion that we have a choice or something.*

To our surprise, **maintaining users' privacy (T1.3 [FG1])** was not an objective that several participants associated with cookie paywalls, and it was only briefly discussed in one focus group. As P1 (FG1) expressed, *you maintain privacy. I think it's about privacy and protecting your data. And you're kind of paying to protect your privacy. And privacy should be a right.* The pay option was also perceived as a way to meet the needs of certain groups of people who care about their privacy, as P2 (FG2) put it: *[...] some people really care about privacy. So by giving them an option, maybe there are some users that they will get to pay that otherwise would just probably leave the site.*

3.2 Fairness of Cookie Paywalls

Another area of discussion, included in the focus group script, was participants' **perception of the fairness of cookie paywalls.** Participants had varied and opposing opinions about the fairness of cookie paywalls. Paywalls were perceived as fair for different reasons and under different conditions. Interestingly, some participants, P1 and P2 (FG1), and P6 and P8 (FG2), even expressed contradictory views, perceiving the paywalls as both fair and unfair depending on contextual factors such as the availability of alternatives or clarity of information. Among the 14 participants, 10 referred to aspects that made cookie paywalls seem unfair, and 8 mentioned reasons for why they found them fair. These counts include overlaps; several participants expressed both perspectives, while others only mentioned fairness or only unfairness.

Offering authentic and original content was the most frequently mentioned justification for the fairness of paywalls (**fair if authentic and original content (T2.4 [FG2, FG3, FG4])**). Participants believed that if the content is original, it cannot be found elsewhere, it is fair to monetize it, as P9 (FG2) put it: *If it's something they had to put effort and work into, then, of course, it's fair that they should have some compensation for their work.* P8 (FG2) similarly stated that if the content is *revised or there's a team behind it and they have certain quality,* it is fair to expect compensation for it.

Some participants believed that no service or (original) content should be free, as companies offering them have costs to cover, making paywalls fair (**fair as nothing comes for free (T2.2 [FG1])**). P1 (FG1) and P3 (FG1) framed it respectively: *I know that these are companies and these are people's jobs. And of course, they should be compensated and paid for it,* and *I don't think things should be free. [...] it's people's jobs. They've worked to create that content.*

Participants believed that paywalls are fair if the options provided are presented honestly and transparently (**fair if transparent (T2.3 [FG1, FG2])**), as P8 (FG2) put it, *they can really understand what they are agreeing to.*

Interestingly, participants had opposing opinions about whether cookie paywalls genuinely offer a choice. Those who believed people are not forced to take any of the options, such as P2 (FG1), who said, *I think they are entitled to put the options in front of us and we either accept or reject [the offer]*, deemed paywalls as fair (**fair as users are not forced to take any options (T2.1 [FG1, FG2, FG3])**). As P7 (FG2) framed it, *it's a business model, when the company does not receive your cookie, you either pay either leave the website [...] I think it's fair.* However, those who believed that people do not truly have a choice and are forced to select one of the two options, without the ability to reject all cookies or at least accept only certain cookies based on their preferences, perceived paywalls as **unfair because forced to make a choice (T2.5)**. As P11 (FG3) put it: *I don't think having to pay or just accept all is fair [...] Everything feels forced. We don't really have a choice.* The perception of a lack of choice, particularly the absence of a "reject all" option to access services or content, was the most frequently mentioned factor in justifying their unfairness.

The requirement to either "accept all" or "pay" was also associated with being forced to give up privacy, as P14 (FG4) framed it: *pay or you don't have your data privacy and I don't like at all.* Additionally, some participants linked this practice to "coercion", as P13 (FG4) explained: *[...] it forces people to actively decide between privacy at a cost and free access with tracking [...] it could also feel like coercion [...].* Similarly, it was compared to "blackmail", particularly when users needed access to essential content or services. As P11 (FG3) described: *They know we're interested [in the information behind the paywall] and we're more likely to accept these absurd conditions. Of course, we're not forced. We can just leave the website, but if we're there, because we probably have to get that information, whatever information it is. So I feel it's a bit like here's a bad option, here's a worse option, you know? So it's almost like blackmailing.*

Additionally, paywalls were also perceived as **unfair as privacy should not be a privilege (T2.6 [FG4])**. In FG4, privacy as a fundamental right was discussed in relation to fairness. Participants believed that privacy should not be treated as a privilege that people must purchase separately. As P14 (FG4) noted, *it feels a bit like a trap [...] why should I have to pay to keep my data private? It kind of makes me think that privacy is being turned into a privilege which is super unfair for me*, especially because, as P13 (FG4) emphasised, *paying for privacy is not a viable option for everyone.*

3.3 Expectations of Cookie Paywalls

Our analysis of the focus groups' data revealed another theme related to *expectations of cookie paywalls (T3)*, as referred below.

The most frequently mentioned expectations across all focus groups were the first two. Participants expressed frustration about being forced to choose between options they did not want and **wished for the existence of the option to**

reject all cookies (T3.1). As P2 (FG1) and P6 (FG2) put it respectively: *[...] I think all cookie banners should have a reject-all option present. They shouldn't be able to lock you down by checking all the boxes,* and *I feel like I'm forced to pay or to accept, in this cookie paywall. I think there should be an option to reject also the cookie.*

Participants expected clearer and more trustworthy information regarding the options presented to them, along with greater control over what they were required to share (**better ex-ante transparency and control of data practices (T3.2)**). Particularly, they wanted to understand exactly what data was being tracked, who would have access to it, and what they would gain if they chose to pay. Additionally, they questioned why service providers required users to accept "all cookies" and why they were not given more control over selecting which cookies to accept. For example, P9 (FG2) believed that *if I have some more information about what's being tracked and what's being taken as data* and *if I knew exactly what was being taken and what was being shared and with who,* they could make more informed decisions.

Participants also emphasised the need for information to be presented in a **trustworthy** manner that did not feel manipulative or aimed at nudging them toward a specific choice. As P1 (FG1) expressed, *that wording about your data will be sold to 300 plus vendors seemed a little bit manipulative and, kind of like a threat or blackmail. So I think wording it in an honest way without making it seem like a threat, your data will be sold, is really important [...]*.

The request for ex-ante transparency was not limited to the "accept" option but also applied to the "pay" option. Participants expected mechanisms to ensure the exclusivity of content. As further discussed in Sect. 3.4, accessing exclusive content/services was one of the strongest motivations for paying when faced with cookie paywalls. However, ensuring that the content was truly exclusive was crucial, as P9 (FG2) stated: *explain or try to explain better what the exclusive content is or what you have to offer, how it's different from other websites and other sources [...]*.

In total, six participants from all the focus groups expected an **additional choice to have contextualised ads only (T3.3)**. They believed that contextualised ads could provide a middle ground between consenting to personalised ads and paying not to be tracked, allowing service providers to monetise while respecting users' privacy. P8 (FG2) also referred to a business model where users *don't have access to all the content and you get contextualized ads.*, and P14 (FG4) mentioned: *[...] So the website would still be monetised, but I wouldn't have to pay neither with my information or with my money.*

Some participants took a step further, believing that **cookie paywalls should not exist (T3.4 [FG2, FG3, FG4])**. They criticised the business model and questioned the necessity of paywalls, arguing that *what is happening is not the way they want to engage with the internet [...] It just feels like it's really taking advantage of people.* (P10 (FG3)). One participant (P5 (FG2)) also pointed out that *there are sites that are running and that are earning money and don't have the cookie paywall. So it's possible to run a site without it.*

3.4 Factors Influencing Users' Pay-or-Ok Decisions in Cookie Paywalls

Participants mentioned numerous, sometimes contradictory, *factors affecting their behaviour/decisions on cookie paywalls*, a theme (*T4*) addressing RQ2. Those factors were said by participants to lead them to either 1) accept all cookies, 2) pay, or 3) leave the website if they deemed the choice unacceptable; although some factors were discussed as leading towards *not paying*, without specifying whether it would mean accepting the cookies or leaving the website. Some factors were impacting participants' decision-making ambivalently: the same factor could be a reason to pay for one participant, and to accept for another. This section only introduces *the most cited factors in our focus groups*, cited across three or four focus groups for a total of at least 10 times.

The most prevalent factor was the **access to exclusive content/service (T4.1)**, heavily mentioned in all focus groups. Most participants valued the possibility to access otherwise gated content, which would interest them, or that they would need (e.g., for educational or professional purposes). P9 (FG2) explains *If it's something very exclusive and I can only see in this website, I will probably pay*, and P6 (FG2) *maybe some information that I will have the access to read it earlier than the others users that they don't pay. So yes, in this scenario also, I will pay*. This factor is a typical example of an ambivalent factor. For instance, for P2 (FG1), the need to access a specific content is first a reason to accept cookies, but ultimately to access the content: *If it's a website that I really don't need to use, I wouldn't use it. And then if I actually needed to use it first, I guess I would accept the cookies and only as a last resort I would pay*. But the decision is often pondered, and some participants, such as P8 (FG2), would first want guarantees on the exclusiveness of content: *if I were to pay, I would like to see what that exclusive content entails, if it's really that it's so safe and interesting*. However, it is important to highlight that in several cases, the exclusive content was the only reason to pay invoked by participants, such as P11 (FG3) *But like I said, if it's something I really need. So that's the only reason why I would still pay*.

The second most prevalent factor was less a factor impacting the decision-making than a blanket refusal to pay for cookie paywalls. Indeed, participants defended across all focus groups that they would **not pay regardless of the situation (T4.2)**. P10 (FG3) resented the model generally speaking *It's like almost like a moral principle or something. I feel, I couldn't on my own. Yeah. Principles, I know I couldn't pay*. When facing various mockups introduced in our scenarios, participants consistently replied *Same I wouldn't, I wouldn't pay, I just accept all*. (P3, FG1, regarding the different types of websites).

However, some factors would get participants more inclined to pay, such as a **cheap/fair subscription price (T4.3)**, a factor often mentioned in combination with other factors. P13 (FG4) details their conception of a fair price as *I would be willing to pay it if the price feels fair for the value*. For P9 (FG2), the price matters, but the content behind the cookie paywall remains crucial: *The price totally makes a difference, of course. But I keep what I said previously. It's* *all about what the content is*. Whereas for P2 (FG1), the price is decisive, but so is the removal of ads (we had given a rough estimation in euros): *for less than €5 a year. It would be nice to not have to see all those ads*. Note that some participants were explicitly relating their choice to their economic situation, such as P12 (FG3) who explains that they would not pay *Well, because I'm very poor*.[6]

Ads were seen as an ambivalent factor: towards consent when participants were **not bothered/influenced by ads (T4.4)**, or towards paying when they wanted to **get rid of (blocking) ads (T4.5)**. P1 (FG1) explains: *normally I accept all still because I'm not really a victim of advertising. I'm not prone to buying things, but I actually like seeing ads that are dedicated to me or personalised for me. I don't mind that*, although they add *I do agree that it's a concern for some people*. P8 (FG2) feels differently and specifies *I don't really like ads, especially if they are intrusive. If I'm reading news or I'm reading a blog or whatever, I don't really like watching any kind of ads.*, a feeling even more prominent in a context where ads cannot be blocked, such as YouTube, which could justify paying.

A feeling of pervasive tracking and data sharing (T4.6) veered participants towards giving consent. This feeling made them feel disempowered, and according to them, made illusory the protection of their data and their privacy. P12 (FG3) had given up on not being tracked: *I would accept because ads and tracking are not such an inconvenience, I am not going to pay 3 or €4 a month just to avoid ads and the tracking, I find it almost impossible. I will be tracked anyway*. According to P7 (FG2), paying for privacy on one website cannot match the data collection of big players: *Well, by my opinion, if you are using the Instagram or the Facebook or the Snapchat or any other messenger, I would say you already are giving your personal data*.

Scenario 5, which investigated a (hypothetical) website transparent about its data practices, backfired and triggered reactance from participants (although the design reflected current practices [33]). Participants experienced a feeling of **perceived manipulation of content/design (T4.7)**. It led some participants to believe that the website may want to trick them into paying by overplaying the risks associated with accepting cookies, and eventually to leave the website as a result. P1 (FG1) expressed that: *Personally, I think the "your data will be shared with 300 plus vendors" I know it's being transparent, but I think it's kind of provocative in a way. They're being transparent and they're being honest. But I think it's written in a way that's going to make people want to pay more. I would personally not visit this website*.

Another important factor that inspired participants not to pay is the **trust in the service provider (T4.8)**. On the one hand, not enough trust in the payment mechanism inspired aversion to it. P3 (FG1) explains: *I more than likely would not pay. It's when you're adding in your card details or giving away your financial information. I have to feel 100% confident..* On the other hand, trust could lead to accepting cookies, a possible explanation being that they feel

---

[6] Recall from the demographics that half of our participants earned an annual net income of less than €16500 a year, for a median net income of €21588 in the EU.

comfortable with data collection which they presumably deem acceptable and non-abusive. P2 (FG1) shares that: *if the website is not trustworthy and I really don't have to access that information, surely I will not accept the cookies and I will probably not even use the website. But if it's something that I really need to see and I actually kind of trust the website. So most likely I will accept the cookies.* From these perceptions, we note that **trust never affected participants in a way that would lead them to pay.**

4 Discussion

This section discusses our findings concerning the research questions (Sects. 4.1 and 4.2), contextualising participants' perceptions, expectations, and decision-making regarding cookie paywalls. We highlight how these perceptions often diverge from the legal and normative assumptions underlying current implementations, especially regarding consent and user autonomy. We conclude by offering design and policy recommendations (Sect. 4.3) to address these gaps and improve the legitimacy and usability of paywall models.

4.1 Cookie Paywalls Through Users' Eyes: Objectives, Choice Architecture, and Design Expectations

Perception of objectives. Most participants viewed cookie paywalls as primarily driven by economic interests (**T1.1**), with websites as the clear financial beneficiaries. Although some mentioned regulatory compliance (**T1.3**) or privacy protection (**T1.2**), these reasons were far less cited. This imbalance suggests that users perceive the model as primarily profit-oriented rather than as a mechanism for ensuring legal compliance or safeguarding their data rights.

Perception of fairness. Fairness perceptions were complex, fluid, and context-dependent. Among the 14 participants, 10 described cookie paywalls as unfair, while 8 found them fair. These numbers include overlaps, as several participants expressed both perspectives depending on the situation. The unfairness was largely tied to the absence of a "reject all" option (**T2.5**) and the sense of coercion. At the same time, some participants justified fairness by pointing to the user's ability to leave the site (**T2.1**).

These contrasting perspectives reflect different interpretive frames: while participants viewed the binary "pay-or-ok" model as unfair, some considered the broader option of leaving the website as a form of fairness. This indicates that cookie paywalls are seen as fair only in a narrow sense, when opting out entirely remains a viable path. However, the prevalent feeling of being forced to choose, or having "no real choice" but to leave, points to a deeper issue: a potential failure to meet the GDPR's requirement for consent to be freely given, as defined in Articles 4(11) and 7.

Moreover, our findings suggest a disconnect between perceived fairness and user behaviour: those who deemed cookie paywalls unfair often refused to pay, while those who considered them fair did not necessarily express willingness to pay likewise. This gap highlights that fairness judgments do not necessarily translate into acceptance or compliance, raising critical concerns about the legitimacy of consent mechanisms under such models.

Expectations. Participants shared a range of expectations about how cookie paywalls should function, spanning issues of transparency, control, and alternatives to the binary pay-or-ok model. While some expectations concerned immediate design choices, others reflected a broader desire for rethinking the underlying model to provide more meaningful options for users.

First, participants wanted greater transparency and control over data practices (**T3.2**). They sought clarity on what data is collected/tracked, who accesses it, what benefits payment offers, and why selective cookie consent is not allowed, i.e. why there is a request to accept "all".

Our study supports the legal requirements of transparency of personal data practices because users also want such information. Under Article 5(1)(a) GDPR, personal data processing must be transparent to users, requiring websites to inform them about the types of data processed, recipients (Art. 14), the associated scope and consequences [14], and risks (Recital 39, GDPR). In practice, however, users often ignore such information, leading to a privacy paradox, where stated intentions and actual behaviours diverge [5].

Strycharz et al. [46] found that while legal information for consent can empower users, it may also reduce perceived risk, leading to a control paradox; increased control over data sharing can raise users' willingness to share.

Presentation and tone also mattered: participants reacted negatively to perceived manipulation in content and design (**T4.7**). While this reaction might have been influenced by our own design choices (see Sect. 3.4), it underscores a key insight: users valued transparency presented with clarity and honesty, not in ways that felt exaggerated or fear-inducing. This highlights that transparency alone is insufficient; how information is framed is equally critical for fostering trust and supporting informed, autonomous decisions.

A notable concern was the statement that "personal data may be shared with 300 vendors". Though legally compliant, our participants perceived it as coercive, particularly when paired with a rigid 'pay-or-ok' structure. Such framing led users to feel pressured to either pay or agree to extensive data sharing, undermining the notion of freely given consent.

These findings suggest that even when transparency requirements are met, users may still feel manipulated, pointing to the need for addressing not only formal compliance but also substantive fairness, and the real impact on user autonomy and rights [29].

Second, many participants (9 out of 14) strongly expected a **"Reject all"** option, which they saw as essential to fairness. They felt pressured by the binary structure of cookie paywalls and wanted the ability to avoid both paying and consenting (**T3.1**). They also called for more granular control over cookie preferences.

Courts and regulators have affirmed the legitimacy of placing a "reject all" button at the first layer of consent [2], which in cookie paywalls would mean rejecting all purposes. However, in practice, rejecting some purposes often triggered the reappearance of the paywall, suggesting users are not truly allowed to opt out. This reflects *privacy theatre* [43], where designs/technologies create the illusion of privacy protection while doing little or nothing to meaningfully safeguard user data. This illusion of choice conceals manipulative design and undermines freely given, meaningful consent. The frustration over limited control and inability to fully customise purposes also relates to GDPR's requirements for granular consent (Recital 32) and purpose specification (Art. 5(1)(b)) [15].

Third, participants expressed interest in **alternative models**, such as accessing content through *contextualised ads* rather than consenting to tracking or paying (**T3.3**). Some saw contextual ads as a privacy-preserving compromise, aligning with the Norwegian Consumer Council's report advocating tracking-free contextualised advertising as both GDPR-compliant and supportive of healthier business models [36].

However, critics warn that contextual advertising may still enable profiling, especially when AI tools analyse content and user behaviour [32]. This enables neuroprogrammatic advertising, which targets individuals based on emotional states and mood profiles, raising concerns about the intrusiveness of these so-called privacy-friendly alternatives. Many vendors combine contextual and personal data [1], blurring boundaries between targeting methods.

Relatedly, Kyi et al. [24] found that users often accept personalised ads not out of preference, but due to a perceived lack of alternatives. These findings question the legitimacy of expanding targeted advertising in any form and reflect a broader discomfort with the inflexible 'pay-or-ok' structure, further discussed in our recommendations (Sect. 4.3).

Finally, a few participants expressed that cookie paywalls should not exist at all (**T3.4**), viewing them as exploitative and fundamentally incompatible with how they believed the Internet should function.

4.2 Drivers of Pay-or-Consent Choices on Cookie Paywalls: Factors Shaping User Decision-Making

Pay decisions are driven by multiple factors in combination. From the results of our study, there was no real 'killer feature', and no unique factor that would sway participants towards paying, and eventually, most responses encompassed *multiple factors* for a conditional answer: a cheap and easy way to subscribe to authentic content on a set of trustworthy websites would trigger a *maybe I will pay*.

Users resent cookie paywalls and would likely never pay. Several participants across several focus groups repeated that they would not pay regardless of the situation (**T4.2**), suggesting a *general sentiment of resentment towards the business model* of cookie paywalls (recall that economic reasons were most invoked by participants), in line with their perception of relative unfairness of cookie paywalls, and the expectation to be able to reject all cookies without detriment. The fact that users consent to tracking to access content, since they cannot pay, could be framed as a sign of economic coercion, which fundamentally undermines the validity of consent under the GDPR.

Access to exclusive content influences users' decisions to pay or to consent. The most impactful factor driving the behaviour of participants was the *access to exclusive content* (**T4.1**), with several participants requesting guarantees behind the exclusiveness of this content. Note that participants were as willing to pay as they were to accept consent to cookies to access content. Several participants implied that, by expecting a "reject all" option, they would prefer not to have to make the choice between paying or consenting to access the desired content. For those with sufficient time, looking for content elsewhere was also mentioned as an alternative, while paying was mostly an option for participants with sufficient financial means; accepting tracking being a sort of *resignation* for those with neither time nor money.

A cheap or fair price factor might influence a few users to pay. Some participants were willing to pay in case of a *cheap or fair price* (**T4.3**). However, this factor was unsurprisingly articulated with their financial means, with less wealthy participants stating that they would not pay *because they are poor*. This economic barrier raises concerns about the scalability of this model: if users are reluctant to pay for one website at the moment of this study, they might not pay for several websites or other types of online services (such as social media) in the future if cookie paywalls become even more prevalent.

This factor should be interpreted in the light of another, albeit less cited factor on the possibility of accessing *multiple services in a single pay-off* (potentially selected by the user) (**T4.17**). Few participants declared that paying for a single website *doesn't make sense* (P14, FG4), while very few suggested that a (cheap) subscription granting access to several websites (P2 (FG1) mentioned 50) could make the offer acceptable. This is currently a reality of several websites granting access up to 500 other websites under a single payoff subscription (see the case of the subscription management platform "Contentpass" used by several German-speaking websites) [8].

In addition, the economic barrier mentioned prompts critical reflection on data protection and privacy as fundamental rights. When assuring these rights become something one must pay for, these models risk introducing or amplifying socioeconomic discrimination. Those with limited financial means are forced to consent and exchange their personal data to access content, while wealthier users can simply buy their way out of tracking. As such, the model divides users into two classes: those who can afford these rights and those who cannot. This has profound implications for the exercise of consent. Consent given under financial pressure, when users might have preferred to pay but could not, is not freely given in the legal sense. This undermines the very foundations of data protection requirements like freely given, informed consent, and the fairness principle, as enshrined in GDPR. These findings challenge the fairness and legitimacy of monetising the right to data protection through paywalls, especially when such systems are deployed at scale.

4.3 Recommendations

Rethinking the business model. Our study indicates that the 'pay-or-ok' model is viewed as profit-driven, widely perceived as unfair, and not enabling users to make a meaningful choice. Willingness to pay emerges only under low pricing and favourable economic conditions. Even flexible models like multi-website bundled prices (e.g. "one subscription unlocks 500 websites") do not assure a paying decision. These findings align with prior work confirming that users consent to tracking nearly 99% of the time [35]. In its current state, the model does not reflect users' expectations, nor the protection of their personal data. This is especially relevant given the increasing prevalence of this model [45]. Regulators must critically reconsider the model's legitimacy in the light of users' expectations, adequately balancing the economic needs of the sectors concerned, the free circulation of information, and fundamental rights. At the minimum, essential services (e.g., political news, education, health) should be protected from these monetisation models that force people to choose between personal (and sensitive) data [49] and access. Ultimately, these findings could support a reflection on how these models risk eroding trust in EU digital law, if users' actual experiences with this model feel systematically rigged. Considering future legislative efforts, we recommend that the future Digital Fairness Act (DFA) [12] explicitly prohibits this model.

Third-option. Several participants suggested an additional choice, such as having *contextualised ads* only, or a *reject all* button (**T3.3** and **T3.1**), as a possible middle ground. These findings align with the recent EDPB opinion [11], which states that offering binary choices "should not be the default way forward". Instead, controllers should provide an equivalent alternative that neither requires a fee nor involves processing personal data for behavioural advertising. Less intrusive advertising models, such as contextual, general, or topic-based advertising, are cited as viable examples. Let us, however, note the following. As pointed out in Sect. 4.1, contextualised advertising does not necessarily lead to a privacy-friendly business model; certain conceptions free of personal data collection (outlined by Forbrukerrådet [36]) may then provide a better alternative than others. Also, the provision of contextualised ads must nonetheless respect the wish of users to be informed about why they see certain ads, be able to be provided with other ads, and their noninvasive integration within interfaces.

Free Trial. Participants proposed the integration of a *free trial* that would make them more inclined to pay. Access to a free trial and previews can be a means to assess whether the content is authentic and original (which is also a factor playing in favour of fairness **T2.4**). This option is actually already available on some cookie paywalls, such as Contentpass (a leading SMP), but not on Freechoice (the other main SMP). The rise of AI-generated content reinforces the appeal of free trial models as an increasing number of websites now offer low-quality articles produced by Large Language Models (LLMs) [38]. Participants saw such content as emblematic of what they would not be willing to pay for, describing it as lacking in effort and human involvement. These concerns highlight a growing scepticism toward automated content and a corresponding expectation that paid content should reflect human labour, editorial oversight, and authenticity.

Criteria for exclusivity and authenticity. Participants request mechanisms to ensure the *exclusivity and authenticity of content*, which would make them perceive cookie paywalls as more fair (**T2.4**). Participants' need for reassurance from organisations regarding privacy-related decisions is a finding in line with previous research [23]. User-facing accountability mechanisms that assure such unique attributes across online services are expected for these models. Hence, regulators must define what constitutes exclusivity and authenticity of services. *Exclusivity* should be understood as offering original reporting, proprietary material, and should not consist merely of aggregated third-party content, subject to independent audits or self-certifications. *Authenticity*, in turn, requires that content be produced by identifiable and credible authors or creators, subject to editorial oversight or quality control. Where AI-assisted content generation is employed, clear labelling and editorial supervision must be ensured.

Subscription management. Trust in service providers heavily affects users' decisions, and users distrust payment mechanisms they perceive as unsafe (**T4.8**), although paying via credit card over encrypted communication – a typical means to pay online – is generally considered safe. Offering familiar and trusted payment options can help boost user trust. In this line, it is relevant to minimise the amount of personal data required for the subscription and to ensure that users can easily cancel subscription renewals [42]. We further highlight the need to examine the role of SMPs, like Contentpass, especially when they bundle access to hundreds of sites and obscure the relationship between users and individual services.

5 Conclusion

This study explored user perceptions and decision-making around cookie paywalls, revealing context-dependent and often ambivalent views. Participants largely perceived cookie paywalls as profit-driven, with fairness assessments shaped by factors, such as the availability of meaningful choices, transparency in data practices, and the authenticity of paid content. While certain conditions like exclusive content, fair pricing, and trusted service providers could, in theory, motivate payment, most participants clearly expressed their reluctance or unwillingness to pay.

A strong expectation for alternatives, such as a "reject all" option or the ability to access content via contextual ads, emerged throughout the discussions. These findings raise important questions about the nature of meaningful consent and the broader implications of monetising the rights to data protection and privacy. When these rights hinge on financial means, there is a risk of reinforcing inequality, potentially challenging the freely given consent requirement under GDPR. Future research could engage with service providers to better understand their motivations and incentives behind implementing cookie paywalls. Capturing the perspectives from both sides could help bridge the gap between user expectations and business realities. In addition, broader and more diverse participant samples, combined with quantitative methods, could help validate and expand on the insights of our study, revealing demographic patterns and further nuances in how users across different contexts perceive and respond to cookie paywalls.

Acknowledgments. This work was supported by the RENFORCE research group and was partially supported by the Wallenberg AI, Autonomous Systems and Software Program (WASP) funded by the Knut and Alice Wallenberg Foundation. We are grateful for the great reflections of Itxaso Dominguez de Olazabal on this model.

A Focus Group Study Materials and Analysis

A.1 Demographic Questions

Here we list the demographic questions our participants were requested to answer. Note that all the questions had a "Prefer not to answer" option and therefore were optional.

1) What is your age? 18–24, 25–34, 35–44, 45–54, 55–64, +65

2) How do you identify yourself? Female, Male, Non-binary

3) What is your latest educational degree/level? Middle School, High School, BSc, MSc, PhD

4) What is your latest educational degree/level? - What is (was) your field of study (if applicable)?

5) How would you rate your confidence in using computers and navigating the internet? 1 = Not confident at all, 2 = Slightly confident, 3 = Moderately confident, 4 = Confident, 5 = Very confident.

6) How would you describe your ability to understand and manage cookie consent banners? 1 = I don't understand cookie banners and find them difficult to manage, 2 = I have a basic understanding of cookie banners but often struggle to manage them, 3 = I understand cookie banners well enough but sometimes need clarification, 4 = I am confident in understanding and managing cookie banners with minimal difficulty, 5 = I fully understand cookie banners and have no issues managing them.

7) What is your current work situation? Employed or self-employed, Looking for a job, Studying, Others 8) What is your monthly income after tax? Less than 15,000 SEK, Between 15,000 and 25,000 SEK, Between 25,000 and 35,000 SEK, Between 35,000 and 45,000 SEK, More than 45,000 SEK.

A.2 Thematic Analysis

First, two authors independently read the transcripts to familiarise themselves with the content and held an initial discussion on excerpts relevant to the research questions, specifically: (1) factors influencing participants' behaviour toward cookie banners and paywalls, and (2) their perceptions and expectations of these mechanisms. Next, both authors individually coded the first focus group

22   V. Morel et al.

based on their discussion, and later refined and reviewed their codes in a joint meeting until they reached a consensus, resulting in a more structured codebook. Using this refined codebook, they proceeded with the remaining focus groups, repeating the process for each until all were analysed and a final, refined codebook was established. Finally, the codes were systematically merged into overarching themes through a collaborative effort.

A.3 Mockups Presented in the Focus Groups

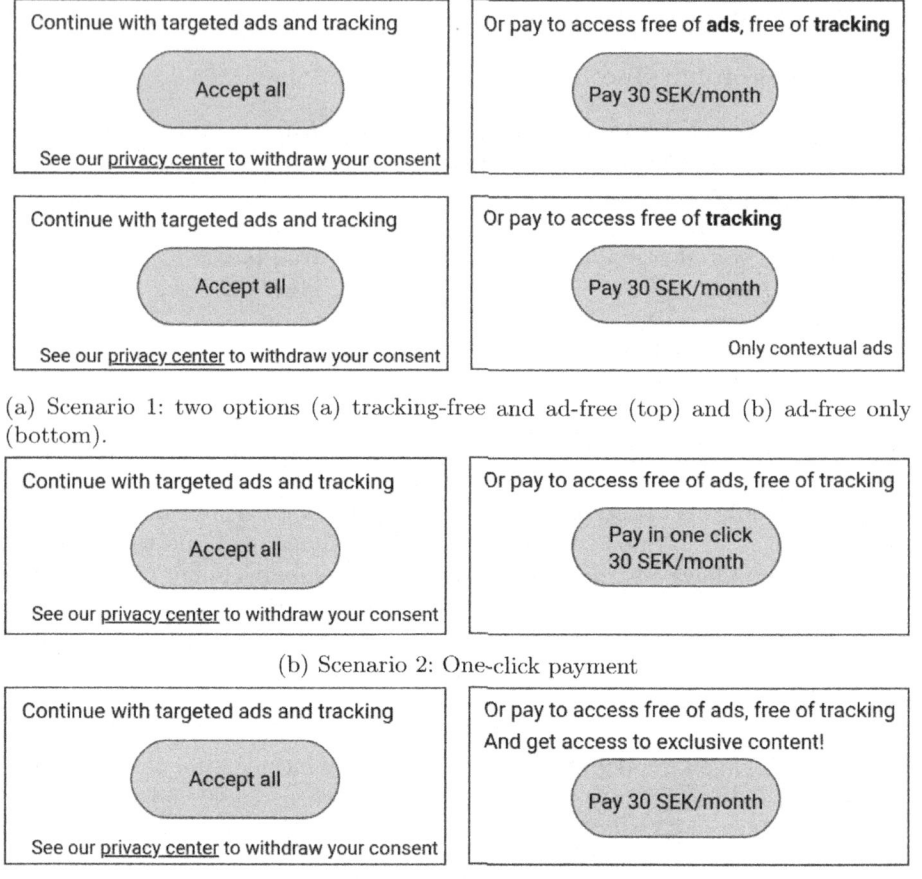

(a) Scenario 1: two options (a) tracking-free and ad-free (top) and (b) ad-free only (bottom).

(b) Scenario 2: One-click payment

(c) Scenario 3: Exclusive content

Fig. 1. Mockups presented in our focus groups.

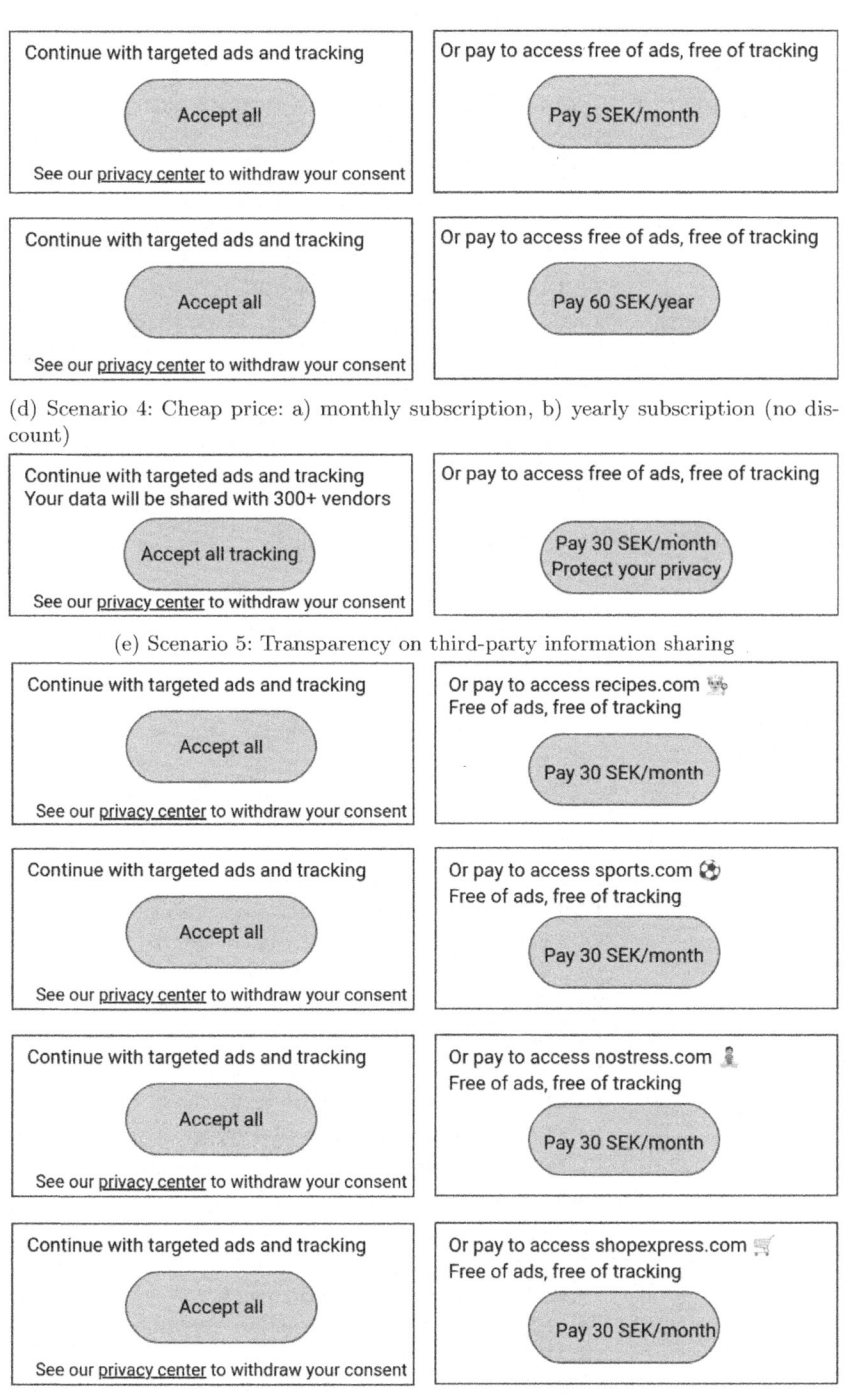

(d) Scenario 4: Cheap price: a) monthly subscription, b) yearly subscription (no discount)

(e) Scenario 5: Transparency on third-party information sharing

(f) Scenario 6: Various types of websites

Fig. 1. (*continued*)

Table 3. Full codebook resulting from our thematic analysis

Themes	Codes
T1 Users' perceptions of cookie paywalls' objective	T1.1 Monetary purpose for the websites - make money either way
	T1.2 To maintain users' privacy
	T1.3 To comply with regulations
T2 Perception of fairness of cookie paywalls	T2.1 Fair as users are not forced to take any options
	T2.2 Fair as nothing comes for free
	T2.3 Fair if transparent
	T2.4 Fair if authentic and original content
	T2.5 Unfair because forced to make a choice (can't reject)
	T2.6 Unfair as privacy should not be a privilege
T3 Expectations of cookie paywalls design	T3.1 A third option - Reject all
	T3.2 Better ex-ante transparency and control of data practices
	T3.3 Additional choice to have contextualized ads only
	T3.4 Cookie paywalls should not exist
T4 Factors affecting behaviour/decisions on cookie paywalls	T4.1 Access to exclusive content/service (regularly)
	T4.2 Not paying regardless of the situation
	T4.3 Cheap/fair subscription price
	T4.4 Not bothered/influenced by ads
	T4.5 Get rid of (blocking) ads
	T4.6 Feeling of pervasive tracking and data sharing
	T4.7 Perceived manipulation of content/design
	T4.8 Trust in the service provider
	T4.9 Feeling of discomfort because of wordings
	T4.10 Limited personal budget
	T4.11 Perceived unreasonable data collection for payment
	T4.12 Information should be free to access
	T4.13 Perceived feeling of safety because of other means in place
	T4.14 Lack of knowledge about cookie collection/tracking
	T4.15 Lack of perceived benefit from paying
	T4.16 Ex-ante transparency on data practices
	T4.17 Single pay-off, multiple services
	T4.18 Aversion towards subscriptions
	T4.19 Perceived sensitivity of context of service/content
	T4.20 Protect their privacy
	T4.21 Resentment of the business model

References

1. Armitage, C., et al: Study on the impact of recent developments in digital advertising on privacy, publishers and advertisers – final report. Publications Office of the European Union (2023). https://doi.org/10.2759/294673
2. Austrian DPA (DSB): A cookie banner's first layer needs to contain a visually equivalent option to reject cookies. https://gdprhub.eu/index.php?title=BVwG_-_W_108_2284491-1
3. Aziz, M.A.B., Wilson, C.: Johnny still can't opt-out: assessing the IAB CCPA compliance framework. Proc. Priv. Enhancing Technol. **2024**(4), 349–363 (2024). https://doi.org/10.56553/popets-2024-0120 https://doi.org/10.56553/popets-2024-0120
4. Bachelet, V.: "pay-or-consent" and emerging trends in digital contract law (2024). https://doi-org.utrechtuniversity.idm.oclc.org/10.54648/erpl2024047
5. Barth, S., Jong, M.D.: The privacy paradox-investigating discrepancies between expressed privacy concerns and actual online behavior-a systematic literature review. Telematics Inform. **34**(7), 1038–1058 (2017)
6. Bielova, N., Santos, C., Gray, C.M.: Two worlds apart! Closing the gap between regulating EU consent and user studies. Harvard JOLT **37** (2024)
7. Braun, V., Clarke, V.: Using thematic analysis in psychology. Qual. Res. Psychol. **3**(2) (2006). https://doi.org/10.1191/1478088706qp063oa
8. Content Pass: contentpass. https://www.contentpass.net/en/publications
9. D'Amico, A., Pelekis, D., Santos, C.T., Duivenvoorde, B.: Meta's pay-or-okay model: an analysis under EU data protection, consumer and competition law. Technol. Regulation **2024**, 254–272. https://doi.org/10.71265/tkk29041 https://doi.org/10.71265/tkk29041 https://doi.org/10.71265/tkk29041
10. Degeling, M., Utz, C., Lentzsch, C., Hosseini, H., Schaub, F., Holz, T.: We value your privacy... now take some cookies: measuring the GDPR's impact on web privacy. In: Proceedings of the 26th Network and Distributed System Security Symposium (2019)
11. EDPB: Opinion 08/2024 on valid consent in the context of consent or pay models implemented by large online platforms. https://www.edpb.europa.eu/system/files/2024-04/edpb_opinion_202408_consentorpay_en.pdf
12. Euronews: EU digital fairness act is for business as much as consumers, says justice commissioner (2025). https://tinyurl.com/4svy5das
13. European Commision: Commission finds apple and meta in breach of the digital markets act. https://ec.europa.eu/commission/presscorner/detail/en/ip_25_1085
14. European Commission: Guidelines on transparency under Regulation 2016/679, WP260 rev.01 (2018). https://ec.europa.eu/newsroom/article29/item-detail.cfm?item_id=622227
15. Fouad, I., Santos, C., Al Kassar, F., Bielova, N., Calzavara, S.: On compliance of cookie purposes with the purpose specification principle. In: 2020 IEEE European Symposium on Security and Privacy Workshops (EuroS&PW). IEEE (2020)
16. Giese, J., Stabauer, M.: Factors that influence cookie acceptance: characteristics of cookie notices that users perceive to affect their decisions. In: 9th International Conference on HCI in Business, Government and Organizations, pp. 272–285 (2022)
17. Gray, C.M., Santos, C., Bielova, N., Toth, M., Clifford, D.: Dark patterns and the legal requirements of consent banners: an interaction criticism perspective. In: 2021 CHI Conference on Human Factors in Computing Systems (2021)

18. Hils, M., Woods, D.W., Böhme, R.: Measuring the emergence of consent management on the web. In: Proceedings of the ACM Internet Measurement Conference, pp. 317–332. IMC '20 (2020)
19. Kampanos, G., Shahandashti, S.F.: Accept all: the landscape of cookie banners in Greece and the UK. In: ICT Systems Security and Privacy Protection (2021)
20. Kollmann, K.: Reconciling "pay or okay" models with the GDPR: the Austrian DPA decision and other recent approaches in Europe (2023). https://doi.org/10.21552/edpl/2023/2/15
21. Krueger, R.: Designing and conducting focus group interviews (2002)
22. Kulyk, O., Hilt, A., Gerber, N., Volkamer, M.: this website uses cookies: Users' perceptions and reactions to the cookie disclaimer. In: EuroUSEC (2018). https://doi.org/10.14722/eurousec.2018.23012
23. Kulyk, O., Renaud, K., Costica, S.: People want reassurance when making privacy-related decisions–not technicalities. J. Syst. Softw. (2023)
24. Kyi, L., Mhaidli, A., Santos, C.T., Roesner, F., Biega, A.J.: It doesn't tell me anything about how my data is used: user perceptions of data collection purposes. In: Proceedings of the 2024 CHI Conference on Human Factors in Computing Systems. CHI '24, Association for Computing Machinery, New York, NY, USA (2024). https://doi.org/10.1145/3613904.3642260
25. Lazar, J., Feng, J.H., Hochheiser, H.: Research Methods in Human-Computer Interaction. Morgan Kaufmann (2017)
26. Leenes, R., Kosta, E.: Taming the cookie monster with Dutch law – a tale of regulatory failure. Comput. Law Secur. Rev. **31** (2015). https://doi.org/10.1016/j.clsr.2015.01.004
27. Ma, E., Birrell, E.: Prospective consent: the effect of framing on cookie consent decisions. In: Extended Abstracts of the 2022 CHI Conference on Human Factors in Computing Systems (2022)
28. Machuletz, D., Boehme, R.: Multiple purposes, multiple problems: a user study of consent dialogs after GDPR. In: Proceedings on Privacy Enhancing Technologies Symposium, vol. 2, pp. 481–498 (2020)
29. Malgieri, G.: The concept of fairness in the GDPR: a linguistic and contextual interpretation. In: FAT* '20: Proceedings of the 2020 Conference on Fairness, Accountability, and Transparency, vol. 36, p. 105374 (2020). https://doi.org/10.1016/j.clsr.2019.105374
30. Matte, C., Bielova, N., Santos, C.: Do cookie banners respect my choice? Measuring legal compliance of banners from IAB Europe's transparency and consent framework. In: 2020 IEEE Symposium on Security and Privacy (SP) (2020)
31. Matte, C., Santos, C., Bielova, N.: Purposes in IAB Europe's TCF: which legal basis and how are they used by advertisers? In: APF 2020 - Annual Privacy Forum, pp. 1–24. Lisbon, Portugal (2020). https://inria.hal.science/hal-02566891
32. von Grafenstein, M., Elisabeth Herbort, N: Regulation of online advertising' (Federation of German Consumer Organisations) (2024). https://www.vzbv.de/sites/default/files/2025-02/vzbv-Gutachten_Expert-Opinion_Grafenstein_Herbort_Online-Advertising.pdf
33. Morel, V., Santos, C., Fredholm, V., Thunberg, A.: Legitimate interest is the new consent-large-scale measurement and legal compliance of IAB Europe TCF paywalls. In: 22nd Workshop on Privacy in the Electronic Society (2023)
34. Morel, V., Santos, C., Lintao, Y., Human, S.: Your consent is worth 75 euros a year-measurement and lawfulness of cookie paywalls. In: Proceedings of the 21st Workshop on Privacy in the Electronic Society, pp. 213–218 (2022)

35. Müller-Tribbensee, T., Miller, K.M., Skiera, B.: Paying for privacy: pay-or-tracking walls. arXiv preprint arXiv:2403.03610 (2024)
36. Myrstad, F., Tjøstheim, I.: Time to ban surveillance-based advertising. The Case Against Commercial Surveillance Online (2021)
37. Nouwens, M., Liccardi, I., Veale, M., Karger, D.R., Kagal, L.: Dark patterns after the GDPR: scraping consent pop-ups and demonstrating their influence. arXiv preprint arXiv:2001.02479 (2020)
38. Orland, K.: Over half of LLM-written news summaries have significant issues–BBC analysis. https://tinyurl.com/yzxxc27z
39. Rasaii, A., Gosain, D., Gasser, O.: Thou shalt not reject: analyzing accept-or-pay cookie banners on the web. In: Proceedings of the 2023 ACM on Internet Measurement Conference, pp. 154–161 (2023)
40. Sanchez-Rola, I., et al.: Can I opt out yet? GDPR and the global illusion of cookie control. In: Proceedings of the 2019 ACM Asia Conference on Computer and Communications Security. pp. 340–351. AsiaCCS '19 (2019)
41. Santos, C., Bielova, N., Matte, C.: Are cookie banners indeed compliant with the law? Deciphering EU legal requirements on consent and technical means to verify compliance of cookie banners. Technology and Regulation (TechReg), pp. 91–135 (2020). https://doi.org/10.26116/techreg.2020.009
42. Sheil, A., Acar, G., Schraffenberger, H., Gellert, R., Malone, D.: Staying at the roach motel: cross-country analysis of manipulative subscription and cancellation flows. In: Proceedings of the 2024 CHI Conference on Human Factors in Computing Systems. CHI '24, Association for Computing Machinery, New York, NY, USA (2024). https://doi.org/10.1145/3613904.3642881
43. Smart, M.A., Sood, D., Vaccaro, K.: Understanding risks of privacy theater with differential privacy. Proc. ACM Hum.-Comput. Interact. **6**(CSCW2), 1–24 (2022)
44. Soe, T.H., Nordberg, O.E., Guribye, F., Slavkovik, M.: Circumvention by design - dark patterns in cookie consent for online news outlets. In: 11th Nordic Conference on Human-Computer Interaction. NordiCHI '20 (2020)
45. Stenwreth, A., Täng, S., Morel, V.: To be or not to be (in the EU): measurement of discrepancies presented in cookie paywalls. arXiv preprint arXiv:2410.06920 (2024)
46. Strycharz, J., Smit, E., Helberger, N., Noort, G.: No to cookies: empowering impact of technical and legal knowledge on rejecting tracking cookies. Comput. Hum. Behav. **120**, 106750 (2021). https://doi.org/10.1016/j.chb.2021.106750
47. Trevisan, M., Traverso, S., Bassi, E., Mellia, M.: 4 years of EU cookie law: results and lessons learned. In: Privacy Enhancing Technologies 2019 (2019)
48. Utz, C., Degeling, M., Fahl, S., Schaub, F., Holz, T.: (Un)informed consent: studying GDPR consent notices in the field. In: Proceedings of the 2019 ACM SIGSAC Conference on Computer and Communications Security (2019). https://doi.org/10.1145/3319535.3354212
49. Wesselkamp, V., Fouad, I., Santos, C., et al.: In-depth technical and legal analysis of tracking on health related websites with Ernie extension. In: Proceedings of the 20th Workshop on Privacy in the Electronic Society (WPES '21). ACM, Seoul, Korea (2021). https://doi.org/10.1145/3463676.3485603

Open Access This chapter is licensed under the terms of the Creative Commons Attribution-NonCommercial-NoDerivatives 4.0 International License (http://creativecommons.org/licenses/by-nc-nd/4.0/), which permits any noncommercial use, sharing, distribution and reproduction in any medium or format, as long as you give appropriate credit to the original author(s) and the source, provide a link to the Creative Commons license and indicate if you modified the licensed material. You do not have permission under this license to share adapted material derived from this chapter or parts of it.

The images or other third party material in this chapter are included in the chapter's Creative Commons license, unless indicated otherwise in a credit line to the material. If material is not included in the chapter's Creative Commons license and your intended use is not permitted by statutory regulation or exceeds the permitted use, you will need to obtain permission directly from the copyright holder.

"Abort the Login": Understanding Phishing Susceptibility Through Warning Design in the Context of 2FA

Agnieszka Kitkowska[(✉)], Jorina Freya Gerken, Zhaoying Wang, and Bruce Ferwerda

Department of Computer Science and Informatics, School of Engineering, Jönköping University, Jönköping, Sweden
{agnieszka.kitkowska,bruce.ferwerda}@ju.se

Abstract. Social engineering attacks are successful due to the exploitative nature of human psychology. Although security solutions, such as 2FA, aim to reduce the severity of attacks, these approaches tend to be insufficient considering sophisticated phishing attacks. In the present paper, we investigate how the design of the 2FA method may influence the likelihood of a login to a malicious website. Through an online experiment with $N = 94$ participants, we show that contrary to common assumptions, warning designs prompting to proceed with login might have a contradicting effect. In contrast, designs that prompt users to abort the login have minimal desired effects. Moreover, we identify that involvement in login activity and confidence in the decision made had further significant effects on the likelihood of login. Our exploratory results contribute to the knowledge of susceptibility to phishing attacks and potential misconceptions about the effects of opinionated design in the context of 2FA.

Keywords: Phishing Susceptibility · Warning Design · 2FA

1 Introduction

Social engineering (SE) is a cyberattack that exploits human behavior to gain access to information or services [6]. Though it involves technology, its success relies on using psychological methods, such as persuasion [6,25]. The European Union Agency for Cybersecurity (ENISA) Threat Landscape 2024 report notes an increase in SE attacks, with phishing and pretexting via email remaining the most common and successful method [6]. Phishing emails mimic legitimate requests [24], often impersonating businesses, referencing current events [6], and exploiting emotions like fear and eliciting urgency [24].

Despite mitigation efforts, phishing remains highly effective. Awareness campaigns have limited impact [23,27]), and attackers quickly bypass new defenses, including two-factor authentication (2FA) [6]. Originally designed to enhance security, 2FA requires users to verify identity using two factors—something they know (e.g., a password), something they have (e.g., a device), or something they are (e.g., biometrics) [17]. The most common form pairs a password with a one-time code sent via SMS, app, or hardware device, ensuring that stealing a password alone is insufficient for access.

However, attackers have found ways to bypass 2FA, including adversary-in-the-middle (AiTM) attacks, which are increasingly available in phishing kits on the Dark Web [5]. In this attack, a victim unknowingly interacts with a fake website that closely mimics a legitimate service. When the victim enters their login credentials, the attacker captures them in real-time and immediately uses them to sign in to the service. Since this triggers a 2FA request, the legitimate service sends the victim a verification prompt or one-time code. If the victim approves the request or enters the code on the fake site, the attacker intercepts it and gains full access to the account [5].

Because many users associate 2FA with strong security, they may assume that a website that utilizes 2FA is legitimate. This false sense of security can make users more likely to trust and interact with a phishing site [22]. Since the only legitimate interaction the victim has during a phishing attack is with the 2FA service, it represents the last possible point of intervention. However, 2FA systems do not have visibility into the website the user is engaging with, making automatic detection difficult.

A potential solution is user-assisted verification. Sun et al. [20] developed a proof-of-concept using photo-based URL verification, where users take a picture of their browser for analysis. While effective, false positives could disrupt urgent tasks. Unlike their approach, which automatically rejects failed verifications, in the present research, we propose using automation to support rather than replace user decision-making.

Our exploratory study investigates how user experience design in a 2FA application can mitigate social engineering attacks, such as phishing, by reducing the likelihood of users logging into phishing websites. Specifically, it examines the impact of combining automated URL verification—based on photo and text recognition [20]—with verification-based warnings to influence user decision-making during 2FA login. The proposed design aims to improve the usability of 2FA by (1) minimizing cognitive effort by automating URL verification, (2) enhancing warning relevance by issuing alerts based on actual risk rather than generic caution, and (3) improving warning effectiveness by applying established research and design principles.

A key focus of the present research is the role of opinionated warning design, which uses visual cues to guide user decisions [7], compared to neutral warnings. Additionally, this study investigates how psychological and individual factors, such as stress, attention, elaboration, involvement, and 2FA frequency, affect users' decisions to proceed or abort login attempts to suspicious websites. Ultimately, the present research answers the following research questions:

RQ1: How do psychological factors (stress, attention, elaboration, involvement) influence users' decisions (i.e., abort or proceed) in 2FA phishing scenarios?
RQ2: How does 2FA frequency impact these decisions (i.e., abort or proceed)?
RQ3: How do opinionated warning designs affect user responses to potential phishing threats?

Although exploratory, our study sheds light on understanding factors that affect decisions around the use of 2FA. In particular:

- We contribute to the body of knowledge on psychological factors that affect the likelihood to proceed with a login to websites, showing that involvement and confidence in decision-making are crucial. However, considering that the attention significantly predicts these traits and that 2FA reduces attention, it is possible that 2FA increases susceptibility to phishing attacks, although more research is needed to confirm that.
- We identified that both too low and too high 2FA use frequencies increase susceptibility, and there may be an optimal frequency where susceptibility is lowest. This suggests that there may be an optimal frequency of 2FA use, and future research should explore this further. Identifying such an optimal level could lead to studies aiming to identify whether different designs or a mixture of different 2FA methods used by one user could lower phishing susceptibility.
- We found that the mechanisms based on opinionated design might not have a desired effect—instead of prompting users to abort login, they were less effective than neutral designs. Such an adverse effect might indicate that the theoretical premise around opinionated design may not work as expected in the context of 2FA logins and phishing attacks. Therefore, we postulate that such methods should be re-evaluated and further research in this specific security context.

2 Related Work

Because phishing exploits human psychology and affects behavior rather than purely technological vulnerabilities [6], effective mitigation must integrate both technical and psychological factors. Designers must account for actual user behavior rather than assuming purely logical decision-making [11]. Therefore, this study examines susceptibility and mitigation strategies in the 2FA context, building on previous research around both technological and psychological aspects of phishing.

2.1 Integrated Information Processing Model of Phishing Susceptibility (IIPM)

The Integrated Information Processing Model (IIPM) explains individual phishing susceptibility through personality-based beliefs, cognition, and information processing [24]. IIPM aligns well with the 2FA phishing process: email phishing represents the first stage, website interaction the second, and 2FA submission the third. Given the continuity of these stages, contextual and situational factors likely remain stable, making IIPM a strong foundation for modeling susceptibility at the 2FA stage. Vishwanath et al. [24] found empirical support for the model, explaining nearly 50% of the variance in phishing susceptibility. However, only attention, involvement, and email load were significant predictors of phishing susceptibility, while knowledge, self-efficacy, and elaboration were not.

In IIPM, phishing susceptibility is measured as the likelihood of responding to a phishing email [24]. In the 2FA context, this translates to the likelihood of proceeding with login. Just as responding to a phishing email signifies susceptibility, proceeding with authentication on a phishing site represents a successful attack. Vishwanath et al. [24] categorized attention into sub-factors, as different email elements (e.g., urgency cues vs. source credibility) influence susceptibility differently. However, in the 2FA context, all interface elements originate from legitimate sources, meaning attackers cannot insert persuasive cues. Since all elements are designed to support users, they should uniformly reduce susceptibility. Therefore, attention is treated as a unidimensional construct. Involvement reflects how personally relevant a message or event appears to a user [24].

2.2 Phishing Mitigation

User vigilance is often recommended to mitigate phishing susceptibility [24], yet maintaining constant alertness is challenging. Effective vigilance requires attention and elaboration, but stress impairs rational thinking, in an economic sense, and recall of security knowledge [21]. Tunnel vision further diverts focus from security cues [2]. Security awareness campaigns and training provide limited long-term effectiveness, as users quickly revert to old habits [23,27]. Therefore, strategies that facilitate alertness and provide situational support are necessary.

Sun et al. [20] introduced a 2FA prototype, PhotoAuth, designed to detect adversary-in-the-middle phishing attacks. In such attacks, the phishing site's URL differs from the legitimate one, but this discrepancy is invisible to the 2FA service due to interception. PhotoAuth addresses this by prompting users to photograph their browser's address bar, using OCR to verify the URL. Their study provided a technical proof of concept, showing that false positives were rare, though potential disruptions to legitimate use cases remain a concern.

Unlike PhotoAuth's strict rejection of mismatched URLs, we propose automation that supports rather than replaces user decision-making. While reintroducing human judgment poses risks, PhotoAuth's method effectively reduces cognitive load. By automating URL verification, it eliminates the need for users to remember, recognize, and analyze security indicators. This approach mitigates phishing susceptibility by reducing attention, elaboration, and stress-related barriers, making security measures more effective in practice.

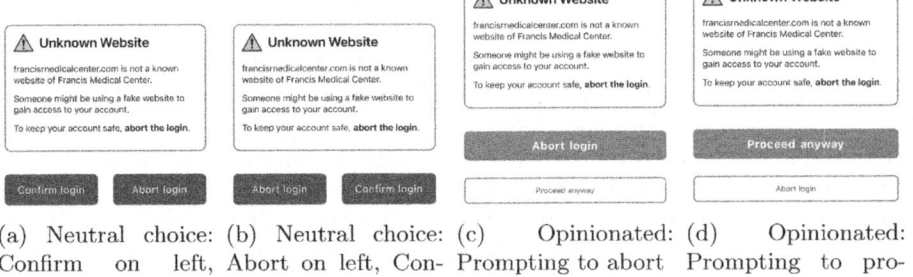

(a) Neutral choice: Confirm on Abort on right
(b) Neutral choice: Abort on left, Confirm on right
(c) Opinionated: Prompting to abort
(d) Opinionated: Prompting to proceed

Fig. 1. Comparison of different warning designs. (a) and (b) show neutral choices, while (c) and (d) represent opinionated prompts.

2.3 Decision-Making Support Using Opinionated Design

Rational thinking tends to decline under high stress, while unconscious choices remain largely unaffected. In fact, research suggests that intuitive decision-making can be even more reliable than rational thought in such situations [21]. This highlights an opportunity for design to support decision-making under stress by leveraging intuitive thinking and incorporating cognitive biases.

Opinionated design, as proposed by Felt et al. [7], similarly to nudging, relies on visual elements to encourage a particular course of action. This approach highlights a preferred choice while making alternative options less prominent. Visual appeal is one method to guide users toward the intended decision. Similarly, Reeder et al. [13] suggest minimizing the visibility of less desirable options and increasing the effort required to select them. Additionally, Felt et al. [7] emphasize that users should be able to grasp the intended action without reading the entire instruction, which reduces the reliance on complex cognitive processes. Since reading itself demands higher-order thinking, simplifying visual communication can enhance usability in stressful situations [21].

By decreasing the need for detailed deliberation, opinionated design can streamline decision-making. The extent to which biases are applied also influences user engagement, potentially increasing involvement depending on their effectiveness.

3 Method

To address our research questions, we conducted a 2 × 4 between-subjects online experiment using SoSci (www.soscisurvey.de). Participants were randomly assigned to two stress groups (with or without stressors) and four warning design groups (Fig. 1) to examine how stress and warning design influenced the likelihood of proceeding with authentication. The stressors were based on an online concentration test that required participants to perform tasks such as counting or summing numbers within a deliberately insufficient time frame, measuring their performance, speed, endurance, and accuracy [12].

The phishing mitigation approach investigated combined automated URL verification, as proposed by Sun et al. [20], with verification-based warnings. The automation handled the tasks of reading, analyzing, and evaluating the URL, reducing the need for higher-order thinking from the user. Warnings were displayed only if the verification failed, aiming to increase the perceived relevance of the information. Four distinct warning designs (Fig. 1) were tested: two opinionated vs. two neutral. Each opinionated design either promoted "proceed" or "abort," enabling the assessment of the influence of visual cues on the user's decision. Additionally, two neutral choice designs were included, identical to the opinionated warnings except for neutral visual cues. This allowed us to compare the effects of the opinionated designs with those that provided neutral choices. The neutral choice designs differed only in the order of the options to control for potential ordering effects.

To give participants a mental context for their interaction with our mockups, we created a fictional scenario in which participants were asked to imagine they had registered with a digital service of their healthcare provider and then received an email claiming that the service had been compromised. We chose the healthcare context because we assumed that the data at risk—medical data— would be perceived as particularly sensitive, increasing motivation to protect it.

When designing the fictional phishing e-mail, we used a common technique: suggesting a threat and offering a solution. Subsequently, the email informed the recipient that there had been a security incident at the online service of their healthcare provider, and their medical data was at risk. We advised them to change their password immediately to protect their data and provided a link directly in the e-mail. This e-mail was shown to participants at the beginning of the scenario, creating a narrative context for the following interactive task.

In the interactive mock-up of a login page (Fig. 2), we used the username from the fictional scenario. The page was prefilled in the login form. We applied phishing indicators by showing an "http" instead of an "https" and using the fictional domain "francisrnedicalcenter.com" in which the "m" (in "medical") had deliberately been replaced by "rn" ("r" and "n"). Using "incorrect and typejacked URLs" is a common technique [2].

3.1 Study Protocol

The study can be divided into three phases (Fig. 3):

Phase 1: After reading through information about the study and acknowledgment of it through consent, participants commenced the study. First, they rated their stress level using the questionnaire's stress scale. They were then randomly assigned to either a stress-induction group or a control group that proceeded directly to the next phase.

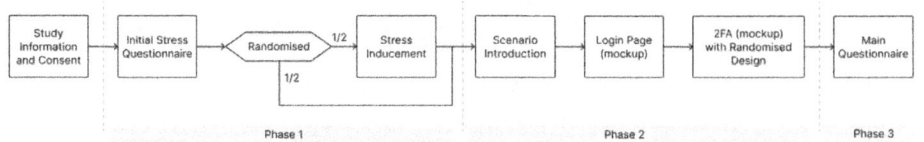

Fig. 2. Login page used in the interactive task. Note the subtle phishing indicators in the URL, such as http and "francisrnedicalcenter."

Fig. 3. Study protocol.

Phase 2: Participants were introduced to a phishing scenario and shown a fake email. They then interacted with a mock login page containing subtle phishing cues (e.g., fake domain, HTTP instead of HTTPS). After entering provided credentials, they scanned a QR code to access a 2FA mock-up, which prompted them to verify the URL by taking a photo. Regardless of their attempt, one of four warning messages was displayed (Fig. 1) in which they chose to proceed or abort.

Phase 3: After the task, participants completed questionnaires. Responses to questionnaires were mandatory, except for demographic questions and an open-ended response in which we asked participants to explain their decision rationale.

3.2 Data Collection

Participants were gathered using convenience sampling via the "sample-size" sub-Reddit (https://www.reddit.com/r/SampleSize/), which has been used for academic research purposes before (e.g., [16]). Additionally, family, friends, colleagues, peers, and their respective networks were utilized. Participants had to be 18+ and fluent in English. No compensation was provided. Participants were required to provide informed consent before taking part in the study.

A total of $N = 94$ valid responses were collected in the study. The participants completed the study in 6:24 min on average. $n = 42$ participants identified as male (44.7%), $n = 34$ as female (36.2%), and the rest preferred not to disclose their gender. No participants selected "non-binary." The majority (54.3%)

was between 25 and 34 years old, followed by the age group 35 to 44 years old (30.9%).

3.3 Measurements

This study examined one dependent variable—likelihood to proceed—and five independent variables: stress, attention, elaboration, involvement, and 2FA frequency. Gender and age were also recorded for descriptive analysis. All questionnaires are presented in the Appendix 6.

1. Likelihood to Proceed: Decision to abort or proceed with login (binary: yes/no),
2. Stress: Measured using the 5-item State-Trait Anxiety Inventory (STAI) [28], focusing on acute stress in the given situation,
3. Attention: Adaptation of the 5-item Mindfulness Attention Awareness Scale (MAAS) [18] to measure situational rather than long-term attention,
4. Elaboration: Adaptation of the Message Elaboration Measure (MEM) [14] to suit concise warnings, ensuring relevance to security messages.
5. Involvement: The 9-item version involvement scale was used [19],
6. 2FA Frequency: Frequency of usage was measured on a 5-point scale ranging from "never" to "every day,"
7. Decision-Making Questions: Additional decision-making questions (5-point Likert scale) were asked to gain deeper insights into user behaviors.

4 Results

4.1 Effect of the Stress Inducement

To test the effect of stress inducement, an independent t-test compared the change in stress levels between induced and non-induced groups. The test showed no significant difference, $t(84) = -0.57, p = 0.57$, failing to reject the null hypothesis. Thus, no evidence supports the effect of stress inducement.

Since neither stressor nor initial stress level were part of the theoretical model and only served to assess inducement effects, they were excluded from the final regression model. A preliminary logistic regression confirmed their insignificance ($p = 0.960$, $p = 0.671$, respectively).

4.2 Logistic Regression

Due to the binary nature of the outcome variable, logistic regression was used. Categorical variables were recoded with dummy variables for the warning designs, using the opinionated design as the reference category.

The regression model included all variables from the theoretical model (stress, attention, involvement, 2FA frequency) apart from elaboration (the scale's reliability was below the required threshold, and we decided to remove it from further analysis) and the likelihood to proceed as the dependent variable. It also included

Understanding Phishing Susceptibility Through Warning Design 37

the warning design treatment and the new construct "confidence in the decision made" as independent variables.

For 2FA frequency, sample sizes for "up to once a month" ($n = 11$) and "up to once a week" ($n = 14$) were small, leading to an uneven distribution. Given the theoretical framework and the small sample size, these two groups were combined into "up to once a week or less," reducing the dummy variables from three to two and increasing the minimum sample size to 25.

Testing Assumptions. Logistic regression assumptions include independence of observations, linearity of the logit, and a minimum sample size of 400, with the smaller outcome group having at least 20 participants. For categorical variables, most cell frequencies should be greater than 5, with no complete or semi-complete separation. For continuous variables, no complete separation should occur, and multicollinearity should be absent [8].

In this study, observations were independent. The overall sample size of 94 was below the recommended 400, but the smaller outcome group (36 participants who proceeded) met the 20-participant threshold. For design, all cell frequencies exceeded 5, and 2FA frequency met the required thresholds.

The Box-Tidwell procedure tested linearity, revealing stress as the only variable with potential nonlinear effects. Adding its interaction term slightly improved the model fit ($\chi^2(1) = 4.25, p = .039$, Nagelkerke R^2 from .557 to .593), but the interaction term itself was not significant ($p = .053$) and showed high multicollinearity ($r(92) = .99, p < .001$). Therefore, no interaction terms were added.

No multicollinearity was found between independent variables. It should be noted that due to the small sample size, results should be interpreted with caution.

Results Logistic Regression. The logistic regression analysis results showed that the overall model was significant with $\chi^2(9) = 49.58, p < .001$, and Nagelkerke $R^2 = .557$. 84% of the predictions were correct for a cut value of .5.

The independent variables "involvement" and "confidence in the decision made" were significant, both having a negative impact on the likelihood to proceed. Higher involvement and higher confidence each reduced the likelihood to proceed.

Two of the dummy variables were also significant, both having a positive impact on the likelihood to proceed. These were the "opinionated design prompting users to abort" and the "neutral design with confirm on the left and abort on the right." Participants were more likely to proceed when presented with these designs than when the opinionated design prompted users to proceed with the login (benchmark category).

Regarding the "frequencies of proceed and abort" across the designs, most participants aborted the login when presented with the opinionated design prompting users to proceed, with 19 aborting and only seven proceeding. In contrast, when the opinionated design prompted users to abort, 15 participants aborted, and 12 proceeded. For the neutral designs, 13 participants aborted, and six proceeded when the "abort" was on the left and "confirm" on the right, while 11 participants aborted and 11 proceeded when the "confirm" was on the left and "abort" on the right (Table. 1).

Table 1. Variables in the Logistic Regression Equation

	B	S.E.	Wald	df	sig	Exp(B)
stress during the interactive task	.075	.567	.018	1	.894	1.078
attention	.481	.439	1.202	1	.273	1.617
involvement	-1.450	.414	12.282	1	.000	.235
confidence in the decision made	-1.300	.534	5.930	1	.015	.273
neutral design: "confirm" left, "abort" right	1.790	.890	4.049	1	.044	5.992
neutral design: "abort" left, "confirm" right	1.061	.965	1.209	1	.272	2.888
opinionated design prompting to abort	1.873	.885	4.478	1	.034	6.511
2FA frequency up to once a day	-1.142	.761	2.254	1	.133	.319
2FA frequency up to once a week or less	1.667	.874	3.640	1	.056	5.295
Constant	7.155	2.729	6.874	1	.009	1281.132

4.3 Qualitative Findings

After the interactive task, participants could optionally provide a reason for their decision to abort or proceed with the login.

Seventeen participants either did not answer or gave non-answers, and four responses were unclear. We read through the short responses to the open-ended questions and identified the main reasons provided by the remaining participants as follows.

- Seven participants proceeded, stating that the scenario was not real or had no consequences (e.g., "It's a survey" or "Doesn't matter").
- Fifteen participants aborted, stating the warning message indicated the website was fake or advised against proceeding (e.g., "The warning reminds me the website is fake").
- Twenty-six participants mentioned the website being fake, with 23 aborting and three proceeding.
- Five participants cited the warning without further detail, with four aborting and one proceeding. The participant who proceeded and one who aborted had seen the opinionated design prompting users to proceed.
- Ten participants referenced a risk or safety concern, with nine aborting and one proceeding.
- Four participants proceeded, citing task-related reasons (e.g., self-initiated authentication or goal achievement).

- Four participants proceeded without specific reasons, expressing indifference (e.g., "Should be fine").
- Two participants cited trust as the reason, with both proceeding to login. One trusted the website because it was sent by a friend (e.g., "I believe she won't cheat me").

5 Discussion

The ENISA Threat Landscape 2024 report highlights phishing as a prevalent and profitable form of social engineering, primarily exploiting human behaviors and cognitive biases [6]. It emphasizes the need to understand factors influencing user susceptibility and potential mitigation strategies, particularly regarding 2FA, an area not previously explored in research. Our study aimed to address this gap by investigating psychological factors and a UX-based mitigation approach. Our findings partially align with the Integrated Information Processing Model proposed by Vishwanath et al. [24]. Specifically, we strongly support the role of involvement, echoing previous studies that identified involvement as a key factor reducing phishing susceptibility. However, our findings on attention differ from those of Vishwanath et al., who identified attention as significantly protective against phishing attacks. In our study, attention showed no significant direct impact when controlling for other factors, possibly because the automation in our 2FA design reduced cognitive demands traditionally placed on users during authentication. Additionally, contrary to previous literature suggesting stress negatively impacts security-related decision-making [21], our results showed no significant stress effect. Lastly, our inability to reliably assess elaboration highlights methodological gaps concerning existing measurement scales, such as the Message Elaboration Measure [14], suggesting further adaptation is necessary for concise security warnings.

The first research question (**RQ1**) examined how psychological factors (stress, attention, elaboration, and involvement) affect users' decisions to proceed or abort logging into a suspicious website [21,24]. Of these factors, involvement significantly reduced the likelihood to proceed, consistent with previous research [24]. Confidence in decision-making also negatively affected the likelihood to proceed. Stress did not significantly impact the decision, potentially due to low stress induction [21]. Attention showed a significant negative effect only in univariate analyses, aligning partially with theoretical predictions [24]. The limited role of attention might reflect the automation of URL verification in our 2FA design. Elaboration was difficult to assess directly, but participants' qualitative feedback indicated active elaboration processes, supported by their frequent references to warning content or recognizing the fake website.

The second research question (**RQ2**) investigated the potential effect of 2FA usage frequency on the likelihood to proceed [3,24]. Although our logistic regression results showed no direct impact, univariate tests suggested low 2FA frequency (up to once a week) increased susceptibility, while moderate usage (once a week to once a day) reduced it. This aligns with theoretical expectations that very low or high frequencies might increase susceptibility, either due to insufficient familiarity or desensitization, respectively [3]. Given that participants interacted with the experimental 2FA only once, habituation or load effects were likely minimal. Thus, future research should explore frequency effects longitudinally across multiple interactions.

The third research question (**RQ3**) investigated the effect of opinionated design on user decisions [7,9,10]. Our findings challenge prior assumptions: participants presented with an opinionated design prompting login continuation were paradoxically more likely to abort, contrary to findings from Felt et al. [7]. Additionally, opinionated designs prompting aborting were less effective than neutral designs. These unexpected outcomes indicate that effectiveness may be context-dependent, suggesting a nuanced interplay of design opinionatedness and psychological factors, such as involvement and decision confidence [10]. Low stress levels might have moderated susceptibility to opinionated designs, emphasizing the importance of considering contextual stress factors in design evaluations [21].

Opinionated designs can be considered a form of dark patterns, as they asymmetrically make it difficult for users to act against the promoted choice. They combine dark patterns of "hidden information" and "aesthetic manipulation" [9], leading to visually obscured important information. While Luguri & Strahilevitz [9] found these strategies effective, our study did not replicate these effects, implying that in the context of 2FA, people might be less susceptible to heuristics and cognitive biases, and instead use rational, in an economic sense, deliberations while making decisions. It is possible that participants would act differently if presented with risk-based authentication warnings. Wei et al. [26] investigated such warnings in the context of changing passwords, and found that presentation of risk levels could positively affect interactions with warnings. However, they also showed that 46% of users disregard warnings, suspecting that they are the actual phishing attempts. To some extent, a similar effect might have had place in our study, hence the unexpected results.

Theoretical frameworks for decision-making, such as that proposed by Löfgren & Nordblom [10], argue that involvement and attention mitigate the impact of opinionated designs. Their study found security concerns influenced decisions, but external involvement factors, such as task completion, may have led participants to proceed despite the abort prompt. In phishing scenarios, this involvement may take precedence, diminishing the effectiveness of opinionated designs.

Additionally, low stress levels in our study may have reduced susceptibility to opinionated designs. The 2FA implementation aimed to reduce attention and elaboration while increasing involvement and lowering stress. Despite its complexity, roughly 40% of participants referenced the warning message content explicitly, suggesting participants evaluated the message beyond its visual presentation.

Overall, our study contributes to the existing body of knowledge by validating certain factors identified in prior phishing susceptibility models (e.g., involvement), challenging others (e.g., attention, opinionated design), and highlighting the need for context-specific adaptation of theoretical frameworks. These direct comparisons illustrate critical nuances in phishing susceptibility within the 2FA context, advocating for tailored security design approaches based on robust psychological insights.

5.1 Practical Implications

Our study contributes to understanding phishing susceptibility and mitigation strategies, particularly within the context of 2FA. The findings have practical implications for both the design of usable 2FA apps and broader efforts to enhance user security.

The results suggest that increasing user confidence in their decisions could help mitigate phishing susceptibility. 2FA implementations should, therefore, aim to bolster users' confidence, potentially by supporting information-seeking behavior. Furthermore, promoting user involvement may also reduce susceptibility, as users who feel more engaged with security processes are less likely to fall for phishing attacks. Situation-aware approaches, such as verification-based warnings, could increase perceived relevance and minimize habituation effects, which may otherwise diminish the effectiveness of security measures [24]. In addition to directly reducing susceptibility, fostering involvement could encourage users to seek more information, reinforcing the importance of supporting information-seeking behavior [4]. This suggests that combining these approaches—confidence-building and increased involvement—could be particularly effective in protecting users from phishing attacks.

On the other hand, relying solely on opinionated design to influence user decisions may not be effective, as it could backfire or even be perceived negatively by users [7]. Users may prioritize the phishing narrative over security considerations in phishing scenarios, making opinionated designs less effective. Thus, alternative design strategies should be prioritized, and any use of opinionated design should be tested for its actual impact on user behavior.

Finally, the study suggests that the frequency of 2FA use and the degree of user involvement can influence susceptibility. Overuse or underuse of 2FA can increase susceptibility, and finding an optimal balance is crucial. The study also points to the potential for habituation effects across various 2FA implementations or even different software products, highlighting the need for a coordinated effort across the industry to mitigate these risks.

5.2 Scientific Contributions

In terms of scientific contributions, we extend existing research by applying it to the 2FA context, offering a new model of phishing susceptibility and mitigation tailored to this area. The findings support the idea that involvement can reduce susceptibility, aligning with previous research on phishing at other stages, such as email [24]. Additionally, confidence in decision-making emerged as a potential new factor influencing phishing susceptibility, warranting further exploration.

Moreover, our study raises questions about the applicability of existing scales, such as the Message Elaboration Measure [15], to the 2FA context. Additionally, our results suggest that opinionated designs may not always influence user decisions as anticipated, and factors like user involvement might alter their effectiveness, indicating the need for further investigation into the interplay between design and user engagement in phishing prevention.

5.3 Limitations and Future Research

The study has several limitations that must be considered. First, participants were recruited through convenience sampling, which limits the generalizability of the results. Despite efforts to diversify recruitment by using Reddit, the low engagement from this platform resulted in a small sample size. This also hindered the mitigation of network-based biases, which was one of the study's objectives.

The stress inducement method did not significantly affect participants' stress levels. While it was based on previous research [1], the timed concentration test may not have been an appropriate stress inducer. The test was modified to avoid participant frustration, potentially making it too easy or short to evoke the desired response. While the ethical considerations were met by avoiding undue distress, the limited effectiveness of the stress inducement calls into question its role in this study.

The study relied on self-reported data, which introduces biases such as social desirability, and participants may report higher involvement than actually exhibited. A lab-based study could have incorporated more objective measures, such as physiological monitoring or eye tracking, to improve data accuracy.

Lastly, participants knew the scenario was fictional, which may have lowered the perceived threat and influenced their decisions. Still, a substantial portion of participants showed engagement with the task, demonstrating a reasonable level of self-efficacy and awareness. Ethical considerations led to choosing a fictional setup, as using a real phishing scenario would have posed significant risks to participants' well-being.

Considering the small sample size, the fictional scenario, and other limitations mentioned above, further research is needed to validate the findings, particularly regarding the potential influence of decision confidence on the likelihood to proceed and the balance between low and high 2FA frequency. Moreover, the newly introduced measure for decision confidence, which showed promising results in exploratory factor analysis, must be further validated.

While the model proposed in this study was informed by prior research, it has not been explored in the 2FA context before. The lack of significance in some susceptibility factors may be due to unaccounted interrelations in the model or suggest that the treatment had a mitigating effect on these factors. Similarly, the absence of significant findings for the opinionated design could be attributed to the combined effectiveness of other aspects of the treatment, such as automation and design principles. Future research should investigate the interplay of these factors and treatment components, examining their individual contributions to phishing susceptibility and mitigation. This could enhance our understanding of how to better protect users from phishing threats and design more usable 2FA solutions.

6 Conclusions

2FA was introduced to enhance security across systems [17]. However, phishing attacks have already circumvented existing 2FA implementations, notably through AitM techniques [5]. The increasing accessibility of Phishing as a Service allows even low-skilled attackers to exploit these vulnerabilities, thereby raising the likelihood of such attacks [5].

In an AitM attack, the 2FA service remains the final line of defense, serving as the only legitimate connection for users after they are redirected to a fraudulent website. This stage is crucial for intervention, and mitigating user susceptibility at this point could play a significant role in preventing substantial harm.

Our exploratory study sought to investigate factors influencing user susceptibility to such attacks and examine potential usable mitigation strategies within the context of 2FA. To our knowledge, this specific angle has not been previously investigated. The study focused on a user experience (UX)-driven mitigation approach for AitM attacks, combining automated URL verification and verification-based warnings. The results indicate that opinionated design might unexpectedly affect decisions around 2FA logins. Further, user engagement and confidence in decisions around authentication might significantly affect phishing susceptibility.

Although our findings are limited by a small sample size and convenience sampling, the results may offer preliminary insights for researchers and practitioners regarding key factors and potential mitigation strategies. Further research is necessary to validate and expand upon these findings.

Compliance with Ethical Standards

Disclosure of Interests. The authors have no competing interests to declare that are relevant to the content of this article.

Appendix A

Full Questionnaires

Initial Stress

Based on the 5-item version of the state component of the State-Trait Anxiety Inventory (STAI) ([28])

5-point Likert items: '1 – Not at all, 2 – Slightly, 3 – Moderately, 4 – Very, 5 – Extremely'

How are you feeling right now at this moment?

1. I feel upset.
2. I feel frightened.
3. I feel nervous.
4. I am jittery.
5. I feel confused.

Open Question After the Interactive Task

For participants who chose to abort the login:
You chose to abort the login. How did you come to this decision?
For participants who chose to proceed with the login:
You chose to confirm the login. How did you come to this decision?

Confidence in the Decision Made

5-point Likert items: '1 âĂŞ Strongly disagree, 2 âĂŞ Disagree, 3 âĂŞ Undecided, 4 âĂŞ Agree, 5 âĂŞ Strongly agree'
Regarding that decision, how much do you agree with the following statements?
1. I was confident in my decision.
2. If I were to come across a similar situation again, I would make the same decision again.
3. I would make the same choice in a real-life situation.
4. I found it difficult to make the decision.
5. I did not think much about the decision.
6. I had an easy time making the decision.
7. I think it was the right decision to make.

Stress During the Interactive Task

Based on 5-item version of state component of State-Trait Anxiety Inventory (STAI) ([28])
5-point Likert items: '1 âĂŞ Not at all, 2 âĂŞ Slightly, 3 âĂŞ Moderately, 4 âĂŞ Very, 5 âĂŞ Extremely'
How were you feeling during the interactive task?
1. I felt upset.
2. I felt frightened.
3. I felt nervous.
4. I was jittery.
5. I felt confused.

Understanding Phishing Susceptibility Through Warning Design

Attention

Adapted from 5-item version of the Mindful Awareness Attention Scale (MAAS) (as cited in [18])
5-point Likert items: '1 âĂŞ Strongly disagree, 2 âĂŞ Disagree, 3 âĂŞ Undecided, 4 âĂŞ Agree, 5 âĂŞ Strongly agree'
How much do you agree with the following statements?
During the interactive task,
1. it seemed I was "running on automatic", without much awareness of what I was doing.
2. I rushed through the activities without being really attentive to them.
3. I got so focused on the goal I wanted to achieve that I lost touch with what I was doing right in the moment to get there.
4. I did the task automatically, without being aware of what I was doing.
5. I found myself doing things without paying attention.

Elaboration

Adapted from Message Elaboration Measure ([14])
5-point Likert items: '1 âĂŞ Strongly disagree, 2 âĂŞ Disagree, 3 âĂŞ Undecided, 4 âĂŞ Agree, 5 âĂŞ Strongly agree'
How much do you agree with the following statements?
When presented with the warning on my phone I was
1. attempting to analyze the statements of the message
2. not very attentive to the implications
3. deep in thought about the message
4. unconcerned with the implications
5. extending a good deal of cognitive effort
6. distracted by other thoughts not related to the message
7. not really exerting my mind
8. doing my best to think about what was written
9. reflecting on the implications made
10. resting my mind
11. searching my mind in response to the implications
12. taking it easy

2FA Frequency

How often do you usually use an app (such as Google Authenticator, Microsoft Authenticator, BankID) to confirm logins in your daily life?
1. Never
2. Up to once a month
3. Up to once a week
4. Up to once a day
5. Up to several times a day

Involvement

Based on Involvement Scale ([19])
5-point semantic differential items, with 1 on the left side and 5 on the right side. Some items were reverse-scored.
To me, logging in securely is

important	unimportant
boring	interesting
relevant	irrelevant
exciting	unexciting
means nothing	means a lot to me
appealing	unappealing
fascinating	mundane
worthless	valuable
involving	uninvolving
not needed	needed

Gender

What gender do you identify yourself as?
1. Female
2. Male
3. Non-binary
4. Prefer not to say

Age Group

How old are you?
1. 18–24 years old
2. 25–34 years old
3. 35–44 years old
4. 45–54 years old
5. 55–64 years old
6. 65 years or older

References

1. Almazrouei, M.A., Morgan, R.M., Dror, I.E.: A method to induce stress in human subjects in online research environments. Behav. Res. Methods **55**(5), 2575–2582 (2023). https://doi.org/10.3758/s13428-022-01915-3

2. Alsharnouby, M., Alaca, F., Chiasson, S.: Why phishing still works: User strategies for combating phishing attacks. Int. J. Hum Comput Stud. **82**, 69–82 (2015). https://doi.org/10.1016/j.ijhcs.2015.05.005
3. Anderson, B.B., Jenkins, J.L., Vance, A., Kirwan, C.B., Eargle, D.: Your memory is working against you: how eye tracking and memory explain habituation to security warnings. Decis. Support Syst. **92**, 3–13 (2016). https://doi.org/10.1016/j.dss.2016.09.010
4. Behe, B.K., Bae, M., Huddleston, P.T., Sage, L.: The effect of involvement on visual attention and product choice. J. Retail. Consum. Serv. **24**, 10–21 (2015). https://doi.org/10.1016/j.jretconser.2015.01.002
5. European Union Agency for Cybersecurity: ENISA threat landscape 2023 – July 2022 to June 2023 (2023). https://doi.org/10.2824/782573
6. European Union Agency for Cybersecurity: ENISA THREAT LANDSCAPE 2024 (2024). https://doi.org/10.2824/782573
7. Felt, A.P., et al.: Improving SSL warnings: comprehension and adherence. In: Proceedings of the 33rd Annual ACM Conference on Human Factors in Computing Systems, pp. 2893–2902. CHI '15, Association for Computing Machinery, New York, NY, USA (2015). https://doi.org/10.1145/2702123.2702442
8. Hair, J.F., Black, W.C., Babin, B.J., Anderson, R.E.: Multivariate Data Analysis, 8 edn. Cengage (2019)
9. Luguri, J., Strahilevitz, L.J.: Shining a light on dark patterns. J. Legal Anal. **13**(1), 43–109 (2021). https://doi.org/10.1093/jla/laaa006
10. Åsa Löfgren, Nordblom, K.: A theoretical framework of decision making explaining the mechanisms of nudging. J. Econ. Behav. Org. **174**, 1–12 (2020). https://doi.org/10.1016/j.jebo.2020.03.021
11. Norman, D.: The Design of Everyday Things. Basic Books (2013)
12. Psychomeda: Konzentrationstest. https://www.psychomeda.de/online-tests/konzentrationstest.html
13. Reeder, R.W., Felt, A.P., Consolvo, S., Malkin, N., Thompson, C., Egelman, S.: An experience sampling study of user reactions to browser warnings in the field. In: Proceedings of the 2018 CHI Conference on Human Factors in Computing Systems, pp. 1–13. CHI '18, Association for Computing Machinery (2018). https://doi.org/10.1145/3173574.3174086
14. Reynolds, R.A.: A validation test of a message elaboration measure. Commun. Res. Rep. **14**(3), 269–278 (1997). https://doi.org/10.1080/08824099709388670
15. Reynolds, R.A.: A validation test of a message elaboration measure. Commun. Res. Rep. **14**(3), 269–278 (1997)
16. Shatz, I.: Fast, free, and targeted: Reddit as a source for recruiting participants online. Soc. Sci. Comput. Rev. **35**(4), 537–549 (2017). https://doi.org/10.1177/0894439316650163
17. Siadati, H., Nguyen, T., Memon, N.: Verification code forwarding attack (short paper). In: Stajano, F., Mjølsnes, S.F., Jenkinson, G., Thorsheim, P. (eds.) Technology and Practice of Passwords, pp. 65–71. Springer (2016). https://doi.org/10.1007/978-3-319-29938-9_5
18. Smith, O.R., Melkevik, O., Samdal, O., Larsen, T.M., Haug, E.: Psychometric properties of the five-item version of the mindful awareness attention scale (MAAS) in Norwegian adolescents. Scand. J. Public Health **45**(4), 373–380 (2017). https://doi.org/10.1177/1403494817699321
19. Solomon, M.R.: Consumer Behavior: Buying, Having, and Being, 13 edn. Pearson, Global Edition (2020)

20. Sun, Y., Zhu, S., Zhao, Y., Sun, P.: Let your camera see for you: a novel two-factor authentication method against real-time phishing attacks. arXiv preprint arXiv.Org (2021https://doi.org/10.48550/arxiv.2109.00132
21. Swindler, K.: Life and Death Design: What Life-Saving Technology Can Teach Everyday UX Designers. Rosenfeld Media, ebook (2021)
22. Tolbert, M.M., Hess, E.M., Nascimento, M.C., Lei, Y., Shue, C.A.: Exploring phone-based authentication vulnerabilities in single sign-on systems. In: Alcaraz, C., Chen, L., Li, S., Samarati, P. (eds.) Information and Communications Security, pp. 184–200. Springer, Cham (2022). https://doi.org/10.1007/978-3-031-15777-6_11
23. Vishwanath, A., Harrison, B., Ng, Y.J.: Suspicion, cognition, and automaticity model of phishing susceptibility. Commun. Res. **45**(8), 1146–1166 (2018). https://doi.org/10.1177/0093650215627483
24. Vishwanath, A., Herath, T., Chen, R., Wang, J., Rao, H.R.: Why do people get phished? Testing individual differences in phishing vulnerability within an integrated, information processing model. Decis. Support Syst. **51**(3), 576–586 (2011). https://doi.org/10.1016/j.dss.2011.03.002
25. Washo, A.H.: An interdisciplinary view of social engineering: a call to action for research. Comput. Hum. Behav. Rep. **4**, 100126 (2021). https://doi.org/10.1016/j.chbr.2021.100126
26. Wei, T., Wang, D., Li, Y., Wang, Y.: Who is trying to access my account? Exploring user perceptions and reactions to risk-based authentication notifications. In: NDSS (2025)
27. Williams, E.J., Hinds, J., Joinson, A.N.: Exploring susceptibility to phishing in the workplace. Int. J. Hum.-Comput. Stud. **120**, 1–13 (2018). https://doi.org/10.1016/j.ijhcs.2018.06.004
28. Zsido, A.N., Teleki, S.A., Csokasi, K., Rozsa, S., Bandi, S.A.: Development of the short version of the Spielberger state-trait anxiety inventory. Psychiatry Res. **291**, 113223 (2020). https://doi.org/10.1016/j.psychres.2020.113223

Open Access This chapter is licensed under the terms of the Creative Commons Attribution-NonCommercial-NoDerivatives 4.0 International License (http://creativecommons.org/licenses/by-nc-nd/4.0/), which permits any noncommercial use, sharing, distribution and reproduction in any medium or format, as long as you give appropriate credit to the original author(s) and the source, provide a link to the Creative Commons license and indicate if you modified the licensed material. You do not have permission under this license to share adapted material derived from this chapter or parts of it.

The images or other third party material in this chapter are included in the chapter's Creative Commons license, unless indicated otherwise in a credit line to the material. If material is not included in the chapter's Creative Commons license and your intended use is not permitted by statutory regulation or exceeds the permitted use, you will need to obtain permission directly from the copyright holder.

Expert Strategies to Assist Laypeople in Making Decisions and Adopting Privacy-Enhancing Technologies

Shirin Shams[1]([✉])[iD], Sebastian Jakob Schillinger[1][iD], and Delphine Reinhardt[2][iD]

[1] Institute of Computer Science, University of Göttingen, Göttingen, Germany
shirin.shams@uni-goettingen.de, s.schillinger@stud.uni-goettingen.de
[2] Institute of Computer Science and Campus Institute Data Science, University of Göttingen, Göttingen, Germany
reinhardt@cs.uni-goettingen.de

Abstract. Despite the availability and advancement of privacy solutions, including *Privacy Enhancing Technologies* (PETs), a gap remains between individuals motivated to protect their online privacy and their actual adoption of PETs. While research has identified a range of discrete factors influencing PET adoption, these insights lack cohesion, limiting their practical applicability. Instead, we interviewed 16 domain experts from Western democratic countries, synthesising fragmented findings to establish strategies for effectively supporting individuals throughout the entire PET adoption process. Grounded in the *Security and Privacy Acceptance Framework* (SPAF), our study focused on three key areas: motivating action, raising awareness, and aligning adoption pathways with users' needs and abilities. Based on our qualitative analysis, we identified a set of 21 recommendations in five categories to be utilised when assisting individuals in their decision-making and adoption of PETs. Our findings emphasise practical recommendations, such as understanding privacy concerns, leveraging risk awareness, offering personalised recommendations, supporting Uptake and maintaining engagement. By combining expert insights with literature findings, our study informs the design of strategies and software assistants that support individuals in the pre-adoption phase and promote the adoption of PET.

Keywords: Usable Privacy · Privacy Enhancing Technologies · Privacy Tools Adoption · Privacy Preserving Technology Presentation

1 Introduction

A variety of privacy-preserving solutions, including *Privacy-Enhancing Technologies* (PETs), are available to help individuals safeguard personal data and mitigate privacy risks. For example, *Virtual Private Networks* (VPNs) are available across platforms to secure internet traffic. At the same time, tracker-blocking extensions can be integrated into web browsers to limit online tracking.

Despite the abundance of these tools, their adoption rate remains strikingly low, even among individuals who express significant concerns about their privacy [7,44,45,56,60,72,90]. For instance, in a study involving 257 participants, more than 80% expressed privacy concerns, yet only 6% had installed privacy-preserving applications on their devices [7]. A more recent study [56] conducted in 2021 confirmed that the complexity of implementation and the vast available tools pose challenges in effective adoption. Further explanation among privacy researchers for the low adoption, including usability challenges, lack of awareness, perceived complexity, or general uncertainty [2,4,7,29,81].

To address this current state, we argue that for users who already exhibit a baseline level of concern or motivation to enhance privacy, such as in [7], a critical next step lies in understanding how to present PETs to them. This involves supporting individuals in navigating known barriers and facilitating more informed and confident decision-making. While existing studies describe available PETs in various domains [6,21,25,42,57] and highlight the different factors involved in PETs adoption [2,10,12,29,78], they offer limited guidance on supporting individuals throughout the journey of understanding risks and mitigation tools specifically in conjunction with individuals' unique needs, concerns, and abilities. As a result, a comprehensive guideline to better present PETs to individuals to enhance the experience and chance of adoption is missing.

To bridge this gap, we focus on the factors and strategies necessary to present PETs in a manner that supports individuals in adopting them. In this study, we hence address the following research question: **RQ:** *What strategies and approaches do experts recommend for presenting PETs to individuals in order to support them throughout the adoption process?* To this end, we leverage the expertise of 16 international domain experts in semi-structured interviews, examining how they engage with people to understand their privacy challenges and subsequently offering PETs to them. This approach enables us to uncover experts' knowledge on themes such as educating individuals about PETs, supporting informed decision-making, and providing tailored recommendations aligned with users' concerns and abilities. Our findings contribute valuable insights for developing a set of recommendations designed to be used for assisting individuals in the process of improving their online privacy practices. Given the scarcity of privacy experts, also acknowledge by themselves (e.g., Expert 5 stated: *"We serve maybe between a dozen and 20 people. There are millions more [...] So, yeah, something that's like an online tool would be really useful"*), we further investigate the potential of a software solution. An online software assistant to support individuals in enhancing their privacy by leveraging expert insights to evaluate its feasibility and inform its design. This work contributes the following:

- We conducted 16 interviews with domain experts, primarily from Western democratic countries, to explore recommendations for supporting individuals in PET adoption. Guided by the Security and Privacy Acceptance Framework (SPAF), the interviews focused on motivation, ability, and awareness. Then, experts discussed a software solution to support users before adoption.

- Our analysis identified five categories with 21 expert-driven recommendations to help individuals enhance their privacy. For instance, the *Understand* category involves learning about users and introducing privacy concepts, while *Streamline options* includes *Personalise* and *Analyse behaviour* (aligning advice with habits). We also outline experts' views on key features, benefits (e.g., reachability), and challenges (e.g., maintenance) of a potential software assistant, acknowledging expert support for all users is unrealistic.
- We contextualised our findings within the literature, especially SPAF, then outlined future directions like user evaluation, potential of a software assistance, and beyond a online assistance.

This paper is structured as: Sect. 2 reviews related work; Sect. 3 details methodology; results appear in Sect. 4; discussion in Sect. 5; and conclusion in Sect. 6.

2 Related Work and Background

This section reviews related work that shaped our study. We cover adoption challenges (Sect. 2.1), user behaviour in privacy adoption (Sect. 2.2), and proposed privacy assistance to support individuals (Sect. 2.3).

2.1 Obstacles in Adopting PETs

Despite the availability of PETs, only a minority leverages them and engages in protecting their privacy, despite their concerns expressed in numerous studies [44,45,72,90]. The prominent explanation for the non-adoption is their lack of usability [2,7,29,48]. Also, a more multi-faceted approach is identified in [2,29,78], suggesting additional factors behind the non-adoption. Examples include citizens' personality traits, privacy concerns, or knowledge. These factors have already been investigated in various attempts to predict individuals' intentions of use, adoption or acceptance of specific PETs [9,10,12,14,15,18,38–40,46,54,63] or PETs in general [52]. Moreover, context is known to be a salient factor in privacy-related decisions [3,5,13,30,53,65–67,83,87,97] and in the adoption of different technologies [20,74,98]. A study on VPN apps examined the impact of various attributes (e.g., rating, price, downloads) on citizens' decisions [84].

Users Informing Themselves. In contrast, our work focuses on the user experience **before adoption**, specifically, the stage where individuals must first inform themselves and choose among options. Even when users are aware of tools [86], misconceptions about their protection remain [91]. Prior studies also highlight the need for better communication about tool capabilities [24,86], underscoring that the state-of-the-art falls short in supporting informed privacy decisions. A recent study (2024) [82] evaluated 69 PET-promoting websites and found that they included only about one-third of the influential factors identified in academic literature, revealing a disconnect between providers and best practices on how to support users in making informed privacy decisions. While both their work and ours aim to support PET adoption, they focus on assessing websites, whereas we engage experts to generate actionable recommendations for guiding individuals through the full privacy improvement process. Similarly, Redmiles et al. (2020) [77] found online privacy advice lacked prioritisation and practicality. In contrast, our expert-informed recommendations provide structured support across all stages of privacy decision-making.

2.2 User Behaviour in Privacy Adoption

Due to the mentioned obstacles and shortcomings, motivated users may even be discouraged from protecting their online privacy. Uncertainty about what to do and encountering multiple barriers increase the risk of inaction [71]. Understanding why users fail to adopt privacy solutions, despite valuing privacy, requires examining behavioural models. The *Fogg Behaviour Model* (FBM) [33] explains behaviour as driven by three factors: motivation, ability, and triggers, which interact to enable or hinder actions across various domains.

The applicability of FBM in the context of privacy and security has been questioned by SPAF model [28] (2022), which argues that privacy behaviours differ due to their unique characteristics: (1) **Preventive nature:** privacy actions aim to prevent future risks, which often lack immediate impact, reducing urgency. (2) **Secondary priority**: privacy-related behaviours are often considered secondary tasks, as first noted in 2004 [31] and overshadowed by more immediate tasks. (3) **Abstract mechanisms:** privacy solutions are complex to average users, leading to confusion and mistrust, further reducing the likelihood of adoption. To address these, SPAF redefines factors by replacing FBM's triggers with awareness, emphasising users' understanding of risks and available protections. SPAF suggests awareness triggers action by helping users recognise threats. SPAF emphasises the importance of educating users about potential privacy risks and solutions, thereby helping to bridge the gap between privacy intentions and privacy behaviours.

Building on SPAF's core factors (motivation, awareness, and ability), we structured our interview questions to explore expert perspectives on supporting individuals in these areas. Considering the recency and comprehensiveness of SPAF, we were unable to find any other comparable alternative. Our study extends beyond SPAF by examining the specific strategies experts employ, providing deeper insight into their practical application. To our knowledge, this is the first study to capture expert-driven approaches for bridging the gap between privacy motivation and behaviour.

2.3 Assisting Users in Privacy Adoption

Ultimately, our goal is to propose a solution that informs citizens in a usable way, reducing barriers for individuals seeking to protect their online privacy but who lack confidence in doing so [11]. While [92] introduces a tool aimed at recommending PETs based on expert and user input, it lacks a comprehensive,

Table 1. Recommendations for Presenting PETs to Individuals: Literature Insights

Theme	Sub-theme	Description
Technology Presentation	Description	Explaining how the PET functions in a clear and user-friendly manner [10,14,73,78]
	Effectiveness	Showing PETs' adoption privacy impact and their accuracy in addressing threats [12,32,54]
	Coverage	Clarifying what the PET protects and its limitations to avoid misconceptions [41,56,78,91]
	Simplicity	Highlighting ease of use and straightforward adoption steps (if applicable) [10]
Internet Connection	Speed	Addressing potential effects of PETs on internet speed [84]
	Stability	Demonstrating PETs' impact on internet reliability [84]
Social and Emotional	Emotion	Motivating by telling stories, presenting fictional future or creating personal relevance [28,63,75]
	Interpersonal	Encouraging adoption by peers, and families [12,28,29,79]
	User feedback	Displaying user reviews and ratings for credibility [84]
Trust	Provider	Providing clear details on provider [39]
	Product	Showing trustworthiness via evidence or certifications [12]
General	Language	Using clear, accessible, and non-technical language [85]
	Price	Facilitating adoption by free versions or trials [84]
	Design and interaction	Offering interactive user-friendly interfaces [64]
	Accessibility	Following guidelines to support users with disabilities [82]

interactive approach to guide individuals through the full privacy improvement process. Additionally, it does not sufficiently tailor recommendations to individual needs and contexts. This underscores the need for a more holistic solution that supports users at every stage, from understanding options to making privacy decisions aligned with their personal concerns. The development of these strategies or software assistants will extend the existing literature on privacy assistants, though our focus is distinct. Prior work largely centers on helping users with tasks such as (1) selecting appropriate audiences for content shared on social networks [51,96], (2) managing access to profile attributes [26,35,36], (3) setting mobile app permissions [49,50,68,88,89,95], and (4) controlling access to Internet-of-Things resources [1,23,27,62,80,99].

Recommendations. We reviewed the literature on supporting the adoption of privacy. Although fragmented, it offered useful insights which we grouped into six themes, summarised in Table 1 detailed as follows:

Technology Presentation covers how PETs should be described and demonstrated to users. Clear explanations of functionality [10,14,73,78], evidence of effectiveness [12,32,54], and transparency about coverage and limitations [41,56,78,91] help reduce misconceptions. Emphasising ease of adoption and use further supports user acceptance [10]. **Internet Connection** addresses performance-related concerns, as users often fear that PETs may reduce browsing speed or stability [84]. Providing empirical evidence can help mitigate these concerns and support adoption. **Social and Emotional** highlights the psychological and social factors influencing PET adoption. Emotional strategies, such as storytelling or future scenarios, help users connect personally to privacy concerns[28,63,75]. Peer and family discussions support adoption through interpersonal diffusion [12,28,29,79], while user feedback, including reviews and ratings, reinforces PET credibility [84]. **Trust** examines the perceived trustworthiness of the provider and the product. Users value transparency about the provider's affiliations and credibility [39], and trust is further strengthened through security certifications, expert reviews, and third-party endorsements [12]. **General** covers cross-cutting factors that support PET adoption. Using clear, non-technical language improves comprehension and approachability [85]. Pricing models such as free or trial versions can reduce entry barriers [84]. Usability and interaction design should ensure intuitive navigation and minimise cognitive load [64], fostering informed decision-making. Lastly, ensuring accessibility for users with physical or cognitive impairments promotes equitable adoption [82].

3 Methodology

To bridge the gap between individuals motivated to enhance their privacy and the available PETs, we aim to develop a comprehensive understanding of how to present PETs to users and effectively guide them through the adoption process. Our initial literature review, as discussed in Sect. 2.3, identified valuable recommendations; however, these findings were fragmented and lacked a cohesive perspective on the entire process. To map out the overall process before engaging with end users, we argue that expert input was essential. Unlike user-centred methods such as user interviews, which may be constrained by participants' limited expertise and lack of a holistic view of the privacy domain, expert perspectives support a broader, well-informed understanding of effective support mechanisms. Hence, we leveraged expert interviews, a widely used method for obtaining in-depth insights [94]. We chose semi-structured interviews, which balance structure and flexibility, allowing discussions to be guided by predefined themes while enabling experts to provide unanticipated insights [16]. Alternative expert-driven methods, such as focus groups, can risk group dynamics influencing individual opinions [47], while surveys may lack the depth needed for qualitative exploration. Therefore, following the approach applied in [29], we decided that expert interviews were the most suitable method for this study. We conducted 16 semi-structured expert interviews, each lasting on average about 50 min (ranging from 32 to 74 min). All interviews were held online in English via the *BigBlueButton* (BBB) video platform provided by our university, during the last quarter of 2023 and the first quarter of 2024.

In the following, we outline the interview design (Sect. 3.1), recruitment and demographics (Sect. 3.2), analysis process (Sect. 3.3), study limitations (Sect. 3.4), and ethical considerations (Sect. 3.5).

3.1 Interview Design and Procedure

Interview Design. As outlined in Sect. 2.2, we drew upon the SPAF [28] to design our interview themes. Our objective was to capture expert perspectives on supporting individuals in the three key factors influencing privacy adoption: motivation, ability, and awareness. We employed a scenario-based interview approach to elicit expert perspectives on supporting individuals (see Appendix A). Experts were asked to imagine a one-on-one consultation with a user seeking to enhance their online privacy, thereby implying a baseline of concern and motivation of the user. To focus on strategic guidance rather than specific tools, the prompt avoided naming any PETs or privacy solutions, instead using an open-ended scenario: "Imagine you want to support an internet user to improve online privacy [...]." This encouraged high-level reflections on privacy adoption strategies. Experts then shared recommendations for supporting user adoption. Given the limited access to expert advice, we also explored the feasibility of a software assistant, such as a website or app, as an alternative to direct expert guidance to help users enhance their privacy. Experts assessed its potential benefits, challenges, and key features. Each section concluded with an open invitation for additional thoughts to deepen understanding of their perspectives.

Procedure. Each interview began with a welcome, followed by an introduction that outlined the interviewer's background, study goals, and procedures for confidentiality and consent. We then collected demographic data (see Appendix B) and proceeded with the interview scenario and questions, concluding by asking for referrals to other potential experts. A pilot interview was conducted to refine the study, improving (a) question clarity and relevance, (b) structure and flow, and (c) feasibility within the allocated time. Data from the pilot were excluded from the final analysis, as they served solely to enhance the interview procedure.

3.2 Recruitment and Demographics

We recruited experts via multiple channels: (a) LinkedIn, (b) email invitations through our research network, (c) outreach to recent authors in usable privacy, and (d) promotion at a usable security and privacy conference. We used purposeful sampling [69] to gain in-depth insights. Experts were defined as individuals with at least two years of experience in privacy or security, following [29]. We explicitly included younger experts to capture fresh and diverse perspectives. We did not compensate expert interviewees as they often participate voluntarily, driven by intrinsic motivation to advance knowledge or inform policy [8], e.g. in [29], also as it minimises bias and enhances authenticity [70]. The final sample size for this study was determined based on thematic saturation, defined as the point at which no new themes or insights emerge from the data, as recommended by Morse [61]. Although prior research suggests that qualitative studies often achieve data saturation with approximately 12 interviews [34,37,93], we extended our data collection to ensure saturation within the specific context of our study. Ultimately, we conducted 16 expert interviews, a sample size aligned

Table 2. Expert Participants Demographics

ID	Gender	Age	Country of residency	Degree	Job title	Experience in field	User involvement in work
E1	F	◐	Germany	PHD	Research Assistant	◐	O
E2	M	◐	Germany	PHD	Research Associate	◐	◐
E3	F	◐	Germany	PHD	Senior Researcher	●	◐
E4	F	O	Germany	Master	Research Associate	◐	●
E5	M	O	UK	Master	PhD Student	O	●
E6	M	O	Germany	Master	PhD Candidate	◐	●
E7	M	◐	Austria	PHD	Professor	●	O
E8	M	O	Netherlands	PHD	Postdoctoral Researcher	◐	◐
E9	M	O	UK	Master	PhD Candidate	O	●
E10	F	◐	Germany	Master	PhD Candidate	O	●
E11	F	◐	Israel	PHD	Assistant Professor	●	●
E12	F	◐	Canada	PHD	Associate Professor	●	●
E13	F	◐	Sweden	PHD	Associate Senior Lecturer	◐	◐
E14	F	●	Sweden	PHD	Professor	●	●
E15	F	O	Germany	Master	Researcher/ Project Lead	O	O
E16	M	O	USA	PHD	Postdoctoral Assistant	O	O
Total	Female=9 Male=7	18-34 O =7 35-49 ◐ =8 50-64 ● =1	8 countries	Ph.D.=10 Master=6		2-5 years O =5 6-10 years ◐ =6 10 plus ● =5	little O =3 Medium ◐ =5 A lot ● =8

with the recommendations of [29]. We tracked saturation during interviews and found little new insight in the final three, indicating thematic saturation.

The demographic information of our participants can be found in Table 2. Our sample comprised seven males and nine females from eight different countries. While almost balanced, our sample reflects the observed higher proportion of females working in usable privacy. As one expert mentioned, precisely five years of experience, 75% of our sample had five or more years of experience in the field, matching with [17,43]. Ten had a Ph.D. degree, and six had a Master's degree. Half reported having a high frequency of user interactions as part of their job, five mentioned a medium frequency, and three reported little interaction. Experts are referred to as "E" followed by their ID as follows.

3.3 Qualitative Analysis

We, two researchers (R1 and R2), transcribed all interviews using the automatic transcript software, *Amberscript*. Then, we proofread and corrected the transcribed results. To analyse the transcriptions, we conducted a qualitative analysis of our data using inductive coding with MAXQDA software. We chose this approach as the starting themes are generated based on the interview content, and this approach is more prone to discovering new insights and themes. We followed established guidelines and common practices for coding semi-structured interviews [19,55]. First, we segmented the transcribed audio recordings into thematic sections based on our interview themes. The primary researcher, R1 (the principal investigator [19]), conducted the first phase of detailed coding using open and in vivo coding techniques. During the iterative refinement process, codes addressing similar topics were merged to enhance coherence, while codes containing multiple distinct concepts were subdivided into separate codes to improve granularity. All codes were categorised into relevant thematic groups following this rigorous refinement. Then, both coders independently coded the first five participants to test the codebook. Both coders were allowed to add, delete, combine or separate codes. After several rounds, a codebook (see Appendix C) consisting of 82 codes was finalised. R1 and R2 then independently coded all transcripts. The coding results were compared using MAXQDA software to identify areas of overlap and discrepancies. To analyse discrepancies, each researcher reviewed codes assigned exclusively by the other coder. First round, each researcher reviewed and validated the other researcher's codes. Unacceptable cases were discussed in a collaborative meeting to reach an agreement.

We achieved an *Inter-Rater Agreement* (IRA) of 95.35% (Kappa = 0.96), which reflects a high level of consistency between the two researchers. The lack of full agreement stemmed from varying interpretations of individual statements. Most of the remaining disagreements involved coding aspects that did not influence the final results. These disagreements typically occurred at the parent code level rather than the final code layer. For example, in one case regarding motivation, one researcher coded the entire response as motivation, while the other identified part of the answer as tailoring down the options. Ultimately, both coded this text segment with different parent codes, as *Personalising*. A smaller subset of disagreements arose from varying interpretations. For instance, the statement *"Hotel websites would change the ordering of things depending on the type of device you went there on. So if you go there on a Mac, they auto sorted. So the more expensive ones are on the top"* (quoted by E12) was coded as *Reveal data collection* by one researcher and as *Raise risk awareness* by another, which in these rare cases we continued with R1, the principal investigator. As noted in prior studies, Kappa values alone can be contentious in complex analyses, as they may not fully capture the depth and context of qualitative coding [19].

3.4 Limitations

This study has several limitations. While centred on expert views, adding user insights would deepen real-world understanding. Future work should validate findings through user studies. The study focused on motivated users, assuming proactive engagement. Yet, society includes a broader range of users, including those with little or no initial motivation to prioritise privacy [11]. We also didn't differentiate between solution types (e.g., simple vs. advanced PETs or device settings), which future work should explore for deeper insights. The study was conducted with experts from Western democracies, and findings should be understood within this context. Privacy in oppressive regimes poses distinct challenges, where tools like VPNs and Tor may be restricted. Research involving diverse cultural and geopolitical contexts [76] is needed for a more inclusive view, especially in high-surveillance or low-literacy environments. Lastly, despite efforts to recruit industry experts, most participants were from academia. While this may limit industry perspectives, academic experts tend to offer structured, context-rich insights that help form recommendations. The sample size (16 participants) should be considered in interpreting the findings.

3.5 Ethical Considerations

Our university *Data Protection Officer* (DPO) expressed a positive opinion on the study. Participants were informed of the study's purpose during recruitment and signed a *General Data Protection Regulation* (GDPR) compliant consent detailing data recording, processing, and storage. At each session, participants were reminded of the study's purpose, withdrawal rights, and confidentiality. Names were later removed, and transcripts were stored in encrypted files.

4 Results

Here, we present key expert recommendations (Sect. 4.1), note additional findings beyond core themes (Sect. 4.2), and summarise results (Sect. 4.3).

4.1 Recommendations for Supporting Individuals

We structured experts' opinions in themes identified during data analysis, resulting in five categories: (1) Understand, (2) Motivate, (3) Streamline options, (4) Support adoption, and (5) Stay Connected. Each category encompasses multiple recommendations, totalling 21, on how to assist individuals in improving their privacy, summarised in Table 3. Then, experts' opinions on a potential software assisting individuals instead of an expert are presented.

Understand. Experts identified three key recommendations for effectively developing an initial mutual understanding to help individuals improve their privacy practices. The first recommendation, *Know your audience*, was emphasised by twelve experts. This involves understanding the users' goals, current online behaviours, and background knowledge. For example, E3 stated, *"I think my first move would be to understand what they know about online privacy. [...] So I think the first thing is to ask the users about themselves"*. An almost similar number of experts highlighted *Provide context* as the next recommendation, which is explaining basic privacy knowledge and potential risks to individuals to provide a context for the session. As E2 mentioned, *"At first, I would need to give them a broad understanding of problems in terms of privacy, going on, on the internet"*. This approach also allows the expert to gauge the user's understanding and reactions to the provided information, enabling a more dynamic approach during the session. By observing how users respond, the expert can adapt their guidance to better align with the user's specific needs, knowledge gaps, or concerns, ensuring more effective support. The final recommendation, *Explore practices*, mentioned by five, assesses users' current privacy practices. As E9 noted, it's key to know *"What their current practices are, how can they be improved, and where do they want to go with that?"* Experts expanded on these recommendations later; here, we include only points related to initial understanding and connection-building.

Motivate. In this category, we grouped the experts' suggested approaches into six key recommendations. *Raise risk awareness* is mentioned by all 16 experts,

Expert Strategies to Assist Laypeople   59

Table 3. Recommendations Set for Supporting Individuals in Improving Their Privacy

Categories	Recommendations	Explanations	Number of Experts
Understand Practices to lay the foundation	Know your audience	gaining an understanding of users' needs, online behaviours, and IT & privacy knowledge	12
	Provide context	explaining foundational privacy knowledge and potential risks	11
	Explore practices	Examining users' current privacy practices	5
Motivate Strategies to encourage users to enhance their online privacy in practice	Raise risk awareness	Highlighting personal and societal risks through example incidents	16
	Showcase simplicity	Showing easy installation and use (if appl.)	13
	Describe technology	providing user-friendly explanation of how the privacy solution works	8
	Reveal data collection	presenting data being collected from potential channels over time and activities	8
	Avoid frightening	preventing fear of threats and of workload needed for their privacy protection	6
	Highlight benefits	illustrating the tangible changes and benefits	3
Streamline options Key considerations for providing options	Personalise	assessing users' needs, concerns, privacy value, preferences, socioeconomic situation, and age concerning IT skills	16
	Analyse behaviour	reviewing hardware (e.g., smart home) and software usage (e.g., visiting websites, social media), and users' current privacy solutions	15
	Acknowledge circumstances	considering users' country, job, disability	6
	Propose usable options	to enable the user to complete the primary task with acceptable quality	5
Support adoption Practices to actively assist users in implementing action	Offer product options	such as VPN products, while explaining the features, as opposed to the concept solution, e.g., VPN, Private Browser	13
	Ensure essentials	crosschecking essential solutions and behaviours which are useful for the majority	9
	Cooperate	in adopting the privacy solution	9
	Offer concept solution	explaining the concept solution (e.g., VPN, Private Browser) rather than specific products; provide product options if requested	7
Stay connected Strategies to stay in touch	Grant resources	sharing educational or news links, users can learn more and stay connected	12
	Share updates	communicating new solutions and news	7
	Follow up	asking if users' need further support	6
	Share contact	such as email or phone number	5

described as demonstrating the potential privacy risk impacts on both personal and societal levels. This involves explaining potential cases of data misuse and their possible impacts on individuals and society. E11 quoted: *"Give them a possible example of what might happen"*. For example, widespread location sharing could serve the interests of data collectors over societal interests. In this regard, E1 mentioned: *"When people get that point of aha moment [...] You could see the difference in the approach [...] So you can see that awareness really makes a difference"*. Next, thirteen experts highlighted *Showcase simplicity*. This involves, where applicable, demonstrating that adopting and using privacy solutions can be straightforward. This would emphasise simplicity, help reduce users' cognitive load, and encourage engagement in privacy-protective behaviours. As E9 mentioned *"I think one of the big barriers to a lot of people using privacy technologies is either real difficulty or the perceived difficulty to it"*. Eight experts emphasised the importance of *Describe technology*, suggesting that explaining how a PET works in a clear, user-friendly way can boost user involvement and motivation to adopt it. This closely aligns with established recommendations in the literature [10,14,73,78]. E14 mentioned, *"Try to motivate and explain the functionality. Yeah. I mean, in the user privacy community, it is also known that the more functional explanations should be fine. And so, not explaining the crypto details. So, it is not a structural explanation but rather a functional explanation on a high level"*. Similarly, *Reveal data collection* was highlighted by eight experts. They noted that showing users how their personal data is collected across different channels over time helps to raise awareness. E12 illustrated this with a practical example of data collection and its personal impact, *"Hotel websites would change the ordering of things depending on the type of device you went there on. So if you go there on a Mac, they auto sorted. So the more expensive ones are on the top"*. This means highlighting the data that can be collected from users when they do not protect their privacy, prompting them to take action. Also, *Avoid frightening* was recommended by six. E6 remarked, *" Generating fear gives the cause stopping through reasoning so they will not think about it [...] What I want is that they start thinking about it"*. A conceptual tension arises here: while enhancing users' awareness of risks is widely advocated, there is simultaneous concern about inducing fear. This raises the question of how these two aims, informing without alarming, can be balanced within user support strategies constructively? *Highlight benefits* were recommended by three experts. Emphasising the benefits of adoption has also been validated by other studies as a key motivator for individuals to enhance their privacy practices. For example, [54] found that perceived effectiveness boosts PET adoption, highlighting the value of showing how a PET addresses privacy concerns.

Streamline Options. Experts identified four key recommendations for tailoring privacy options to individuals. All participants emphasised *Personalise* as a key factor for refining PETs to be suggested, indicating that PET options should be crafted based on an individual's needs, goals, and privacy values rather than general criteria. E6 noted, *"Because if it's not tailored to the specific case, to the specific person, to the specific scenario of applications, it will just not work."* Additionally, age was considered a factor in personalising, though most experts agreed it is relevant only when it impacts IT skills, with particular attention recommended for teenagers and the elderly. These groups may need more tailored guidance, as teenagers often require support to develop privacy awareness in their formative years, while elderly individuals may face challenges navigating modern technologies. This means that age-specific interventions should align with the user's familiarity and comfort with digital platforms. Next, *Analyse behaviour*, recommended by 15 experts, involves examining users' online activities, a task that can be complex. Experts suggested several approaches to achieve this, including analysing hardware usage (e.g., smartwatches, smart home devices), assessing software interactions (e.g., frequently visited websites or applications), and exploring current privacy practices. Additionally, *Acknowledge circumstances* refers to accounting for factors such as a user's country of residence, job, or physical and mental disabilities, recommended by six experts to take into account when assisting as it may influence privacy needs. Lastly, *Propose usable options* was recommended by five experts. For instance, E6 highlighted the importance of offering solutions that are effective yet unobtrusive, stating, *"it needs to be an effective solution that does not impact the efficiency of what they want to do."* Similarly, E5 emphasised the need for recommending passive solutions, explaining that privacy tools should work seamlessly without interrupting the user's workflow by mentioning *"[...] something that you kind of use passively"*. These underscore the importance of usability and simplicity in privacy solutions.

Support Adoption. To support adopting privacy solutions in practice, 13 experts mentioned *Offer product options*. This means presenting users with a selection of commercial products, such as recommending particular VPN products, rather than merely suggesting the type of solution needed. Experts highlighted that providing concrete product suggestions simplifies decision-making and increases the likelihood of adoption, as users are less likely to face the burden of independently researching and shortlisting suitable products. In 2022, [73] demonstrates that when asked about known PETs, most lay public participants predominantly identified tools with different primary functionalities than privacy protection, indicating a lack of awareness of available solutions, further emphasising the need for providing users with a selection of products. Experts emphasise the value of giving options to users as it is essential to provide flexibility in decisions by offering various product options instead of prescribing a single solution. E5 states, *"I think if I can give more specific solutions [commercial products], that is probably best. [...] to help themselves a bit more and not just use this one tool you give them. You know, it's what's that of saying, give a man a fish head for a day. You teach him to fish; he will be fed for life. It's basically that for privacy"*. E5 further likened this to the proverb about teaching a person to fish, suggesting that privacy support should empower individuals to make informed decisions while offering flexible solutions to suit their needs. *Ensure essentials*, mentioned by nine experts, refers to cross-checking essential protection solutions and behaviours that are helpful for most people. Additionally, the same number of experts recommend to *Cooperate* along with users for adopting the selected solution. E8 quoted: *"I would try to install it on the spot and show how it works"*. E5 also quoted: *"We could just leave them with instructions, but I think they do appreciate just a little bit of hand-holding"*. Lastly, seven experts mentioned *Offer concept solution*, which means suggesting the general type of privacy technology (e.g., VPN or private browser) without endorsing specific products. This stands in contrast to *Offer product options*, which entails presenting concrete tool choices to users. Experts who supported both approaches emphasised that the appropriate strategy should be guided by the individual's context, needs, and preferences. As E16 noted: *"I think we should show both solutions [product options and concept solution] to them. Or I would, depending it* *on the person"*. This gives rise to an important question: What are the comparative advantages and limitations of offering conceptual solutions versus specific product options in effectively supporting users' privacy-related decisions?

Stay Connected. As illustrated by E13, privacy protection often requires ongoing support beyond a single session. The experts proposed different recommendations for staying connected. E13 quoted: *"Obviously privacy is not something set in stone. It's dynamic. We change our privacy preferences over time. When I'm 20, I'm probably thinking about this construct differently when I'm using Facebook than when I'm using Facebook when I'm 35. I'm already a different person. So we would still need to have a way to convince the user that it's worth spending time on making those adjustments from time to time"*. As a result, we identified four recommendations supporting this aspect. The first recommendation is *Grant resources*, mentioned by 12 experts, which involves sharing educational materials that enable users to stay informed independently. This means that providing these resources makes individuals more likely to remain engaged with privacy support over time and engage in further privacy-enhancing behaviours. Additionally, *Share updates*, noted by seven experts, involves sending users periodic updates as a direct way to maintain a connection. Six experts recommended *Follow up*, checking in to reinforce engagement, for example, E2 noted: *"I could also ask them to report on how things [previous solutions] have worked out for them"*. Experts also suggested sharing contact info to ensure users can seek help when needed. Finally, *Share contact* information, such as email address, was suggested to ensure users can seek help when needed. E2 quoted: *"I would offer them to just contact me if any further questions arise"*, and E5 said: *"making yourself quite approachable and available [for staying in contact]"*.

Software Assistant. We categorised expert views on the potential of a software assistant into key elements, benefits, and challenges.

Elements. Experts emphasised personalisation, recommendation, and awareness as key elements. Ten experts mentioned a personalisation element for the software that gathers users' needs, preferences, online behaviour, and privacy goals. E3 explained, *"So just ask what the most important things people do online and what they don't do. So like online shopping, online banking, reading, new social networking, and so this would be, I guess, also the first step in this tool"*. An equal number of experts mentioned a recommendation element for the software that provides tailored suggestions based on the information gathered through personalisation. Nine experts highlighted the importance of an awareness element to educate users on privacy risks and mitigation strategies. Additionally, four experts recommended incorporating interactive elements such as gamification and multimedia to enhance engagement. E15 expressed, *"I would always go for gamification"* while E7 suggested, *"[utilising] video because people don't read web pages anymore"*. Three experts suggested solution checklists; two stressed prioritising them for effective user action. E6 noted, *"Prioritisation needs to depend on what is the most dangerous thing that can happen to them right now"*.

Advantages. Experts identified the scalability and technological strengths as key advantages. Half of the experts emphasised the software's ability to reach a broad audience simultaneously, provide immediate support, and operate independently of geographical constraints as critical features. As E5 stated, *"We [experts] serve maybe between a dozen and 20 people. There are millions more. It is not a local area. And probably a lot of them would appreciate this kind of information. So, yeah, something that's like an online tool would be really useful"*. E11 further noted, *"[N]ot everyone knows the experts [...] so people can just reach out to that platform"*. Additionally, six experts highlighted the technical strengths of the software. They mentioned it could streamline privacy improvement by linking users directly to relevant resources and solutions. E9 pointed out, *"[Users] be able to go at their own pace and learn what they want"*. Moreover, the tool fosters a judgment-free environment, encouraging users to seek assistance without fear of criticism. E10 remarked, *"[M]aybe I need to find a way to visit porn websites without everyone knowing it. And I would probably shy away from talking about that with my friends, but I can talk about that with the software"*. These features position the software assistance as an inclusive and reachable alternative to expert consultations.

Challenges. Experts identified several challenges. Seven experts noted that some individuals might not use it due to a preference for human interaction or a lack of awareness of its existence. E8 remarked, *"There are people who would probably just not enjoy talking to the robot [assistant tool]"*. Seven experts emphasised the need for continuous maintenance to address evolving privacy threats and mitigation strategies and incorporate user feedback, acknowledging the associated costs. E3 stated, *"[T]he landscape of privacy-enhancing tools changes quite a lot. And the question is, who is going to maintain the software to be up to date?"* Trust emerged as a concern, with six experts noting users may doubt recommendations or fear privacy risks. Usability and technical barriers were also raised, stressing the need for a user-friendly, stable, unbiased, and accessible platform. These challenges highlight areas requiring attention.

4.2 Additional Findings

Although many privacy-preserving technologies are available [24] and the scenario was intentionally open-ended, experts mainly mentioned widely available PETs like VPNs, ad blockers, private search engines, privacy-focused browsers, Tor, and encrypted communication tools. This implies their focus was on broad strategies rather than specific tools. Additionally, although reported by one or two experts, the following offers practical guidance on specific aspects.

Start with Simple Solutions: E3 stressed beginning with straightforward and implementable solutions to boost confidence and reduce perceived difficulty. **Provide Manageable Options:** E1 and E8 advised presenting users with a limited, manageable set of solutions during each session. This prevents overwhelming users and fosters a more focused adoption process. **Leverage Peer Support Networks:** E11 emphasized the effectiveness of peer-to-peer support.

A 2022 study [58] demonstrated this through an app aiding older adults with help from friends, family, or community volunteers. **Consider Caregiver Responsibilities:** E3 and E11 stressed that any privacy improvement strategies must account for individuals' responsibilities toward children or the elderly. **Integrate Gamification:** E10 and E15 suggested incorporating gamification into the adoption process. This approach could make the experience more engaging by introducing elements of fun and achievement. **Multi-Tool Approach:** E14 underlined the necessity of informing users that maintaining privacy requires a combination of tools and behaviour rather than relying on a single solution.

4.3 Summary

The analysis of the gathered information resulted in five categories of recommendations. Among these recommendations, *Raise risk awareness* and *Personalise* were highlighted by all experts, underscoring the critical importance of tailoring privacy solutions to individual needs and effectively communicating potential risks to drive engagement to encourage widespread adoption. Experts also suggested that a software solution could effectively empower more individuals in diverse locations at any time to enhance their privacy. However, they noted that not being used, maintenance, and trust are challenges that must be addressed.

5 Discussion

This section compares findings (Sect. 5.1) and outline future directions (Sect. 5.2).

5.1 Comparing with Existing Works

By addressing our research question (*What strategies and approaches do experts recommend for presenting PETs to individuals throughout the adoption process?*), our study offers actionable recommendations aligned with the three SPAF factors [28], which guided our work (see Sect. 2). For awareness and motivation, experts highlighted *Raise risk awareness* and *Showcase simplicity* as central strategies. Regarding ability, *Personalise* and *Analyse behaviour* emerged as key, underscoring the need to tailor solutions to individuals. These findings demonstrate how SPAF principles can be operationalised through experts' practical guidance. They also address gaps found in recent studies; for instance, the analysis of 69 PET-promoting websites [82] showed most provided static, non-personalised, one-way information. In contrast, our experts stressed the importance of tailored support based on user behaviour. As E9 noted, *"It can't just be, here's a bunch of tools [...] Obviously a lot of PETs aren't one size fits all."* Similarly, [77] identified a crisis in advice prioritisation, with users struggling to make informed privacy choices. Our findings address this through expert-backed strategies for streamlining options and supporting user decision-making. In sum, our work builds on SPAF [28] and complements prior research [77,82] by offering expert-driven measures to support individuals throughout the privacy adoption.

Comparing with Literature Recommendations. The comparison between expert insights and literature recommendations (outlined in Sect. 2.3) revealed shared priorities and notable differences. Both emphasise simplicity, trust, and clear explanations. However, experts offered a more comprehensive, process-oriented approach beyond the initial presentation to include long-term engagement. They stressed a structured progression: starting with understanding users' privacy knowledge and habits, and continuing with sustained support. Notably, the *Understand* category, which encompasses warming up interactions and assessing current practices, is largely absent from the literature. Experts also introduced *Avoid frightening* as a key to reducing user hesitation, another overlooked aspect. While personalisation and behavioural analysis were seen as essential by all experts, these were underrepresented in prior research. Experts further noted that privacy adoption is an ongoing process, which the literature seldom addresses. Literature-based insights remain valuable for PET presentations, offering guidance on elements such as provider details and user feedback, although less emphasised by experts. Together, expert and literature insights complement each other, supporting more effective, user-centred PET adoption strategies.

5.2 Future Directions

User Evaluation. The next step is to test these recommendations in the lab with diverse users differing in motivation, literacy, and privacy concerns. **Privacy Software Assistance.** Based on the scarcity of experts and insights from this study, we see potential for a privacy software assistance, such as a website or app, to provide support to a broad segment of society at any time and location. By incorporating expert recommendations, the tool should be designed to capture users' requirements and concerns, subsequently suggesting PETs, promoting engagement and adoption. We advocate a user-centred design approach, starting with understanding user behaviour, integrating expert insights, and refining the tool through iterative development and usability testing. **Beyond Software Assistance.** Beyond software assistants, expert recommendations can be implemented through various channels and actors, such as privacy champions [59], peer educators [22], social supporters [58], and partnerships with NGOs and advocacy groups. They can be integrated into existing programs, supported by open-access toolkits, and scaled through train-the-trainer models.

6 Conclusion

Our research contributes to addressing the ongoing challenge of bridging the gap between individuals' motivation to protect their privacy and the actual adoption of PETs. Through interviews with 16 experts, we gained 21 actionable recommendations on how individuals can be supported. The proposed recommendations highlight strategies, such as streamlining privacy options through tailored suggestions and behavioural analysis, to facilitate PET adoption. This work provides a practical foundation for designing strategies and software to support users, ultimately promoting greater adoption of PETs and enhanced privacy outcomes.

Acknowledgments. We thank our participants for sharing their expertise. This work is funded by the Deutsche Forschungsgemeinschaft (DFG, German Research Foundation), referenced as 505982147. OpenAI was used partially for text editing.

Disclosure of Interests. The authors have no competing interests to declare that are relevant to the content of this article.

Appendix

Appendix A Interview Scenarios and Questions

Scenario: Imagine you want to support an internet user in improving their online privacy in a one-on-one (online or in-person) session, like a consulting session, or helping friends and family members who are not experts in this area. These individuals come to you because of their interests, meaning they probably have minimal motivation and IT skills. Take a moment to think of this imaginary session. Think of how you would, in general, organise such a session; we are not focused on a specific product to be recommended, but on the process you take. **Overall Approach:** - 1. What would be your main agenda for such a session? - 2. How would you structure the session? **Motivation, Awareness and Ability** - 1. To motivate users to take privacy solutions in practice, would you have any specific strategy? (- Do you think showing what data is possibly collected from users can play a motivational role for them? - Do you believe telling the potential risk they are running by not protecting their privacy can play a motivational role? - Would you explain these risks in personal impact, societal impact, or both to increase motivation? - Do you think mentioning the ease of usage for privacy solutions can be motivational?) - 2. How do you determine the most suitable privacy solutions to suggest to an individual from all potential options? - 3. Would you think knowing about users can be beneficial for you to provide better solutions? Why? (If yes, what would you like to know about a user?) - 4. Would you rather try to give direct solutions (exact tool) or explain the solutions on a general level? Why? - 5. Would you see benefits in asking participants to install the solution immediately in the session? Why? - 6. What would you do to motivate the user to stay connected to you to receive further privacy advice even after the session? - 7. Would you suggest any information resources to individuals where they can learn more about online privacy by themselves (e.g., websites, videos)? **Software Assistant Tool Scenario. Scenario:** Instead of a one-to-one person session, imagine an online assistance tool that aims to support individuals in improving privacy. Something like a webpage or an application that people use to get out of the maze of massive online information and have assistance in improving their online privacy. - 1. Do

Expert Strategies to Assist Laypeople   67

you see any specific advantages in having such a tool available for individuals? Why? - 2. Do you see any specific disadvantages or risks in having such a tool? Why? - 3. To enhance such an assistance tool's efficacy in supporting individuals, what, in your opinion, should be the ideal user interaction flow?

Appendix B Demographic Questions

What is the highest university degree you have achieved? - Which country are you based in? - What is your current job or study title? - To what level does your work or study involve citizens' interaction with privacy or security? - How long have you been in the privacy or security sector (work and study)? - How do you describe your gender identity? - Which age group do you belong to?

Appendix C Codebook

Table 4 and Table 5 present the codebooks used for qualitative analysis.

Table 4. Codebook used for qualitative data analysis - software assistance

Them	Code
Modules and Features	Information Resources – General checklist – Recommendation – Prioritising – Education and awareness – Should be personalised – Redirect to a human – Chatbot, gamification, video and audio – Motivation – Example (current solutions) – Trust in the tool itself
Advantages	Yes, such a tool helps – People access (scalable) – Time (scalable) – Location (scalable) – Link to resources – Link to adoption – Broader recommendations – Judgment-free – Automatic audit
Disadvantages	Usability, accessibility, technical – Quality of recommendations – People do not use it and are not aware of it – Experts are more comfortable – Maintenance and reliability – Improvement potentials

Table 5. Codebook used for qualitative data analysis - main

Them	Code
Overall Approach	Emotion Consideration – Users' current privacy strategies, tools – Receiving user concerns, needs and goals – Users' current understanding of privacy – Teaching the privacy basics to users – Learning about users' online behaviour and devices – Giving risk awareness to the user – Explaining the technology (privacy solution) and its advantages to the user – Providing recommendation to user – General advice for everybody – Answering users' specific questions – Users' argument for not taking action (adopting privacy solution)
Motivation	Show users tangible changes and benefits (of adoption) – Prevent fear and frightening users – Easiness and complication of use – Impact level (personal, society) – Show users tangible changes
Awareness	User awareness (general) – Risk awareness – Showing users the data being collected from them (ways and possibilities) – Explain the technology solution to users – Give users examples
Recommendation Refining	Job of the user – Disability of user – Manageable portion of solution for users – Physical location – Quality and usability of privacy solution – User's current privacy practices – Personalising – Responsibility for children or the elderly – Age of user – Offering a general list of solutions – User concerns, questions and goals – User online behaviour – Start with an easy recommendation – IT knowledge of user – The software users use – The hardware users use
Solutions Type	Give users both concept and concrete solutions – Give users concrete options to choose – Depends on the user or situation (to give a direct solution or just a concept) – Act (adopt the solution) – Users' right away (in the session) – Give the available options and features
Education	Giving education resources to the user – Do not give education resources to the user – Depending on the user and if users want education resources – Depending on education resources (types and characteristics)
Maintain Engagement	Open questions at the end – Sharing the expert contact (expert must be approachable) – Necessity of regular update – Enjoyable events and community base – Sharing privacy news – Expert follow up on user – Feedback session for this session privacy tasks – Fix a time for the next meeting – Give the user the reliability feeling

References

1. Abdi, N., Ramokapane, K.M., Such, J.M.: More than smart speakers: security and privacy perceptions of smart home personal assistants. In: Proceedings of the USENIX Conference on Usable Privacy and Security (2019)
2. Abu-Salma, R., Sasse, M.A., Bonneau, J., Danilova, A., Naiakshina, A., Smith, M.: Obstacles to the adoption of secure communication tools. In: Proceedings of the IEEE Symposium on Security and Privacy (2017)
3. Acquisti, A., Brandimarte, L., Loewenstein, G.: Privacy and human behavior in the age of information. Science (2015)
4. Adams, A., Sasse, M.A.: Users are not the enemy. Commun. ACM (1999)
5. Altman, I.: The Environment and Social Behavior: Privacy, Personal Space, Territory, and Crowding. ERIC (1975)
6. Argyrakis, J., Gritzalis, S., Kioulafas, C.: Privacy enhancing technologies: a review. In: Proceedings of the Electronic Government: Second International Conference (2003)
7. Assal, H., Hurtado, S., Imran, A., Chiasson, S.: What's the deal with privacy apps? A comprehensive exploration of user perception and usability. In: Proceedings of the 14th International Conference on Mobile and Ubiquitous Multimedia (2015)
8. Beauchamp, T.L., Childress, J.F.: Principles of biomedical ethics. Edicoes Loyola (1994)
9. Benenson, Z., Girard, A., Krontiris, I.: User acceptance factors for anonymous credentials: an empirical investigation. In: Proceedings of the Workshop on the Economics of Information Security (WEIS) (2015)
10. Benenson, Z., Girard, A., Krontiris, I., Liagkou, V., Rannenberg, K., Stamatiou, Y.: User acceptance of privacy-ABCs: an exploratory study. In: Proceedings of the 2nd Human Aspects of Information Security, Privacy, and Trust (2014)
11. Boerman, S.C., Kruikemeier, S., Zuiderveen Borgesius, F.J.: Exploring motivations for online privacy protection behavior: insights from panel data. Commun. Res. (2021)
12. Bracamonte, V., Pape, S., Kiyomoto, S.: Investigating user intention to use a privacy sensitive information detection tool. In: Symposium on Cryptography and Information Security (SCIS) (2021)
13. Brandimarte, L., Acquisti, A., Loewenstein, G.: Misplaced confidences: privacy and the control paradox. Soc. Psychol. Pers. Sci. (2013)

14. Brecht, F., Fabian, B., Kunz, S., Mueller, S.: Are you willing to wait longer for internet privacy? In: Proceedings of the European Conference on Information Systems (ECIS) (2011)
15. Brecht, F., Fabian, B., Kunz, S., Mueller, S.: Communication anonymizers: personality, internet privacy literacy and their influence on technology acceptance. In: Proceedings of ECIS (2012)
16. Brinkmann, S.: Unstructured and semi-structured interviewing. The Oxford handbook of qualitative research (2014)
17. Busse, K., Schäfer, J., Smith, M.: Replication: no one can hack my mind revisiting a study on expert and {Non-Expert} security practices and advice. In: Fifteenth Symposium on Usable Privacy and Security (SOUPS) (2019)
18. Cabinakova, J., Zimmermann, C., Mueller, G.: An empirical analysis of privacy dashboard acceptance: the Google case. In: Proceedings of the European Conference on Information Systems (ECIS) (2016)
19. Campbell, J.L., Quincy, C., Osserman, J., Pedersen, O.K.: Coding in-depth semistructured interviews: Problems of unitisation and intercoder reliability and agreement. Sociol. Methods Res. (2013)
20. Caulfield, T., Ioannidis, C., Pym, D.: On the adoption of privacy-enhancing technologies. In: Zhu, Q., Alpcan, T., Panaousis, E., Tambe, M., Casey, W. (eds.) GameSec 2016. LNCS, vol. 9996, pp. 175–194. Springer, Cham (2016). https://doi.org/10.1007/978-3-319-47413-7_11
21. Cha, S.C., Hsu, T.Y., Xiang, Y., Yeh, K.H.: Privacy enhancing technologies in the Internet of Things: perspectives and challenges. IEEE Internet Things J. (2018)
22. Chang, H.H., Wong, K.H., Lee, H.C.: Peer privacy protection motivation and action on social networking sites: privacy self-efficacy and information security as moderators. Electron. Commer. Res. Appl. (2022)
23. Colnago, J., et al.: Informing the design of a personalized privacy assistant for the Internet of Things. In: Proceedings of the Conference on Human Factors in Computing Systems (CHI) (2020)
24. Coopamootoo, K.P.: Usage patterns of privacy-enhancing technologies. In: Proceedings of ACM CCS (2020)
25. Curzon, J., Almehmadi, A., El-Khatib, K.: A survey of privacy enhancing technologies for smart cities. Pervasive Mob. Comput. (2019)
26. Darwish, R., Ghazinour, K.: A novel approach for studying privacy behavior in social media. In: IEEE International Conference on Computational Science and Computational Intelligence (2017)

27. Das, A., Degeling, M., Smullen, D., Sadeh, N.: Personalized privacy assistants for the Internet of Things: providing users with notice and choice. IEEE Pervasive Comput. (2018)
28. Das, S., Faklaris, C., Hong, J.I., Dabbish, L.A., et al.: The security & privacy acceptance framework (SPAF). Found. Trends Privacy Secur. (2022)
29. De Luca, A., Das, S., Ortlieb, M., Ion, I., Laurie, B.: Expert and {Non-Expert} attitudes towards (secure) instant messaging. In: Proceedings of the 12th Usable Privacy and Security (SOUPS) (2016)
30. Derlega, V.J., Chaikin, A.L.: Privacy and Self-disclosure in Social Relationships. J. Soc. Issues (1977)
31. Dourish, P., Grinter, R.E., Delgado De La Flor, J., Joseph, M.: Security in the wild: user strategies for managing security as an everyday, practical problem. Pers. Ubiquit. Comput. (2004)
32. Fishbein, M.: A Theory of Reasoned Action: Some Applications and Implications (1979)
33. Fogg, B.J.: A behavior model for persuasive design. In: Proceedings of the 4th International Conference on Persuasive Technology (2009)
34. Fugard, A.J., Potts, H.W.: Supporting thinking on sample sizes for thematic analyses: a quantitative tool. Int. J. Soc. Res. Methodol. (2015)
35. Ghazinour, K., Matwin, S., Sokolova, M.: Monitoring and recommending privacy settings in social networks. In: Proceedings of the Joint EDBT/ICDT Workshops (2013)
36. Ghazinour, K., Matwin, S., Sokolova, M.: Yourprivacyprotector, a recommender system for privacy settings in social networks. Int. J. Secur. Privacy Trust Manag. (2013)
37. Guest, G., Bunce, A., Johnson, L.: How many interviews are enough? An experiment with data saturation and variability. Field Methods (2006)
38. Harborth, D., Pape, S.: Examining technology use factors of privacy-enhancing technologies: the role of perceived anonymity and trust. In: Proceedings of AMCIS (2018)
39. Harborth, D., Pape, S.: How privacy concerns and trust and risk beliefs influence users' intentions to use privacy-enhancing technologies-the case of tor. In: 52nd Hawaii International Conference on System Sciences (2019)
40. Harborth, D., Pape, S., Rannenberg, K.: Explaining the technology use behavior of privacy-enhancing technologies: the case of Tor and Jondonym. Privacy Enhancing Technol. (2020)

41. Herbert, F., et al.: A world full of privacy and security (MIS) conceptions? Findings of a representative survey in 12 countries. In: Proceedings of the ACM Conference on Human Factors in Computing Systems (CHI) (2023)
42. Heurix, J., Zimmermann, P., Neubauer, T., Fenz, S.: A taxonomy for privacy enhancing technologies. Comput. Secur. (2015)
43. Ion, I., Reeder, R., Consolvo, S.: "... No one can hack my mind": comparing expert and non-expert security practices. In: Eleventh Symposium On Usable Privacy and Security (SOUPS) (2015)
44. Klasnja, P., Consolvo, S., Choudhury, T., Beckwith, R., Hightower, J.: Exploring privacy concerns about personal sensing. In: Proceedings of the 7th Pervasive Computing (2009)
45. Kokolakis, S.: Privacy attitudes and privacy behaviour: a review of current research on the privacy paradox phenomenon. Comput. Secur. (2017)
46. Krontiris, I., Benenson, Z., Girard, A., Sabouri, A., Rannenberg, K., Schoo, P.: Privacy-ABCs as a case for studying the adoption of pets by users and service providers. In: Proceedings of APF (2015)
47. Krueger, R.A.: Focus Groups: A Practical Guide for Applied Research. Sage Publications (2014)
48. Lee, L., Fifield, D., Malkin, N., Iyer, G., Egelman, S., Wagner, D.: A Usability Evaluation of Tor Launcher. PoPETs (2017)
49. Liu, B., et al.: To Deny, or Not to Deny: A Personalized Privacy Assistant for Mobile App Permissions. FTC PrivacyCon (2016)
50. Liu, B., et al.: Follow my recommendations: a personalized privacy assistant for mobile app permissions. In: Proceedings of the 12th Symposium on Usable Privacy and Security (SOUPS) (2016)
51. Liu, C., Zhu, T., Zhang, J., Zhou, W.: Privacy intelligence: a survey on image privacy in online social networks. ACM Comput. Surv. (2022)
52. Mangiò, F., Andreini, D., Pedeliento, G.: Hands off my data: users' security concerns and intention to adopt privacy enhancing technologies. Italian J. Mark. (2020)
53. Marx, G.T.: Murky conceptual waters: the public and the private. Ethics Inf. Technol. (2001)
54. Matt, C., Peckelsen, P.: Sweet idleness, but why? How cognitive factors and personality traits affect privacy-protective behavior. In: 2016 49th Hawaii International Conference on System Sciences (HICSS). IEEE (2016)
55. Mayring, P., et al.: Combination and integration of qualitative and quantitative analysis. In: Forum Qualitative Sozialforschung/Forum: Qualitative Social Research (2001)
56. Mehrnezhad, M., Coopamootoo, K., Toreini, E.: How can and would people protect from online tracking? Proc. Privacy Enhancing Technol. (2021)

57. Melzi, P., Rathgeb, C., Tolosana, R., Vera-Rodriguez, R., Busch, C.: An overview of privacy-enhancing technologies in biometric recognition. ACM Comput. Surv. (2024)
58. Mendel, T., Toch, E.: Meerkat: a social community support application for older adults. In: CHI Conference on Human Factors in Computing Systems Extended Abstracts (2022)
59. Menges, U., Hielscher, J., Kocksch, L., Kluge, A., Sasse, M.A.: Caring not scaring- an evaluation of a workshop to train apprentices as security champions. In: Proceedings of the 2023 European Symposium on Usable Security (2023)
60. Miltgen, C.L., Peyrat-Guillard, D.: Cultural and generational influences on privacy concerns: a qualitative study in seven European countries. Eur. J. Inf. Syst. (2014)
61. Morse, J.M.: The significance of saturation (1995)
62. Nah, F., Tan, C.H.: HCI in Business: A Collaboration with Academia in IoT Privacy (2015)
63. Namara, M., Wilkinson, D., Caine, K., Knijnenburg, B.P.: Emotional and practical considerations towards the adoption and abandonment of VPNs as a privacy-enhancing technology. Proc. Privacy Enhancing Technol. (2020)
64. Nielsen, J.: Enhancing the explanatory power of usability heuristics. In: Proceedings of the Human Factors in Computing Systems (SIGCHI) (1994)
65. Nissenbaum, H.: Privacy as contextual integrity. Wash. L. Rev. (2004)
66. Nissenbaum, H.: Privacy in Context: Technology, Policy, and the Integrity of Social Life. Stanford University Press (2009)
67. Nissenbaum, H.: Respecting context to protect privacy: why meaning matters. Sci. Eng. Ethics (2018)
68. Olejnik, K., Dacosta, I., Soares Machado, J., Huguenin, K., Khan, M.E., Hubaux, J.P.: SmarPer: context-aware and automatic runtime-permissions for mobile devices. In: IEEE S&P (2017)
69. Palinkas, L.A., Horwitz, S.M., Green, C.A., Wisdom, J.P., Duan, N., Hoagwood, K.: Purposeful sampling for qualitative data collection and analysis in mixed method implementation research. Administration and policy in mental health and mental health services research (2015)
70. Patton, M.Q.: Qualitative Research & Evaluation Methods: Integrating Theory and Practice. Sage Publications (2014)
71. Pfleeger, S.L., Sasse, M.A., Furnham, A.: From weakest link to security hero: transforming staff security behavior. J. Homeland Secur. Emergency Manag. (2014)
72. Phelps, J., Nowak, G., Ferrell, E.: Privacy concerns and consumer willingness to provide personal information. J. Public Policy Mark. (2000)
73. Racine, E., Skeba, P., Baumer, E.P., Forte, A.: What are PETs for privacy experts and non-experts. In: Proceedings of the Symposium on Usable Privacy and Security (2020)

74. Rad, M.S., Nilashi, M., Dahlan, H.M.: Information technology adoption: a review of the literature and classification. Univ. Access Inf. Soc. (2018)
75. Rader, E., Wash, R., Brooks, B.: Stories as informal lessons about security. In: Proceedings of the 18th Symposium on Usable Privacy and Security (2012)
76. Raman, R., Abdalla Mikhaeil, C., James, T., Venkatesh, V.: Cultural differences in the adoption of privacy-enhancing technologies. AMCIS TREOs (2024)
77. Redmiles, E.M., et al.: A comprehensive quality evaluation of security and privacy advice on the web. In: Proceedings of the 29th USENIX Security Symposium (2020)
78. Renaud, K., Volkamer, M., Renkema-Padmos, A.: Why doesn't jane protect her privacy? In: Proceedings of the 14th International Symposium om Privacy Enhancing Technologies (2014)
79. Rogers, E.M.: Diffusion of Innovations the Free Press of Glencoe. NY (1962)
80. Seymour, W., Kraemer, M.J., Binns, R., Van Kleek, M.: Informing the design of privacy-empowering tools for the connected home. In: Proceedings of the CHI Conference on Human Factors in Computing Systems (2020)
81. Shams, S., Reinhardt, D.: Vision: supporting citizens in adopting privacy enhancing technologies. In: Proceedings of the European Symposium on Usable Security (2023)
82. Shams, S., Reinke, S., Reinhardt, D.: Left alone facing a difficult choice: an expert analysis of websites promoting selected privacy-enhancing technologies. In: Proceedings of the 29th Nordic Conference on Secure IT Systems (NordSec) (2024)
83. Solove, D.J.: Introduction: privacy self-management and the consent dilemma. Harv. L. Rev. (2012)
84. Sombatruang, N., Omiya, T., Miyamoto, D., Sasse, M.A., Kadobayashi, Y., Baddeley, M.: Attributes affecting user decision to adopt a virtual private network (VPN) app. In: Meng, W., Gollmann, D., Jensen, C.D., Zhou, J. (eds.) ICICS 2020. LNCS, vol. 12282, pp. 223–242. Springer, Cham (2020). https://doi.org/10.1007/978-3-030-61078-4_13
85. Stokes, J., et al.: How language formality in security and privacy interfaces impacts intended compliance. In: Proceedings of the Human Factors in Computing Systems (CHI) (2023)
86. Story, P., et al.: Awareness, adoption, and misconceptions of web privacy tools. Proc. Privacy Enhancing Technol. (2021)
87. Stutzman, F.D., Gross, R., Acquisti, A.: Silent listeners: the evolution of privacy and disclosure on Facebook. J. Privacy Confidentiality (2013)
88. Tan, H.Z., Zhao, W., Shen, H.H.: A context-perceptual privacy protection approach on Android devices. In: IEEE International Conference on Communications (ICC) (2018)

89. Tsai, L., et al.: Turtle guard: helping Android users apply contextual privacy preferences. In: SOUPS (2017)
90. Udo, G.J.: Privacy and security concerns as major barriers for e-commerce: a survey study. Inf. Manag. Comput. Secur. (2001)
91. Ur, B., Leon, P.G., Cranor, L.F., Shay, R., Wang, Y.: Smart, useful, scary, creepy: perceptions of online behavioral advertising. In: Proceedings of the 8th Symposium on Usable Privacy and Security (SOUPS) (2012)
92. Van Schaik, P., Renaud, K.V.: PEDRO: Privacy-Enhancing Decision suppoRt tOol. Preprints (2024)
93. Vasileiou, K., Barnett, J., Thorpe, S., Young, T.: Characterising and justifying sample size sufficiency in interview-based studies: systematic analysis of qualitative health research over a 15-year period. BMC Med. Res. Methodol. (2018)
94. Volkamer, M., Renaud, K.: Mental models-general introduction and review of their application to human-centred security. In: Number theory and cryptography: Papers in honour of Johannes Buchmann on the occasion of his 60th birthday (2013)
95. Wijesekera, P., et al.: Contextualizing privacy decisions for better prediction (and protection). In: Proceedings of the CHI Conference on Human Factors in Computing Systems (2018)
96. Xu, A., Zhou, Z., Miyazaki, K., Yoshikawa, R., Hosio, S., Yatani, K.: DIPA2: an image dataset with cross-cultural privacy perception annotations. In: Proceedings of the ACM IMWUT (2024)
97. Xu, H., Teo, H.H., Tan, B.C., Agarwal, R.: The role of push-pull technology in privacy calculus: the case of location-based services. J. Manag. Inf. Syst. (2009)
98. Yang, S., Lu, Y., Gupta, S., Cao, Y.: Does context matter? The impact of use context on mobile internet adoption. Int. J. HCI (2012)
99. Zibuschka, J., Horsch, M., Kubach, M.: The ENTOURAGE Privacy and security reference architecture for Internet of Things ecosystems. Open Identity Summit (2019)

Open Access This chapter is licensed under the terms of the Creative Commons Attribution-NonCommercial-NoDerivatives 4.0 International License (http://creativecommons.org/licenses/by-nc-nd/4.0/), which permits any noncommercial use, sharing, distribution and reproduction in any medium or format, as long as you give appropriate credit to the original author(s) and the source, provide a link to the Creative Commons license and indicate if you modified the licensed material. You do not have permission under this license to share adapted material derived from this chapter or parts of it.

The images or other third party material in this chapter are included in the chapter's Creative Commons license, unless indicated otherwise in a credit line to the material. If material is not included in the chapter's Creative Commons license and your intended use is not permitted by statutory regulation or exceeds the permitted use, you will need to obtain permission directly from the copyright holder.

Emerging Risks from Upcoming Technologies, Misunderstandings, and Regulatory Derogation

Interfacing Human Brains: What Could Go Wrong?
Research Paper

Marta Beltrán^(✉) ⓘ

Agencia Española de Protección de Datos (AEPD), Madrid, Spain
mbeltran@aepd.es
https://www.aepd.es/en

Abstract. The proliferation of Brain Computer Interfaces (BCIs), which enable direct interaction with the human brain, poses significant yet underexplored threats to privacy and data protection. These neurotechnologies process neurodata, highly sensitive information with the potential to reflect an individual's mental state. This paper critically examines the potential negative consequences of using BCIs, considering the neurodata lifecycle from acquisition to deletion. The analysis highlights the unique risks posed by neurodata processing, coming from the difficulty individuals face in understanding and controlling the information collected, its potential for linking or identification, and the ability to decode and even modify inner mental states such as thoughts and emotions. A comprehensive understanding of associated threats is crucial as BCIs are deployed in diverse sectors, including healthcare, workplace, education, entertainment, marketing, and safety. This paper proposes a comprehensive and systematic threat model specifically designed to identify privacy and data protection threats unique to BCIs. In addition, the paper discusses the produced threat model to offer practical recommendations and point out possible safeguards, drawing on existing data protection frameworks while also identifying critical gaps that need to be addressed to ensure the responsible and compliant design, development, deployment and use of BCIs and the adequate protection of data subjects' rights and freedoms. The analysis presented in this paper provides crucial insights for researchers, providers, policymakers, and the public regarding the potential impacts of interfacing human brains and the urgent need for robust safeguards.

Keywords: Brain Computer Interface · Neurotechnology · Neurodata · Data protection · Privacy risk management · Threat model

1 Introduction

The landscape of human-computer interaction is rapidly evolving. Innovative neurotechnologies and Brain-Computer Interfaces (BCIs) now offer new ways to directly connect the human brain with devices [31], or even with other brains

[32,37]. Driven by advances in cognitive science and engineering, these tools are spreading across healthcare, workplace, education, entertainment, marketing, and safety. While these domains offer great benefits, they also bring new risks, especially regarding privacy and data protection [44,46].

Data processed by these neurotechnologies, often termed neurodata, constitutes a distinct category of information derived from the structure, activity and functioning of the brain [33]. Such data may reveal details about individuals' cognitive states, emotions, intentions, and predispositions. Unlike conventional personal data, neurodata possesses a direct connection to the individual's mental processes, raising questions about mental privacy, cognitive liberty, and mental integrity. The ability to gather, decode, interpret, and even modify neural signals in real time represents a significant development beyond traditional data processing and may expose individuals' thoughts and feelings to external scrutiny and manipulation [22]. The sensitivity of neurodata highlights the necessity of proactively identifying and addressing the impacts on data subjects' rights and freedoms.

This paper aims to contribute to this critical discussion by developing a comprehensive threat model for BCIs and the processing of neurodata. The main contributions of this paper are: 1) Analysing existing BCI application domains to understand the lifecycle of neurodata, from its acquisition to its deletion, and its potential data protection implications. 2) Proposing a comprehensive and systematic threat model to identify privacy and data protection threats specific to BCIs and neurodata processing. 3) Discussing the produced model to offer practical recommendations, point out possible safeguards or identify gaps that need to be worked on.

The rest of this paper is structured as follows. Section 2 summarises the legal and ethical frameworks for neurodata processing, related work on privacy-preserving BCIs and privacy threat modelling, outlining the motivation for this research. Section 3 provides a foundational understanding of neurodata and its processing lifecycle, identifying the usual stages from collection to deletion. Section 4 presents our systematic threat model, derived using the LIINE4DU methodology. Section 5 provides recommendations to foster responsible innovation in neurotechnology while safeguarding fundamental rights. Section 6 concludes by summarising our key findings and emphasising the ongoing need for vigilance and proactive measures.

2 Related Work and Motivation

2.1 On the Legal and Ethical Framework

Addressing the privacy of BCIs effectively requires a thorough understanding of the existing legal and ethical landscape, as well as ongoing discussions surrounding the need for specific regulations and principles for neurotechnology and neurodata processing.

Neurodata is personal data (information relating to an identified or identifiable natural person, the data subject). Therefore, current data protection frameworks, such as the General Data Protection Regulation (GDPR) and Convention

108, are relevant to the processing of neurodata regardless of the technologies or media chosen [43]. All their principles and requirements must be complied with when processing neurodata under these or other equivalent regimes.

Numerous ethical considerations beyond these legal issues surround the design, development, deployment and use of neurotechnology and the processing of neurodata [5,6,12,44]. The first is autonomy and agency because neurotechnologies could influence or manipulate an individual's thoughts, feelings, and decisions, impacting their freedom and capacity to act. The second is discrimination and bias; biased algorithms could lead to discriminatory outcomes based on neurodata, reinforcing existing societal inequalities or creating new forms of neurodiscrimination. The third is societal impact: the widespread adoption of neurotechnologies could have significant implications, including potential shifts in our understanding of identity, consciousness, dignity, and what it means to be human.

In response to the unique challenges posed by neurotechnology and neurodata processing, the concept of neurorights has emerged. Different foundations, expert groups and regulatory frameworks have proposed several fundamental neurorights [15,45], mainly: the right to mental privacy, the right to personal identity, the right to free will, the right to equal access to mental augmentation and the right to protection from algorithmic bias.

While the idea of codifying specific neurorights at the level of human rights is gaining traction, a debate persists about whether new rights are necessary or if existing human rights frameworks can be interpreted and adapted to address these concerns. Some argue that existing rights, such as the right to privacy (Articles 7 and 8 Charter of Fundamental Rights, CFR), freedom of thought (Article 10 CFR), and the right to physical and mental integrity (Article 3 CFR), already provide a protective shield. The Council of Europe, for example, suggests that a multi-level governance approach, including the interpretation and application of the existing rights, might be a more productive approach [16].

2.2 On Brain Computer Interfaces' Privacy

BCIs involve processing neurodata, such as electroencephalogram (EEG) signals, which may reveal personal health or mental information. The lack of established privacy standards in BCI technology further exacerbates the already mentioned concerns, requiring research on security and privacy-preserving methods. Few works are focusing on security [4,23] and, specifically, on privacy of BCIs [41].

Some of them present an offensive approach, proposing or analysing attacks on BCI systems and applications [17,27,28]. Concerning the defensive approach, recent proposals suggest adopting privacy-by-design frameworks and system-engineering methodologies to systematically address privacy and security concerns in BCIs [20].

Solutions such as secure multiparty computation (SMC) or data perturbation have been proposed in previous research to protect EEG data by making it identity-unlearnable while maintaining BCI functionality [2,28,29]. Federated learning is also a promising approach, as it decentralises training and keeps data on the originating device. This method is feasible for motor imagery BCI tasks [10]. Furthermore, privacy-preserving generative adversarial networks [7] and deep compression learning techniques [24] can be used to reduce communication costs and protect against reconstruction attacks by generating synthetic data for training or transforming neural signals into irreversible hash values. Transfer learning approaches [38] and privacy-preserving domain adaptation techniques, such as the Augmentation-based Source-Free Adaptation [40], have also been explored in previous research.

Finally, work devoted to analysing the public perception or attitude towards the sensitivity of neurodata and its collection, such as [14] or [19], should be mentioned. This kind of research highlights the broader societal and ethical context that drives the need for technical mechanisms for privacy preservation in BCIs such as those mentioned before.

2.3 On Privacy Threat Modelling

Threat modelling is a methodical approach aimed at identifying, analysing, and communicating threats, and their potential countermeasures, while protecting valuable assets. It provides an organised depiction of all the details that influence the safety, security or privacy of assets such as software applications, systems, networks or business operations [42]. While conventional threat modelling focuses on safety and security issues, privacy or data protection threat modelling specifically targets risks associated with the collection, recording, organisation, structuring, storage, modification, retrieval, consultation, utilisation, disclosure through transmission, dissemination, or other methods of making personal data available, as well as alignment or combination, restriction, deletion, or destruction of personal data.

The most widely used privacy-specific threat modelling method is LINDDUN [39]. It was designed to help identify and mitigate privacy threats in software systems. LINDDUN follows the same principles as the well-known cybersecurity threat modelling method STRIDE and tries to answer the same four questions: What are we building? What can go wrong? What are we going to do about it? Did we do a decent job?

While LINDDUN is a robust and mature framework for privacy threat modelling (used in the past for BCI in [20]), it does not always directly map to specific data protection principles and requirements. While it helps identify privacy threats, translating these into regulatory compliance measures can be challenging. This is the reason why the LIINE4DU framework has been recently proposed, focusing on protecting rights and freedoms, as well as regulatory compliance (concerning GDPR), and based on slightly different threat categories [1,3].

2.4 Motivation

The motivation to produce a privacy and data protection threat model for BCIs is driven by the rapid advancements and increasing accessibility of neurotechnologies, which enable the collection and processing of neurodata.
Several factors contribute to the urgency of this research. Firstly, brain-interface technologies have moved beyond clinical use and are entering mainstream consumer markets as wearable devices [8]. These devices are capable of collecting massive amounts of data directly from the brain, often effortlessly and with high data density. Secondly, the processing and decoding of this raw neurodata are crucially dependent on Artificial Intelligence (AI) systems, which enable the interpretation of brain activity to reveal insights into emotions, memories, thoughts, and intentions [11]. And finally, as already discussed, neurodata possesses unique characteristics and sensitivities compared to traditional forms of personal data [5,13,20,30]. The use of BCIs and neurodata processing can lead to various harms, including compromised mental privacy through the aggregation of data, the potential for unauthorised access and cyberattacks ("brainjacking") that could lead to data theft or manipulation of devices, and the risk of implicit coercion or manipulation of individual behaviours, particularly in contexts with power imbalances like the workplace or through consumer neuroenhancement [26]. Furthermore, neurodata processing can inadvertently expose detailed personal information, even when collected for unrelated purposes, and may impact an individual's subjective experience and personal identity. The ability to decode mental states, such as imagined images and words, further underscores the potential for extracting confidential brain data and its potential misuse.

This combination of widespread accessibility, vast data collection capabilities, and powerful AI-driven processing creates a new reality with significant challenges. The potential impacts underscore the critical need for research that anticipates and models privacy threats specific to BCIs and neurodata processing, informing the development of appropriate safeguards, technical standards, or even regulations.

No previous work has produced a privacy and data protection threat model tailored explicitly to BCI use cases, applying a combination of systematic threat modelling and privacy engineering tools. Such a systematic threat modelling approach, employing the proper methodologies is imperative because it provides a structured process for identifying, understanding, and communicating potential threats; it is essential for proactively designing privacy-preserving data processing; it establishes actionable guidelines for the detection, evaluation and mitigation of specific risks; it is crucial for effective Data Protection Impact Assessments (DPIAs) and it enables the development of tailored mitigation strategies rather than generic solutions. In summary, it fosters a proactive approach to privacy by anticipating and addressing potential issues before they become significant problems. This systematic method is crucial, given the immaturity of current practices, standardisation, and regulation, ensuring that BCIs are designed, developed, deployed respecting fundamental rights and freedoms.

3 Neurodata Lifecycle

Neurodata refers to data originating directly from the structure, activity and functioning of the brain and the central nervous system. Neurodata is primarily collected (but not exclusively) through neurotechnological devices including Brain-Computer Interfaces (BCIs). BCIs collect and analyse information directly from the brain, which often serves as a prerequisite for their operation.

A prominent method for collecting neurodata is Electroencephalography (EEG), which records brain activity through electrodes capturing voltage fluctuations caused by ionic current flows within neurons. Other brain imaging techniques also contribute to the acquisition of neurodata such as Structural Magnetic Resonance Imaging (MRI), Functional Magnetic Resonance Imaging (fMRI), Magnetoencephalography (MEG) or Functional Near-Infrared Spectroscopy (fNIRS).

Local BCIs collecting neurodata with all these techniques can be non-invasive (placed outside the body using glasses, visors, or headbands) or invasive (surgically implanted in the brain or near it). Remote BCIs, which are not in direct contact with the person's body but are located at a distance (so the person may not be aware of their existence), are still an immature technology [25].

Once collected, whatever the type of technology used, raw neurodata undergoes processing and analysis, often involving machine learning or Artificial Intelligence (AI) systems. These systems can process the raw neurodata to generate decoded neurodata, providing interpretations of the data subject's cognitive, affective, or conative state. This processing can involve identifying specific brain activity patterns associated with different mental processes. Developing sophisticated algorithms continuously enhances the decoding power of neurotechnologies, increasing the ability to interpret complex neural signals.

Previous work [9] has identified three different neurodata processing categories, focusing on their objectives and data flow. The first (category 1), processing focused on gathering neurodata that provides direct knowledge or predictions about the person's physical health or fitness, problem-solving, reasoning, decision-making, comprehension, memory retrieval, perception, language, emotions, and other cognitive functions. The second (category 2), processing focused on gathering neurodata that enables the control of an external application or device. And the third (category 3), processing focused on gathering neurodata that allows the subject's stimulation or modulation, achieving closed-loop neurofeedback. This means that signals from the brain are used to generate new signals, which are then fed back to the brain.

Considering the above, the lifecycle of neurodata can be broadly outlined in the following stages for all use cases and application domains:

1. Collection/Acquisition: The initial capture of neural signals from the brain and neurodata using BCIs and neurotechnological devices (invasive, non-invasive or remote in the future).
2. Processing/Analysis: Pre-processing, data management and applying algorithms, often AI-powered, to interpret and decode the neurodata.

3. Interpretation/Output Generation: The derivation of meaningful insights (knowledge or predictions) about the individual's mental state, intentions, emotions, etc. or the generation of instructions, commands and cues, depending on the use case.
4. Application/Use: The utilisation of the interpreted neurodata. Knowledge or predictions are displayed or visualised as individual or collective metrics, reports, etc. through dashboards, interfaces or messaging applications (category 1), instructions are communicated or sent to the controlled external artefacts (category 2) or training parameters are shared with the data subjects as visual or audio cues or direct brain stimulation or modulation (category 3).
5. Transmission/Storage: The transfer and storage of the collected raw neurodata; generated knowledge, predictions, instructions, commands, cues or intermediate and final results.
6. Deletion/Retention: The erasure of neurodata, including management decisions concerning retention periods and deletion methods.

The increasing availability of direct-to-consumer BCIs further expands the landscape of neurodata collection beyond clinical or research settings. Current BCI architectures exhibit a spectrum in terms of where these stages are executed. For example, considering consumer devices, at one extreme, the wearable component focuses on recording or stimulating/modulating neural activity, and the raw neurodata collected is transmitted, often wirelessly, directly to remote cloud services for storage and processing. Cloud infrastructure offers significant storage and computing capacity, which is usually necessary for computationally intensive tasks such as decoding raw neurodata and generating outputs, frequently utilising AI systems for this processing. In this remote extreme, nearly all functions beyond data capture are handled by cloud services. At the other extreme, while computationally challenging for a purely wearable device, a substantial part of the BCI functionality can be supported by a local device, such as a mobile phone or personal computer, connected wirelessly or via a wired connection to the wearable. In this scenario, the wearable captures data, and the local device handles significant processing, data management, and user interaction. However, the prevailing case is a hybrid model where the wearable BCI device records raw neurodata and transmits it to a connected local device, such as a smartphone or PC. This local device can handle initial processing, run companion applications for user interface and control, and manage data. The local device sends data to remote cloud services for more complex processing, analysis, long-term storage, or features requiring more significant computational resources. In general, this is the case considered in this paper because it is the most common nowadays

Understanding these stages, regardless of where they are executed, is essential for identifying potential weaknesses and developing a comprehensive threat model that addresses the privacy and data protection implications of BCIs and neurodata processing. The Data Flow Diagram (DFD) produced is derived directly from these stages (Fig. 1). This knowledge allows us to answer the first question asked when performing threat modelling, What are we building?

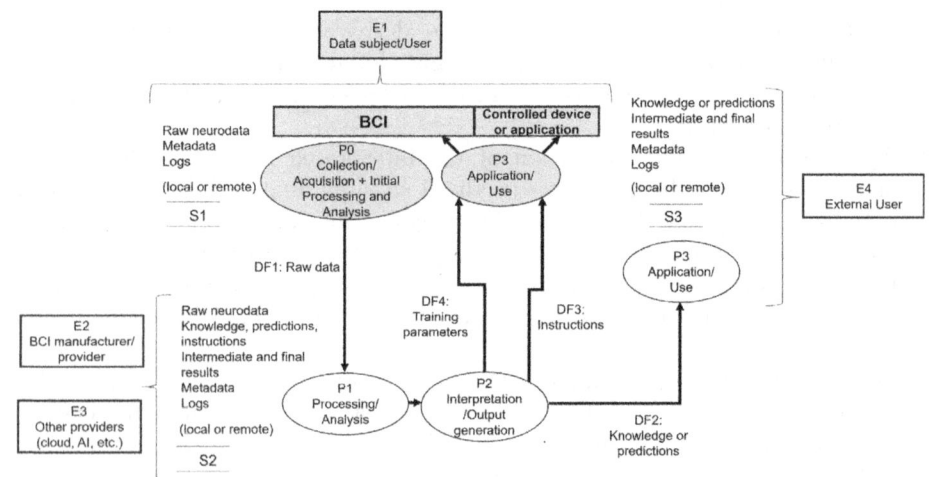

Fig. 1. Data Flow Diagram.

Entity E1 is the data subject using the BCI and, in some use cases, the user of the outputs. Entity E2 is the BCI manufacturer or provider. E3 is any other provider involved in processing, such as cloud, database, or AI providers. E4 is any external user of the results, like a professor, supervisor, or physician, who is not the data subject. Each entity has its own storage, local or remote. Storage providers could be included as entities in the DFD, with new data flows. However, these are omitted for simplicity based on our assumptions.

Three main processes that require computation map to stages in the neurodata processing lifecycle. P1 is the Processing/Analysis stage. P2 is the Interpretation/Output Generation stage. P3 is the Application/Use stage. When the output concerns physical health, fitness, or cognitive predictions, an external user (E4) is usually involved. In contrast, if the processing controls an external application or device, the data subject is usually the user. The same applies in closed-loop neurofeedback cases. For this reason, P3 is duplicated in the DFD; its execution and related data flows depend on the use case (data subject context vs external user context).

To complement these stages, P0 has been included in the DFD, concerning the Collection/Acquisition stage and the initial processing and analysis operations performed locally, within the BCI itself.

As a result of the stages and processes outlined above, all data flows from DF1 to DF4 have been identified in this research as essential when using BCIs. The BCI collects data directly from the data subject's brain in P0. This collected data, which can be categorised as raw or primary neurodata (such as brain waves and images), requires further processing to become usable. Raw neurodata (or part of them) may be transmitted from the BCI after executing P0 to different providers in DF1. DF2, DF3, and DF4 represent the transmission of outputs in the different use case categories: generated knowledge or predictions in category

1, instructions or commands in category 2 and neurostimulation or neuromodulation cues in category 3.

The DFD has been produced considering the following assumptions:

1. The produced threat model is focused exclusively on the rights and freedoms of the data subject.
2. All elements of the DFD that are the responsibility of the different entities are sufficiently protected against malicious insiders and cyberattacks (for example, misleading stimuli attacks or adversarial attacks), as well as the communications between them. There is a trusted boundary that groups the essential elements for neurodata processing within E1 on the one hand (data subject, BCI, controlled device or application, storage and local communication) and in E2, E3 and E4 on the other.
3. The processes within the DFD are appropriately implemented and perform the function for which they are designed.
4. The elements appearing in the DFD cannot be impersonated.

In this way, threats related to security are not modelled (a different and complementary modelling process would be needed), but are exclusively associated with privacy and data protection.

4 Threats to Privacy and Data Protection

The DFD and the assumptions presented in the previous section have been validated in different use cases and serve as a basis for following the LIINE4DU methodology [1] and answer the second question: What can go wrong?. The objective is to identify the main privacy threats associated with BCIs and the neurodata processing they enable.

This modelling approach has been tailored to the maturity level of the use cases and their availability. Current use cases, such as monitoring fatigue in assembly line workers, hands-free gaming, measuring sleep quality or assessing attention in educational environments, have been modelled directly in a lab, allowing for the precise mapping of actual neurodata acquisition, processing, storage, and transfer using real devices like portable EEG headsets. On the other hand, prototype use cases, which often involve clinical use cases (very often involving invasive BCIs) and hypothetical BCI systems or envisioned future applications, have been desk-modelled on paper, reflecting proposed architectures and speculative data flows for broader or less-developed neurotechnology scenarios. This distinction ensures a comprehensive and anticipative threat analysis across both tangible and emergent BCI applications. Furthermore, across consumer and clinical devices and systems.

The rest of this section presents the threats elicited in each of the categories established by the selected methodology, LIINE4DU: Linking, Identifying, Inaccuracy, Non-repudiation, Exclusion, Detecting, Data breach, Deception, Data disclosure and Unawareness and Unintervenability.

4.1 Linking

This threat involves associating different data items or a data subject's actions to learn more about a data subject or group. It is the ability to determine if two or more items are related without knowing the actual identity of the data subject [1].

Even if individuals are not initially identified during neurodata collection/acquisition, they can be linkable due to the unique nature of their neurodata, their "brain fingerprint". This allows for the association of different brain signal recordings from the same data subject, given the unique pattern of a single person's brain structure, activity, and functioning. The more data is collected (in terms of volume and variety) and the more detailed it is, the easier it is to find unique patterns for linking.

The uniqueness allows individuals to be distinguished for various purposes, such as profiling. Fine-grained raw data from a BCI can link particular data items to specific individuals. Still, the riskiest scenario happens when this data is related to the context (metadata in the form of shown stimuli, precise synchronisation information, logs, etc.) because the information that can be extracted from raw brain signals alone is limited. Patterns or inferences derived from neurodata are more risky; they can be used to link data not intended to be linked, such as Internet or video game activity or participation in social events, due to the analysis of specific BCI responses.

In addition, combining different neurodata and performing inferences can create a profile considered a "brain phenotype", understood as the set of observable or measurable characteristics of an individual's brain, as reflected in their neurodata. These phenotypes can provide insights, correct or incorrect, into categories or types of traits or factors that characterise an individual. Furthermore, the same BCI response can establish a relationship between a group of people (sharing knowledge, memories or emotions, etc.)

Therefore, brain fingerprints can serve as a unique identifier for a data subject, allowing items (such as brain recordings) to be linked to this individual. In contrast, brain phenotypes or the analysis of specific BCI responses enable all data subjects with certain characteristics to be associated with a particular group.

E2, E3 and E4 may materialise this threat. In addition, any other entity could also materialise this threat if storage elements are remote and consumed as a service from an external provider, from the provider's infrastructure, or after a data breach (see the Data breach threat later in this section). The materialisation of Linking threats can magnify the impact of other threats, such as Identifying or Non-repudiation. Suppose different actions can be linked to the same data subject (by materialising Linking). In that case, the ability to match those actions to an identity or to attribute them to that subject will be strengthened.

4.2 Identifying

This threat involves learning a data subject's identity directly (through the processing of identifiable information or leaks, for example) or indirectly (through deduction or inference, for example) [1].

As mentioned, neurodata is inherently linked to an individual and can be a unique identifier. The current concept of anonymisation might not function effectively for neurodata due to its unique connection to the individual. Even if an individual is not identified during the collection/acquisition of neurodata, they can be (re)identified later because brain waves are unique to each person. This may compromise anonymity in different scenarios, for example, when accessing products or services. What is considered anonymous today might not be tomorrow due to technological development. Reidentification attacks have become increasingly sophisticated, capitalising on progress in machine learning and AI systems [18,35].

In summary, combining neurodata with other explicit data or metadata can reveal an individual's identity. This threat can be materialised by E2, E3, or E4 and by other entities accessing different storage elements in the DFD.

4.3 Inaccuracy

This threat involves using obsolete, incorrect, incomplete, biased, or low-quality data, which may lead to erroneous decisions or actions, potentially causing inconvenience or even harm to the data subject [1]. For example, due to misdiagnosis, wrong instructions or commands or poorly calibrated modulation.

Neurodata, which is not verified or tested for completeness, consistency, timeliness, validity, etc., is a source of inaccuracy in BCI applications. Neurodata is complex and mixed, containing signals from multiple processes and activities at different levels of detail. To make this information useful, decoding is required to isolate each signal and associate it with a specific function or neural activity. The reliability and accuracy of the sensors/actuators within the BCI, as well as the translation algorithms, may pose a significant threat.

One of the primary concerns is brain plasticity, which refers to the brain's ability to adapt and change over time. These changes can impact the accuracy of neurodata, making it obsolete. Brain structure changes over time, particularly in individuals between 5 and 30 years of age, who are in a period of significant brain plasticity. These age ranges overlap with those targeted by systems using neurodata for learning and gaming, for example.

Uncertainties and measurement errors associated with specific data collection methods in P0, especially those using non-invasive or innovative sensors, must be considered. Consumer-grade neurotechnology devices are prone to signal artefacts that corrupt the signal and falsify results. These devices often record more muscle artefacts than brain activation due to electrode placement over facial muscles. Furthermore, non-invasive neurotechnologies, which are applied superficially on the scalp, can only record and stimulate cortical regions, not deeper brain areas. The brain signal, which is very weak (in the range of μV), must pass through the scalp, dura mater, skin, and hair. During this passage, the electrical signals from muscles, which are much stronger, can easily overlay and disturb the delicate brain signals. The recorded data may be unreliable if these artefacts and noise are not correctly filtered before executing P1, P2 or P3.

There are also concerns about how neurodata is analysed, interpreted and used (P1, P2, P3). Data enrichment or analysis can lead to the derivation of sensitive information that may not be accurate or reliable. Even with advances in machine learning and AI, which can analyse large amounts of neurodata, decoding relies on probabilistic, statistical algorithms that are not always effective in real-world scenarios. The decoded neurodata and generated outputs might be interpreted too broadly or speculatively, leading to inaccurate conclusions about the individual. Interpretations of neurodata might lack sufficient contextual understanding, leading to misrepresentations of the data subject's mental state or intentions.

Biased data or AI models used in neurodata processing can also result in inaccurate outcomes. A system that fails to account for individual differences can lead to inaccurate results. For example, using a dataset with predominantly male subjects can result in biased outcomes for women.

There is a growing concern about the replicability of neuroscientific findings. Lab results are not always applicable (accurate enough) in real-world conditions. Brain patterns can change in response to environmental conditions or the person's mood at the time. What was accurate in one situation may not be accurate in another. In addition, the absence of ground truth data (a set of verified, authoritative labels or measurements that serve as the reference standard for computational methods) significantly impacts BCI applications' accuracy by introducing challenges in model training, validation, and bias detection.

Finally, it has to be considered that Inaccuracy threats might have irreversible impacts in neuromodulation scenarios (DF4). Because neuromodulation directly interacts with the brain's plastic and dynamic nature, incorrect or unintended writing to the brain (neurofeedback) can lead to profound and lasting changes. Individuals undergoing brain stimulation or modulation have reported personality changes, increased impulsivity, apathy, distortions of self-representation, and feelings of self-estrangement, with some even questioning their own identity and decision-making capacity [21,34,36].

E2, E3 or E4 can materialise this threat. Concerning the entity with the data controller role, Inaccuracy threats make it very difficult to comply with the necessity principle, specifically, to pass the effectiveness test. This test needs to demonstrate that the processing is essential and more effective than alternative, less intrusive options.

4.4 Non-repudiation

This threat involves the ability to attribute a claim to the data subject (something they know, are or do) when this impacts their fundamental rights and freedoms [1].

Neurotechnology, particularly when combined with AI, is becoming increasingly capable of decoding information from neurodata, including thoughts, motor intentions, mental states, feelings, semantic content, and perceptual content. This ability to interpret neural signals means that what was once purely internal and inaccessible can be translated into processable and storable data. The uniqueness and directness of the connection between neurodata and the individual it represents is highlighted as a novel characteristic. While the interpretation models might have inaccuracies, the raw data comes directly from the data subject's brain, potentially revealing information not even known to the individual or outside their conscious control, including subconscious thoughts.

It allows the translation into data form of previously unrecordable aspects of the individual, potentially giving insight into real-time brain processes related to personality, mood, behaviours, thoughts, or feelings. The threat of non-repudiation implies that the interpretation derived from this data, once recorded, can be presented as evidence of a mental state or knowledge at a specific time that the individual cannot convincingly deny. The raw data provides the source for these inferences.

In summary, the combination of decodability, the direct link to internal states (including subconscious ones), and the existence of a record based on this data leads to the loss of plausible deniability. If neurodata can reveal what a person is thinking, feeling, or perceiving, they might be unable to deny this information later. This could lead to individuals being held accountable based on these previously private, internal states. The potential for compelled testimony or use in legal settings is a related concern.

It is essential to mention the combination of this threat with the Inaccuracy one. If inaccurate inferences about an individual's thoughts, intentions, or mental states are made, these could be used to attribute actions or responsibilities to them that do not align with their actual volition. The increasing use of AI in BCI use cases introduces a principle of indeterminacy, making it difficult to determine whether a behavioural output was genuinely performed by the user or influenced by algorithmic components, with significant repercussions for legal and moral responsibility, including in criminal law. For example, imagine a situation where a person is held accountable for something that an inference says they did or thought, even if the underlying data or its interpretation were flawed.

This threat can be materialised by E2, E3 or E4 and other entities accessing different storage elements in the DFD.

4.5 Exclusion

This threat involves unintentionally or deliberately failing to adequately serve a data subject, hindering their participation or involvement in physical or digital life [1].

Data subjects should not be discriminated against based on the data collected or processed with BCI. As neurotechnology and AI become capable of decoding and interpreting neural information, this data can be used to make correlations with certain personality traits of an individual or even for highly reliable biometric identification due to the uniqueness of a person's brain activity. Discrimination based on a person's brain phenotype could arise, indicating features such as a predisposition to dementia, mental health status, personality traits, cognitive performance, intentions, or emotional states. Neurodata provides information that might not be visible, allowing discrimination based on something the individual has no control over, similar to concerns raised by genetic information. Neurotechnology should not exacerbate or amplify pre-existing inequalities or create new inequalities based on cognitive or other neurobiological features.

Using neurodata for profiling or predictive purposes in decision-making, especially in high-risk activities, poses significant risks. The potential use of neurodata to tailor experiences and to decide which content to serve or which ads to show based on granular profiles may have severe implications. However, the use of this method to predict criminal offences could directly question the right to the presumption of innocence. These applications rely on creating profiles based on neural characteristics, which opens the door to potential discrimination if these profiles lead to adverse treatment. Impacts of this threat are more significant when combined with Inaccuracy or Non-repudiation; they could contribute to discrimination if individuals are held accountable for actions or states attributed to them based on potentially biased interpretations of their neurodata, for example.

Adopting the complementary approach, fair access to BCI could be considered a right (non-discrimination). The benefits of therapy or improvements to sensory and mental capacity through neurotechnology should be equitable. Data subjects should not be discriminated against in their access to these benefits on any grounds such as sex, race, colour, ethnic or social origin, genetic features, etc.

This threat can be materialised by E2, E3, or other entities accessing different storage elements in the DFD, but mainly by E4, the entity that applies or uses the generated outputs.

4.6 Detecting

This threat involves deducing the existence of data items or a data subject's actions through observation [1]. In this case, detectability is the ability to discern whether an item of interest exists in the data subject's brain.

While fully decoding the semantic content of thoughts is currently challenging and can be considered an unrealistic capability for current consumer technology, neurotechnology can reveal statistically significant correlations between neurodata and mental states. Detectability focuses on this ability to discern the presence of something, rather than necessarily the full content, such as thoughts, memories, intentions, feelings or emotions, cognitive states and processes, specific knowledge, attitudes or reactions to stimuli (attention, philias, or phobias, for example), arousal state (being awake, focused, or relaxed), etc.

The mere knowledge of the existence of these internal states or information, even without full access to their content, can be highly sensitive. For example, detecting the presence of patterns associated with particular emotional states, cognitive performance levels, or potential predispositions to neuropsychiatric disorders is profoundly personal and can have significant consequences. Neurodata can reveal information not even known to the individual or outside their conscious control. Again, the combination of this threat with Inaccuracy needs to be considered, given that individuals face the risk of being misrepresented by their own brain data without the means to effectively challenge or deny inferences that are not truly themselves.

This threat can be materialised by E2, E3 or E4 and other entities accessing different storage elements in the DFD.

4.7 Data Breach

This threat involves the destruction, loss, alteration, and unauthorised disclosure of, or access to, personal data through mistakes, malicious insiders, or cyberattacks [1].

Neurodata processing may involve many devices, infrastructures, and services, and it can occur in various settings, including health, education, entertainment, and the workplace, thereby increasing exposure to potential data breaches and challenging the storage limitation principle. In such complex architectures, neurodata might be retained longer than necessary for the specified purpose, increasing the risk of potential misuse or breaches over time.

Massive neurodata databases created by the collection of neurodata pose a significant risk. Various factors, including cyberattacks (due to the sensitivity of the data, which makes them an attractive target), insider threats, and human error, can lead to breaches. Despite its less BCI-specific nature, the impact of materialising a Data breach threat is profoundly magnified when it involves neurodata.

Breaching raw neurodata poses significant risks. Even if it is initially uninterpreted or the interpretation capabilities are limited at the time of the breach, the raw data contains the potential for future decoding and interpretation.

Breaching processed, analysed, or interpreted neurodata, inferences drawn from it, or outputs is arguably even more immediately harmful. This threat refers to unauthorised disclosure or access to conclusions, predictions, or insights derived from raw neural signal processing. Examples include information about cognitive functions, mental health status, personality traits, intentions, emotional states, potential predispositions to disorders, and reactions to stimuli. As mentioned, this can lead to Linking, Identifying, Exclusion, and other threats. And when combined with any form of Inaccuracy, it can result in significant harm.

This threat can be materialised by any actor on any of the data flows, processes or storage elements in the DFD.

4.8 Deception

This threat involves intentionally attempting to influence, coerce or manipulate the data subject into making unintended, unwilling and potentially harmful decisions, often against their best interests [1].
Neurodata processing can reveal a person's most intimate thoughts, feelings, and preferences. Others could exploit this data to deceive an individual. Neurodata is unique to each individual and can be used to create extremely personalised profiles. This feature can be exploited to target individuals with highly effective deceptive techniques. Additionally, the complexity of BCI and related technologies makes it more challenging for individuals to comprehend the implications of neurodata processing. This lack of understanding can make them more vulnerable to deception.

This threat could be materialised, for example, through the manipulation of preferences, behaviours, or emotional responses. Neurodata processing may help identify susceptibility to certain stimuli or messages. This capability raises concerns about entities using these insights to tailor communications and potentially alter behaviour or decisions subtly and unethically. In addition, insights derived from neurodata about an individual's predispositions or state could put those with access to this data in a powerful position to manipulate people using dark, deceptive, persuasive or addictive design patterns, using targeted strategies for each individual.

BCI-based systems could predict and influence a data subject's decisions by processing neurodata. This capability challenges the concept of mental self-determination and free will, a fundamental principle underlying other freedoms. The use of neurotechnology can threaten personal identity and agency by modulating behaviours in unwanted or unconsented ways. There are concerns about implicit coercion, especially in contexts such as the workplace, where refusing to use a neural interface may lead to disadvantage.

Finally, neurofeedback systems could be designed to manipulate a person's brain activity towards desired outcomes. The opacity in technology development, particularly the lack of transparency about what is being decoded and modified, could allow systems to shape neural activity in non-transparent ways that benefit the operator/user rather than the data subject.

This threat can be materialised, mainly by E2 (the BCI manufacturer or provider) and E4 (applying or using the generated results).

4.9 Data Disclosure

This threat involves the excessive collection, storage, processing, or sharing/transferring of personal data [1]. The uncertainties and complexity around BCI and neurotechnologies make gathering more neurodata than necessary for a specific purpose, unjustified processing or uncontrolled sharing/transfer likely.

BCI can effortlessly collect large amounts of neurodata during P0, challenging compliance with the data minimisation principle. This may involve the continuous collection of data, often passively gathered during the ordinary use of

BCIs. The data subject might not be aware that the device's primary purpose is not data collection, leading to information being gathered that individuals may not realise they are sharing. Neurotechnology products record vast quantities and varieties of neurodata, and the high data density of this information can inadvertently expose detailed personal details even when collected for unrelated purposes. The difficulty in pre-emptively filtering purpose-specific data from the dynamic flow of neural signals means a large amount of redundant information can be collected. This effortless and potentially unknown collection of large volumes of highly personal data inherently increases the risk of this data being disclosed in ways unintended by the data subject, infringing the principle of fairness.

Neurodata can be generated subconsciously and often involuntarily. Due to its involuntary nature, individuals may not have direct control over the information disclosed by their neurodata, making them vulnerable to unintended disclosure. Brain data is mostly elusive to conscious control and thus cannot always be intentionally secluded. The inability of individuals to pre-emptively control what specific information is collected from the dynamic flow of brain signals exacerbates this vulnerability to unintended disclosure. For example, a medical condition to an insurance company, an emotional state to an employer, or an innovative idea to an employer.

Neurodata collected for one purpose may be used for another, unintendedly. Or there might be incentives to repurpose data or share it with third parties. Given the difficulty in filtering purpose-specific information during collection, redundant data beyond the initial purpose may be gathered and used later. The richness of neurodata and its potential for aggregation with other data sources means that data collected for one seemingly innocuous purpose could be combined or re-analysed to draw sensitive conclusions not intended by the data subject when they agreed to data collection. This potential for secondary use challenges the principle of purpose limitation, which is difficult to apply effectively to the dynamic nature of neurodata.

All these threats can be materialised by E2, E3 or E4 and other entities accessing different storage elements in the DFD.

4.10 Unawareness and Unintervenability

This threat involves insufficiently demonstrating compliance or informing, involving, or empowering data subjects in the processing of their personal data [1]. As mentioned before, due to BCI's intrinsic and involuntary nature, individuals may not realise the extent to which their data is being collected and processed.

Neurodata could be collected in P0 without the explicit and informed consent of the data subject, particularly with the increasing prevalence of direct-to-consumer neurotechnologies. This could happen through ambiguous terms of service or a lack of clear information about data collection practices.

Individuals may be unable to manage their data (including data access rights and preferences) or verify the accuracy of the information. BCI data, due to its complexity and difficulty in understanding, makes it challenging for individuals to exercise their rights, such as access or rectification. Data subjects may be unable to receive data about themselves in a commonly used machine-readable format and to exercise their right to data portability. Individuals generally lack the necessary technical means to process their raw BCI data.

Verifying the accuracy of neurodata is particularly challenging because it is dynamic and relies on complex interpretation models, meaning that data that is accurate in one context may not be accurate in another. Controllers may also hold unconscious data that the individual is unaware of. Additionally, individuals cannot object to how their data is used, and BCI-based systems do not provide the required fine-grained control.

Furthermore, data subjects may not be able to revoke consent for the processing. While individuals have the right to erasure and withdraw consent, controllers might still retain or use derivatively linked data, including unconscious data that the individual was unaware of. For neuromodulation applications (such as cognitive enhancement), simply deleting data may not address the lasting changes or consequences, suggesting a need for options to reverse or discontinue enhancements to uphold autonomy.

Finally, the black-box nature of some AI algorithms can make it difficult for data subjects and even controllers to understand how neurodata is being processed and what inferences are being made, hindering transparency and accountability.

Specially concerning are the emerging "clone" or "resurrection" technologies, creating avatars from an individual's neurodata even after death, due to the inherent inability of individuals to exercise actual control or provide ongoing consent in these use cases, especially within the second group. The individual, once deceased, is fundamentally unable to meaningfully exercise informational self-determination over how their brain activity or mental states (cognitive, affective, conative, perceptual, sensory) are used to reconstruct their digital identity. The mental states, memories, and personality traits reconstructed for the digital entity could be based on inferences and interpretations that the original person could neither understand, verify, nor contest. The prospect of preserving human memory on a storage device raises the question of whether the individual ever truly understood or consented to the complete and potentially unforeseen uses of such a comprehensive digital archive of their inner life. An individual can be reduced to an instrument in the hands of others, even after death, with their digital likeness being subject to manipulation or exploitation without their consent.

All these threats can be materialised by E2, E3 or E4 and other entities accessing different storage elements in the DFD.

5 Discussion

It is essential to remember that personal data processing in which the latter threats of the acronym LIINE4DU (certain Data Breaches, Deception, Data

Disclosure and Unawareness and Unintervenability) can be materialised directly, entails breaches of the GDPR. After carrying out the threat modelling process, we have drawn some relevant conclusions in this regard.

Vendors of consumer neurotechnology are frequently observed to make unsubstantiated or only loosely corroborated claims about their devices' capabilities, such as improving mental well-being, sleep or cognitive performance, creating a significant discrepancy between what is promised and what is scientifically demonstrated. In addition, the accuracy of consumer devices (non-invasive) is often limited compared to medical devices (invasive), usually involving a trade-off between data quality and factors such as physical appearance or price. However, despite these technical limitations and questionable efficacy, the threats to data protection and privacy associated with these devices remain significant, and in some cases, are even exacerbated by the deception and unfairness inherent in misleading marketing messages and design, as well as in predatory practices that seek to collect more data to improve technology or propose new use cases.

The lack of transparency regarding how BCIs work contributes to a black-box fallacy, making it difficult for data subjects to assess credibility and understand neurodata processing. The inadequate regulatory framework for consumer neurotechnologies, coupled with power imbalances and phenomena such as the privacy paradox, means that individuals may feel compelled to accept undesirable terms and risks to access technology, leading to potential exploitation through profiling, targeted marketing, or discrimination. The transfer of reputation from validated medical neurotechnology to less-validated consumer devices further obscures these risks.

Some BCI applications collect a tremendous amount of data for future uses, even when device reliability is questioned now. Privacy policies can be vague, unspecific, or inconsistent, failing to clearly state what data is collected, for what purpose, and with whom it is shared, leaving data subjects unaware or unable to intervene. Practices such as unnecessary data collection and processing beyond stated purposes, or retaining data longer than needed, occur. Furthermore, due to complicated processes, low vendor response rates, and deceptive design patterns, individuals face significant difficulties in exercising their data rights, such as accessing or deleting their data.

Existing legal systems, designed before the advent of consumer neurotechnology, face challenges in adequately addressing the unique nature of BCIs and their implications for privacy and data protection. While human rights principles and existing data protection laws provide a foundation to deal with the threats identified in the previous section, there is debate about the adequacy of current legislative tools. We propose different regulatory options here trying to answer the third question within the threat modelling process, What are we going to do about it?.

One approach is adapting existing general data protection laws to cover neurotechnology and neurodata processing. In this sense, mandating Data Protection Impact Assessments (DPIAs) for neurodata processing can be considered necessary. This approach would consider neurodata processing high-risk by default, aligning with risk-based approaches that are very often recommended for new technologies or processing activities. Furthermore, neurodata may be considered a special category of sensitive data within frameworks such as the GDPR (Article 9) or the Convention 108+ (Article 6).

Another policy option is creating a dedicated legal framework specifically for BCIs and neurotechnologies, potentially referred to as a "Neurotechnologies Act". A specific law could enable a risk-based classification of neurotechnologies, similar to the approach taken for AI within the European Union, with varying levels of regulatory scrutiny based on risk levels (e.g., invasive vs. non-invasive, consumer vs. medical use). This approach could include identifying unacceptable risks or red lines for specific applications.

Consumer protection laws should also be examined as relevant existing legislation. Adhering to existing technical standards for medical devices and potentially adapting them for neurotechnology suggests a role for certification and standardisation. Collaboration with standardisation bodies and private entities to develop a consumer rights-oriented approach should also be considered.

Additionally, market surveillance is a relevant policy option, particularly in the context of preventing the unchecked deployment of potentially harmful technologies. The EU AI Act serves as a model for regulating new technologies; it already classifies specific AI-related systems as high-risk and will have implications for AI systems that process neurodata. The risk evaluation approach under the AI Act, which currently focuses on technology-centred risk, could be adapted to include a human-centred risk evaluation that considers the impact of the entire ecosystem of technologies and the effects of long-term usage.

Beyond these general approaches around rights and freedoms, consumer protection, or market regulation, regulating the use of neurotechnology in particular domains, such as healthcare, work, education, entertainment, marketing, or safety, may be essential. Allowed and prohibited uses for different contexts, potentially linked to risk assessments, could be established by this kind of laws.

In addition to regulatory frameworks, responsible innovation and self-regulation by private entities are essential components of the multi-level governance of neurotechnology. Private sector actors are increasingly recognising the importance of embedding ethical considerations and human rights principles into their design, development, deployment and use of BCIs and neurodata processing. This includes adhering to professional standards, ensuring activities respect privacy and dignity, and responding transparently to feedback. Initiatives are being undertaken to develop ethical guidelines for neurotechnology, with a primary focus on high-risk applications. Recommendations include establishing standards and best practices for the technical, ethical, legal, and social aspects, promoting market entry based on sufficient evidence of safety, quality, and efficacy, and developing rigorous procedures for monitoring product safety and security.

Technical standards are indispensable for the compliant and responsible design, development, deployment and use of neurotechnologies, ensuring safety, security, and privacy throughout their lifecycle. While general standards exist, the unique characteristics of neurotechnology (differentiating between invasive and non-invasive, with the former being riskier at this point) highlight the need for specific technical considerations around BCIs and other neurotechnologies.

Finally, a critical challenge is the concept of everlasting privacy, stemming from the fact that raw neurodata collected today, even if seemingly benign, could be subject to increasingly powerful decoding algorithms in the future, potentially revealing intimate thoughts, intentions, or other mental states not currently decodable. In this sense, the importance of privacy and data protection by design and by default must be highlighted. In addition, the development and adoption of privacy-enhancing technologies (PETs) and other technical solutions should be explored to address specific privacy concerns related to the decoding of mental states. Considered strategies may include techniques such as differential privacy, federated learning, homomorphic encryption, secure multi-party computation, and tools for selective filtering of neurodata.

6 Conclusions

The rapid rise of Brain-Computer Interfaces (BCIs) and other neurotechnologies brings urgent privacy and data protection issues. BCIs enable direct brain-to-digital system communication and the direct collection of neural activity. This information is uniquely sensitive, potentially revealing thoughts, emotions, and intentions, often unconsciously. As BCIs move beyond clinical applications into healthcare, workplace, education, entertainment, marketing or safety, their use will expand. This will grow neurodata processing, posing risks not addressed by current regulations or technical safeguards.

This paper presents a systematic privacy threat model for BCIs and neurodata processing. The model has been developed using the LIINE4DU methodology. It helps identify privacy threats across the BCI lifecycle, from acquisition to deletion. Systematic analysis reveals the challenges of applying traditional data protection concepts to current and future use cases. Concepts such as anonymity, accuracy or control are hard to apply to the complex and dynamic nature of neurodata processing.

Addressing threats from the model requires a multi-faceted approach. Efforts should focus on evolving regulatory landscapes and ongoing research into organisational and technical measures. Existing frameworks provide a starting point but struggle with the uniqueness of neurodata processing. The legal frameworks need to be updated. This may involve changing data protection, consumer, or market laws. Alternatively, dedicated neurotechnology legislation may be needed. Simultaneously, identified threats should guide the proposal of specific, actionable organisational and technical measures. These measures should rely on core principles such as data protection by design and by default. Ongoing research is essential to guide these legal and technical developments and help create strong, evidence-based safeguards.

Future research should expand the threat model at both ends. On one hand, it should address Brain-to-Brain (BtB) interfaces. These new and sophisticated neurotechnologies enable direct brain-to-brain communication and support bidirectional information flow. On the other hand, research should consider biosensor technologies that do not directly interface with the brain. Examples include eye-tracking, voice analysis, or skin conductance. Such biosensors can still infer sensitive mental data, revealing thoughts, emotions or intentions and further broadening the landscape of neurodata processing.

Acknowledgments. This study was funded by the Agencia Española de Protección de Datos (AEPD), the Spanish Data Protection Authority. The authors want to thank the entire AEPD team and specifically the staff of the Innovation and Technology Division for their involvement in this project and all their generous comments and contributions.

Disclosure of Interests. The authors declare that they have no known competing financial interests or personal relationships that could have appeared to influence the work reported in this paper.

References

1. AEPD: An introduction to LIINE4DU 1.0: A new privacy & data protection threat modelling framework. https://www.aepd.es/guides/technical-note-introduction-to-liine4du-1-0.pdf (2024)
2. Agarwal, A., et al.: Protecting privacy of users in brain-computer interface applications. IEEE Trans. Neural Syst. Rehabil. Eng. **27**, 1546–1555 (2019). https://doi.org/10.1109/TNSRE.2019.2926965
3. Beltrán, M., de Salvador, L.: Implications of age assurance on privacy and data protection: a systematic threat model. In: Privacy Technologies and Policy - Proceedings of the 12th Annual Privacy Forum. Lecture Notes in Computer Science, vol. 14831, pp. 1–22. Springer (2024). https://doi.org/10.1007/978-3-031-68024-3_1
4. Bernal, S.L., Celdrán, A.H., Pérez, G., Barros, M.T., Balasubramaniam, S.: Security in brain-computer interfaces. ACM Comput. Surv. **54**, 1 – 35 (2019). https://doi.org/10.1145/3427376
5. Brown, C.M.L.: Neurorights, mental privacy, and mind reading. Neuroethics **17**(2), 34 (2024). https://doi.org/10.1007/s12152-024-09568-z
6. Collins, B., Klein, E.: Invasive neurotechnology: a study of the concept of invasiveness in neuroethics. Neuroethics **16**(1), 11 (2023). https://doi.org/10.1007/s12152-023-09518-1
7. Debie, E.S., Moustafa, N., Whitty, M.: A privacy-preserving generative adversarial network method for securing EEG brain signals. In: Proceedings of the International Joint Conference on Neural Networks, pp. 1–8 (2020). https://doi.org/10.1109/IJCNN48605.2020.9206683
8. Edelman, B.J., et al.: Non-invasive brain-computer interfaces: state of the art and trends. IEEE Rev. Biomed. Eng. (2024). https://doi.org/10.1109/RBME.2024.3449790
9. EDPS and AEPD: Techdispatch 1/2024 - Neurodata. https://www.edps.europa.eu/data-protection/our-work/publications/techdispatch/2024-06-03-techdispatch-12024-neurodata_en (2024)

10. Floreani, E.D., Chau, T.: Towards privacy preserving BCIs: profiling the feasibility of federated learning for motor imagery brain-computer interfaces. In: Proceedings of the IEEE International Conference on Systems, Man, and Cybernetics, pp. 3067–3072 (2023). https://doi.org/10.1109/SMC53992.2023.10394136
11. Gilbert, F., Russo, I.: Mind-reading in AI and neurotechnology: evaluating claims, hype, and ethical implications for neurorights. AI Ethics **4**(3), 855–872 (2024). https://doi.org/10.1007/s43681-024-00514-6
12. Goering, S., Brown, T., Klein, E.: Neurotechnology ethics and relational agency. Philos Compass **16**(4), e12734 (2021). https://doi.org/10.1111/phc3.12734
13. Hallinan, D., Schütz, P., Friedewald, M., De Hert, P.: Neurodata and neuroprivacy: data protection outdated? Surveill. Soc. **12**(1), 55–72 (2014). https://doi.org/10.24908/ss.v12i1.4500
14. Huang, S., et al.: US public perceptions of the sensitivity of brain data. J. Law Biosci. **11**(1), lsad032 (2024). https://doi.org/10.1093/jlb/lsad032
15. Ienca, M.: On neurorights. Front. Hum. Neurosci. **15**, 701258 (2021). https://doi.org/10.3389/fnhum.2021.701258
16. Ienca, M.: Common Human Rights challenges raised by different applications of neurotechnologies in the bio (report commissiones by the Committee on Bioethics of the Council of Europe. https://rm.coe.int/report-final-en/1680a429f3 (2024)
17. Jiang, X., Zhang, X., Wu, D.: Active learning for black-box adversarial attacks in EEG-based brain-computer interfaces. In: Proceedings of the IEEE Symposium Series on Computational Intelligence, pp. 361–368 (2019)
18. Jwa, A.S., Poldrack, R.A.: The spectrum of data sharing policies in neuroimaging data repositories. Hum. Brain Mapp. **43**(8), 2707–2721 (2022). https://doi.org/10.1002/hbm.25803
19. Kablo, E., Arias-Cabarcos, P.: Privacy in the age of neurotechnology: investigating public attitudes towards brain data collection and use. In: Proceedings of the 2023 ACM SIGSAC Conference on Computer and Communications Security, pp. 225–238 (2023)
20. Kapitonova, M., Kellmeyer, P., Vogt, S., Ball, T.: A framework for preserving privacy and cybersecurity in brain-computer interfacing applications. ArXiv (2022). https://doi.org/10.48550/arXiv.2209.09653
21. Klaming, L., Haselager, P.: Did my brain implant make me do it? Questions raised by DBS regarding psychological continuity, responsibility for action and mental competence. Neuroethics **6**(3), 527–539 (2010). https://doi.org/10.1007/s12152-010-9093-1
22. Landau, O., Cohen, A., Gordon, S., Nissim, N.: Mind your privacy: privacy leakage through BCI applications using machine learning methods. Knowl. Based Syst. **198**, 105932 (2020). https://doi.org/10.1016/j.knosys.2020.105932
23. Landau, O., Puzis, R., Nissim, N.: Mind your mind. ACM Comput. Surv. **53**, 1–38 (2020). https://doi.org/10.1145/3372043
24. Li, H., et al.: Privacy computing using deep compression learning techniques for neural decoding. Smart Health (2021). https://doi.org/10.1016/j.smhl.2021.100229
25. Liao, K., et al.: Exploring the intersection of brain-computer interfaces and quantum sensing: a review of research progress and future trends. Adv. Quantum Technol. **7**(1), 2300185 (2024). https://doi.org/10.1002/qute.202300185
26. Marazziti, D., et al.: Neuroenhancement: state of the art and future perspectives. Clin. Neuropsychiatry **18**(3), 137 (2021). https://doi.org/10.36131/cnfioritieditore20210303

27. Martinovic, I., Davies, D., Frank, M., Perito, D., Ros, T., Song, D.: On the feasibility of side-channel attacks with brain-computer interfaces. In: Proceedings of the 21st USENIX Security Symposium, pp. 143–158 (2012)
28. Meng, L., et al.: EEG-based brain-computer interfaces are vulnerable to backdoor attacks. IEEE Trans. Neural Syst. Rehabil. Eng. **31**, 2224–2234 (2023). https://doi.org/10.1109/TNSRE.2023.3273214
29. Meng, L., Jiang, X., Jia, T., Wu, D.: Protecting multiple types of privacy simultaneously in EEG-based brain-computer interfaces. In: Proceedings of the IEEE International Conference on Systems, Man, and Cybernetics, pp. 2894–2899 (2024). https://doi.org/10.1109/SMC54092.2024.10832088
30. Moore, A.D.: Privacy, neuroscience, and neuro-surveillance. Res. Publica. **23**(2), 159–177 (2017). https://doi.org/10.1007/s11158-016-9341-2
31. Mridha, M., Das, S., Kabir, M.M., Lima, A.A., Islam, M.R., Watanobe, Y.: Brain-computer interface: advancement and challenges. Sensors **21** (2021). https://doi.org/10.3390/s21175746
32. Nam, C.S., Traylor, Z., Chen, M., Jiang, X., Feng, W., Chhatbar, P.Y.: Direct communication between brains: a systematic Prisma review of brain-to-brain interface. Front. Neurorobot. **15**, 656943 (2021). https://doi.org/10.3389/fnbot.2021.656943
33. Naufel, S.N., Klein, E.: Brain–computer interface (BCI) researcher perspectives on neural data ownership and privacy. J. Neural Eng. **17** (2019). https://doi.org/10.1088/1741-2552/ab5b7f
34. Pham, U., et al.: Personality changes after deep brain stimulation in Parkinson's disease. Parkinson's Dis. **2015**(1), 490507 (2015). https://doi.org/10.1155/2015/490507
35. Ravindra, V., Grama, A.: De-anonymization attacks on neuroimaging datasets. In: Proceedings of the International Conference on Management of Data, pp. 2394–2398 (2021)
36. Sarica, C., et al.: Human studies of transcranial ultrasound neuromodulation: a systematic review of effectiveness and safety. Brain Stimul. **15**(3), 737–746 (2022). https://doi.org/10.1016/j.brs.2022.05.002
37. Vakilipour, P., Fekrvand, S.: Brain-to-brain interface technology: a brief history, current state, and future goals. Int. J. Dev. Neurosci. **84**(5), 351–367 (2024). https://doi.org/10.1002/jdn.10334
38. Wu, D.: Accurate, secure and privacy-preserving brain-computer interfaces: keynote address. In: Proceedings of the IEEE/ACIS 23rd International Conference on Computer and Information Science, pp. 1–1 (2023). https://doi.org/10.1109/ICIS57766.2023.10210238
39. Wuyts, K., Joosen, W.: LINDDUN privacy threat modeling: a tutorial. CW Reports (2015)
40. Xia, K., Deng, L., Duch, W., Wu, D.: Privacy-preserving domain adaptation for motor imagery-based brain-computer interfaces. IEEE Trans. Biomed. Eng. **69**, 3365–3376 (2022). https://doi.org/10.1109/TBME.2022.3168570
41. Xia, K., et al.: Privacy-preserving brain–computer interfaces: a systematic review. IEEE Trans. Comput. Soc. Syst. **10**, 2312–2324 (2023). https://doi.org/10.1109/TCSS.2022.3184818
42. Xiong, W., Lagerström, R.: Threat modeling-a systematic literature review. Comput. Secur. **84**, 53–69 (2019). https://doi.org/10.1016/j.cose.2019.03.010
43. Yilmaz, S.S., Seval, H.D.: Mind over matter: examining the implications of machine brain interfaces on privacy and data protection under the GDPR. Eur. J. Priv. Law Technolo. (2022). https://doi.org/10.57230/ejplt222ssyhds

44. Yue, C.: Privacy and ethical concerns of brain-computer interfaces. In: Proceedings of the IEEE International Conference on Metaverse Computing, Networking and Applications, pp. 134–138 (2023). https://doi.org/10.1109/MetaCom57706.2023.00036
45. Yuste, R., Genser, J., Herrmann, S.: It's time for neuro-rights. Horizons **18**, 154–164 (2021)
46. Zhang, T.K.: Perspective and boundary exploration of privacy transfer dilemma in brain–computer interface-dimension based on ethical matrix. Philosophies (2024). https://doi.org/10.3390/philosophies9010010

Open Access This chapter is licensed under the terms of the Creative Commons Attribution-NonCommercial-NoDerivatives 4.0 International License (http://creativecommons.org/licenses/by-nc-nd/4.0/), which permits any noncommercial use, sharing, distribution and reproduction in any medium or format, as long as you give appropriate credit to the original author(s) and the source, provide a link to the Creative Commons license and indicate if you modified the licensed material. You do not have permission under this license to share adapted material derived from this chapter or parts of it.

The images or other third party material in this chapter are included in the chapter's Creative Commons license, unless indicated otherwise in a credit line to the material. If material is not included in the chapter's Creative Commons license and your intended use is not permitted by statutory regulation or exceeds the permitted use, you will need to obtain permission directly from the copyright holder.

Anonymity-Washing

Szilvia Lestyán[1,2(✉)], William Letrone[3], Ludovica Robustelli[3], and Gergely Biczók[4]

[1] Inria, Saclay, France
szilvia.lestyan@inria.fr
[2] Institut national d'études démographiques, Aubervilliers, France
[3] DCS, Nantes University, CNRS, Nantes, France
{william.letrone,ludovica.robustelli}@univ-nantes.fr
[4] CrySyS Lab, Budapest University of Technology and Economics, Budapest, Hungary
biczok@crysys.hu

Abstract. Anonymization is a foundational principle of data privacy regulation, yet its practical application remains riddled with ambiguity and inconsistency. This paper introduces the concept of anonymity-washing—the misrepresentation of the anonymity level of "sanitized" personal data—as a critical privacy concern. While both legal and technical critiques of anonymization exist, they tend to address isolated aspects of the problem. In contrast, this paper offers a comprehensive overview of the conditions that enable anonymity-washing. It synthesizes fragmented legal interpretations, technical misunderstandings, and outdated regulatory guidance and complements them with a systematic review of national and international resources, including legal cases, data protection authority guidelines, and technical documentation. Our findings reveal a lack of coherent support for practitioners, contributing to the persistent misuse of pseudonymization and obsolete anonymization techniques. We conclude by recommending targeted education, clearer technical guidance, and closer cooperation between regulators, researchers, and industry to bridge the gap between legal norms and technical reality.

1 Introduction

Anonymization is widely regarded as a crucial tool for protecting privacy in an era of big data processing. Theoretically, it serves as a means to mitigate risks associated with the misuse of personal data by ensuring that individuals can no longer be identified. In practice, however, anonymization remains an imprecise science, often misunderstood and misapplied. Many datasets that are presented as anonymized continue to pose significant re-identification risks due to improper techniques or evolving technological capabilities. This gap between the intended function of anonymization and its real-world implementation has led to growing concerns about *anonymity-washing* – a phenomenon in which organizations claim to have achieved strong privacy protections through anonymization while failing

© The Author(s) 2026
N. Arastouei et al. (Eds.): APF 2025, LNCS 16183, pp. 102–126, 2026.
https://doi.org/10.1007/978-3-032-07574-1_5

to provide meaningful safeguards. Note that anonymity-washing is a specialized form of *privacy-washing*[1] [21].

The General Data Protection Regulation (GDPR) establishes anonymization as a mechanism through which personal data can be rendered outside the scope of data protection laws. Recital 26 of the GDPR defines anonymization as the process by which data is *"rendered anonymous in such a manner that the data subject is not or no longer identifiable."* However, the absence of clear, practical guidance on how to achieve this standard has resulted in inconsistent implementations and legal uncertainties. Many organizations either overestimate the effectiveness of their anonymization processes or struggle to comply due to conflicting regulatory interpretations. Additionally, courts have recognized that anonymization is never absolute – what is considered anonymous[2] today may become identifiable tomorrow as technology advances. Despite the importance of anonymization, the regulatory and educational landscape remains fragmented and inadequate. On one end of the spectrum, legal guidelines provide high-level definitions and compliance requirements but lack technical specificity. On the other end, academic research offers rigorous, mathematically grounded approaches to anonymization that are often inaccessible to practitioners who do not have advanced expertise in statistics or computer science. This disconnect has left engineers, data scientists, and policymakers without the necessary tools to implement anonymization effectively. The result is widespread reliance on outdated or insufficient methods—such as k-anonymity and l-diversity—that have been repeatedly shown to fail against modern re-identification attacks [56].

Furthermore, anonymity-washing is exacerbated by inconsistent regulatory interpretations across jurisdictions. The European Union has exercised significant global influence on data privacy regulation, with many countries modelling their laws after the GDPR. However, even within the EU, national data protection authorities and courts have issued conflicting opinions on what constitutes effective anonymization, leading to uncertainty among organizations attempting to comply. Beyond Europe, frameworks such as the United States' de-identification standards under the Health Insurance Portability and Accountability Act (HIPAA) and the California Consumer Privacy Act (CCPA), Japan's Act on the Protection of Personal Information (APPI), and emerging guidelines such as the Brazilian General Data Protection Law, the *Lei Geral de Proteçao de Dados* (LGPD), further demonstrate that approaches to anonymization lack uniformity at the international level, making cross-border data governance exceedingly complex.

Another critical factor enabling anonymity-washing is the lack of accessible educational resources for practitioners. Engineers and software developers responsible for implementing anonymization frequently lack adequate training and rely on either high-level legal guidelines or complex, research-oriented papers

---

[1] a particularly timely research theme, see https://www.dagstuhl.de/en/seminars/seminar-calendar/seminar-details/25112.

[2] In this paper we use the word *anonymous* whenever we cite or reference a text that has used the same expression.

that do not offer practical guidance. Several regulatory bodies and experts have called for clearer standards, including the European Data Protection Board (EDPB), national data protection authorities (such as the National Commission for Information Technology and Civil Liberties in France (CNIL) and the Federal Commissioner for Data Protection and Freedom of Information (BfDI) in Germany), and research institutions. Yet, despite these calls for action, practitioners continue to report difficulties in accessing concrete, actionable information on how to apply anonymization techniques effectively.

In light of these challenges, this paper argues that ambiguities in regulatory guidance, outdated technical approaches, and gaps in practitioner education may lead to anonymity-washing. While prior works have addressed specific aspects of the problem—such as legal critiques of anonymization under data protection law [18,79,84,89], technical limitations of anonymization techniques [1,25,27,36,56,68], or even highlighting key misunderstandings [35]— these contributions offer only a partial view of the broader landscape. In contrast, our work provides a comprehensive analysis of the multiple, interrelated issues underlying anonymity-washing. We expand on the existing literature by integrating a wide range of sources, including legal cases, regulatory interpretations, and technical guidelines, while offering a systematic critique of technical documentation. Furthermore, we provide an international perspective that, to our knowledge, has not been previously compiled in a single work.

First, in Sect. 2 we introduce the concept of anonymity-washing and situate it within the broader landscape of privacy discourse. In Sect. 3, we examine the legal foundations and the regulatory ambiguity surrounding anonymization. Next, Sect. 4 presents an overview and critique of technical guidelines and educational resources, highlighting the gaps practitioners face. Section 5 explores the practical implications of anonymity-washing, including legal cases and implementation failures. Finally, Sect. 6 offers recommendations and concluding reflections on how to address the risks of anonymity-washing through clearer guidance and improved institutional coordination.

2 Contextual Elements

2.1 Anonymization Terminology

The anonymization landscape is complex, with multiple laws advocating for different requirements. But many points of contention stem from the terminology surrounding the topic of anonymization. To begin, it is interesting to look at the terminology developed by the International Organization for Standardization (ISO), as it constitutes the main standard-setting body with international influence. Several ISO standards touch on the topic of data anonymization. These global standards have recognized the importance of anonymization in various contexts. ISO/IEC 29100:2024(en) establishing a common privacy terminology, defines anonymization as a

> "[A] process by which personally identifiable information (...) is irreversibly altered in such a way that a [**data subject**] (...) can no longer

be identified directly or indirectly, either by the PII controller alone or in collaboration with any other party."

The same document defines pseudonymization as a

"[A] process applied to personally identifiable information (PII) (3.7) which replaces identifying information with an alias."

The other term, "de-identification", is usually considered more neutral and broader than anonymization, although sometimes conflated with the latter [20, 57]. Indeed, according to ISO, "de-identification" refers to

"[A] process of removing the association between a set of identifying attributes (3.14) and the data subject (3.4)."[3].

It results that anonymization implies the highest degree of privacy, while the more specific process of pseudonymization is a step below anonymization in terms of re-identifiability. In contrast "de-identification" is the general term describing the process through which data is made confidential[4]. While some jurisdictions mostly follow the ISO terminology, others, unfortunately, do not [2,91]. An example is the fact that the term "de-identification" is not even used within the EU's GDPR, while several important US instruments, such as the HIPAA [93] and the CCPA [19] use it in place of anonymization. In the same vein, Nigeria and Malawi's Data Protection Acts do not use the term "anonymization", despite referring to both "de-identification" and "pseudonymization" in their statutes [2]. In contrast, Japan's *Act on the Protection of Personal Information*, much like the EU, does not refer to de-identification. Finally, a cursory look at the relevant literature in social science reveals that authors themselves appear to have subscribed to different terminologies [20, 56].

Beyond word choice, there seems to be no equivalence between the terms when they are used to refer to data records that have undergone the appropriate treatment to exempt data controllers and processors from their obligations under data protection laws. That is to say, the tolerance level towards identifiability tends to vary across jurisdictions [2]. Discrepancies sometimes exist within a single legal system, as in the US, where re-identifiability tolerance may vary depending on the nature of the data contained in a record, and the projected use of the record [57]. In the EU, the situation is no less confusing, as "anonymization" suffers from conflicting interpretations [36] (see details in Sect. 3).

Take-away

These variations and inconsistencies make it difficult for practitioners to understand and determine the required level of protection, hindering the understanding and adequate application of anonymization techniques.

---

[3] ISO/IEC 20889:2018(en) Privacy enhancing data de-identification terminology and classification of techniques. See also, the more recent ISO/IEC 5207:2024(en) Information technology – Data usage – Terminology and use cases.

[4] Note that the technical terminology could be used slightly differently; here we are discussing only the legal definitions.

2.2 "Anonymity-Washing" as the Misrepresentation of Actual Confidentiality Levels

Due to interpretative instability, the terms that compose the anonymization terminology should not necessarily be taken at face value. Not only are practitioners affected by the confusion in the terminology, but individuals are affected as well, as they may put more trust in information processes than they should. In order to better understand this effect, we must look at interpretations of *privacy-washing*. In the course of an analysis on questionable data practices of tech industry giants, Girucci gives the following definition [21]:

"The purposeful conflation of security with privacy, the disregarding of more granular definitions of privacy (social vs. institutional privacy as well as data types including explicit, implicit, aggregated, and inferred), and a general reliance on offline privacy expectations that are no longer applicable to online spaces.".

Despite its provocative tone, the term privacy-washing is more than a mere rhetorical device. Indeed, privacy-washing can accurately describe situations where data privacy guarantees deviate from the standards to which the concerned entities purportedly committed. Evidently, the concept of privacy-washing is broad: it can cover a variety of subjects like cybersecurity and third-party data sharing. This paper is focused on privacy-washing in the anonymization context because deceptive privacy representations in this context are highly likely. In fact, while the anonymization vocabulary taken at face value is unambiguous, it does little to convey the actual fragility [79] of current anonymization methods:

"The way companies and the media talk about de-identified data matters, and data holders regularly play fast and loose with the concept of anonymity. The terms "anonymous" and "anonymization" simply overpromise. They create expectations of near-perfection and lull people into a false sense of security" [84].

Data controllers could be tempted to exploit the complexity within current data privacy terminology to mislead data subjects regarding the safety and confidentiality of their data, resulting in anonymity-washing. In essence, anonymity-washing refers to situations involving the misrepresentation of anonymity levels of a data record. Recently, the Federal Trade Commission (FTC), as the main agency dealing with consumer protection in the US, dealt with anonymity-washing cases. In a recent communication, the FTC warned that unwarranted claims of anonymity could constitute deceptive consumer practices, reiterating that pseudonymous identifiers in the form of hashing do not constitute anonymization, as some businesses have claimed:

"Companies should not act or claim as if hashing personal information renders it anonymized. FTC staff will remain vigilant to ensure companies are following the law and take action when the privacy claims they make are deceptive"[55].

Remark, how this highlights the manipulative aspect of anonymity-washing.[5] In the EU, potential anonymity-washing cases have been scrutinized by data protection authorities, and some practices have been challenged in Court. For instance, the Italian Data Protection Authority (Garante) recently sanctioned the Italian National Institute of Statistics for its failure to deploy the necessary measures to avoid re-identification of the data it used for statistical analysis. In its order, the Italian authority explained [58];

"Simply having organizational measures or ethical codes is not enough to satisfy data protection principles."

In this case, data controllers claimed to have upheld data protection principles while the data subjects remained, in fact, easily re-identifiable from their data records.

The question of intentionality behind deceitful anonymity statements deserves a brief focus, as the term "washing" implies an intentional action, motivated by a paucity of resources, time constraints, or uncertain goals regarding projected uses of data records. Except that intention in this context can be difficult to prove. Sometimes, anonymity-washing cases are so blatant that the willingness to deceive leaves no doubt. Other times, anonymity-washing is harder to prove and therefore appears incidental, giving the impression that data controllers and/or processors are acting in good faith while deploying weaker solutions. There is, of course, a risk of mischaracterization. Still, it may never be possible to prove with a high degree of confidence that a data controller and/or processor acted in good faith, since defendants are likely to claim to be acting in good faith when notified, and in the course of legal proceedings.

> **Take-away**
>
> Anonymity-washing is a subset of privacy-washing, which refers to the misrepresentation of the anonymity level of data. The phenomenon is exacerbated by several factors, including unclear terminology.

3 Overview of Regulatory Guidance on Data Anonymization

On 25 July 2024, the European Commission published its second report on the implementation of the GDPR [45]. One of the key issues highlighted in the report is the persistence of differing interpretations among national data protection authorities, which undermines the uniform application of the GDPR. This discrepancy gives rise to legal uncertainty; thus, businesses are confronted

---

[5] It bears noting that the FTC's view on hashing is consistent with the practices in the EU, where hashing constitutes a method of pseudonymization that does not suffice on its own, in making data records fall outside the GDPR's scope, due to the likelihood of privacy harms that may result from sharing the records.

with divergent administrative requirements across different Member States. In this regard, the Commission seeks to reiterate its request, previously made in 2020 [41], to support practitioners by providing clearer guidance and materials to facilitate GDPR compliance. This issue is particularly pertinent in the context of anonymity washing, as the Commission has reported in [42]:

> "Some stakeholders also consider that certain data protection authorities and the Board adopt interpretations that deviate from the risk-based approach of the GDPR, [and] (...) mention as areas of concern: (i) the interpretation of anonymization; (...)". [As a result, the report] "underline[s] the need for additional guidelines, in particular on anonymization and pseudonymization (...)".

3.1 EU Regulations

The abrogation of Directive 95/46/EC [39] (Data Protection Directive or DPD) and the adoption of the GDPR did not affect anonymization. This is confirmed by the endorsement of the Working Party 29's (WP29) Opinion 5/2014 on anonymization by the European Data Protection Board (EDPB), which is still in the process of preparing an updated version [87]. In its Opinion 5/2014 on anonymization [5], WP29 recalls the ISO definition of anonymization[6] and that the simple removal of identifiers from personal data does not make the anonymization process irreversible. Account should be taken of all"reasonable means"(including computational power and technological evolution) to re-identify anonymous data. These points are addressed by Recital 26 of the GDPR, stating that :

> "Account should be taken of all the means reasonably likely to be used, such as singling out, either by the controller or by another person, to identify the natural person directly or indirectly. To ascertain whether means are reasonably likely to be used to identify the natural person, account should be taken of all objective factors, such as the costs of and the amount of time required for identification, taking into consideration the available technology at the time of the processing and technological developments."[7]

Before deciding on an anonymization method, an anonymization test must be performed to evaluate the risks (singling-out, linkability, and inference). WP29 provides an assessment of the guarantees and shortcomings of each technique from the two main families of anonymization (generalization and randomization) based on these risks. However, several research papers have shown that the

---

[6] ISO 29100:2024.
[7] The previous directive 95/46/EC, which the WP29 Opinion 5/2014 referred to, was not as detailed. It contained a general reference to reasonable means that are likely to be used to re-identify the data (without including the notion of 'singling out') and relied on codes of conduct to encourage anonymization practices.

analyses provided by WP29 have weak points, and they do not consider these techniques valid [25,31,73,74,82,86][8].

More recent guidelines have been adopted by the EDPB on issues related to data anonymization, but they do not contain additional advice. On 17 December 2024, the EDPB published guidelines on the anonymization of AI models [43]. It states that whenever models are trained on personal data, they cannot be considered anonymous. The reason is that many studies on these models have demonstrated their capacity to "regurgitate" part of their training datasets [8]. The EDPB stated that a model is considered anonymous only when, based on appropriate documentation, personal data cannot be inferred either directly (by statistical inference, including the probabilistic functioning of the model) or indirectly (within a user's prompt). If the risk of "regurgitation" of personal data persists, a deeper analysis is needed[9].

Sénéchal criticizes the lack of a threshold of the risk of "regurgitating" personal data and the lack of a distinction between the different AI models in these guidelines in [92] (for example, the general-purpose AI models [46] and the ones posing systemic risks. This is problematic since anonymization is difficult to implement, especially with unstructured data [94], which are essentially used to train general-purpose AI models [95]. Additionally, the question of whether the data can be separated from the model remains unanswered. It is also not known whether the anonymization of the model implies that of the data it contains.

The EDPB also adopted on 16 January 2025, guidelines on pseudonymization [44], in which it recalls the GDPR definition set out in article 4(5). The Board stressed that, although pseudonymization secures data, whenever the reattribution of data to a natural person (by linking pseudonyms to additional data) remains possible, the GDPR applies. It recalls that even if the original data are deleted, pseudonymized data become anonymous only if all requirements are met. It is interesting to note that the *guidelines do not provide further information on anonymization requirements*. This is regrettable for two reasons: first, updated guidelines on anonymization have yet to be issued; and second, as the Spanish Data Protection Authority has pointed out, confusion between anonymization and pseudonymization remains a common misunderstanding among data controllers [35].

---

[8] For example, the k-anonymity technique does not prevent the risk of singling out, contrary to the conclusions of WP29.
[9] The following aspects are required for verification: the source of the data, their preparation and minimization, the training method, the analysis of the model, the resistance of the model to cyber attacks, and the documentation provided.

> **Take-away**
>
> Guidelines on anonymization need to be updated (as they have not been since 2014). The information provided by the EDPB on pseudonymization and anonymization of AI models does not resolve the contradictions of its previous guidelines and the practical difficulties controllers are confronted with when implementing anonymization protocols in real life.

3.2 Anonymization Regimes Beyond the EU

The uncertainties resulting from the changing interpretation within the EU undermine the so-called "Brussels effect", when non-EU states take inspiration from the EU's laws for building their own legal regime. Data flows often involve entities located in different jurisdictions, including non-EU countries [69, 72]. Moreover, data protection laws usually have some extraterritorial effects, which means that multiple regimes are sometimes applicable simultaneously. Hence, it is vital to ensure that legal regimes on anonymization do not contradict each other. Yet, a survey conducted by the OECD in 2019 found that

"uncertainty regarding legal privacy regimes" and *"incompatibility of legal regimes"* topped the list of the main challenges to cross-border data flows [78].

Anonymization guidelines are present in data protection regimes across the globe. There are differences, however, in the approaches and the overall granularity levels exhibited by the relevant frameworks. Notably, some data protection regimes, such as in Japan [66] and the US [93], come with relatively detailed guidance on how to achieve the expected levels of anonymization and how to handle the data [7, 81]. Concerning data transfer between the EU and the USA, the previous Privacy Shield, which was adopted on the basis of the European Commission's decision that the USA's level of personal data protection was equivalent to that of the EU, [38], was replaced by a revised Privacy Framework, after the EU Court of Justice overturned it [49] In contrast, other regulatory frameworks, such as in Brazil [16], are not particularly prescriptive and require additional input. At the same time, several jurisdictions have initiated efforts to modernize their approaches to data protection, including anonymization. For example, Brazil's national data protection authority, the ANDP, is set to clarify what measures could be implemented to ensure anonymity in accordance with its LGPD in the upcoming years [4]. A call for public participation in that effect has been published in early 2024. In 2023, the Data Security Council of India (DSCI) published a roadmap considering possible orientations for a national data anonymization regime [29]. At the intra-state level, in Québec, the *Regulation respecting the anonymization of personal information* was published in 2024 [83]. The text is very prescriptive and seeks to clarify the distinction between anonymity and pseudonymity, aligning with the EU's view. In the EU, the EDPB is expected to publish new guidelines on anonymization later this year. It is expected that the new guidelines will fix the inconsistencies introduced by the WP29 Opinion 5/2014 on anonymization, thereby clarifying the dominant approach at the EU level [36].

Anonymization is still a maturing field. Valuable guidelines on anonymization are often released after the publication of the main body of law. Hence, recent data protection laws such as China's *Personal Information Protection Law*, or India's *Digital Personal Data Protection Act*, will need to be complemented with guidelines on anonymization [72,88]. Furthermore, while precise anonymization parameters are still not consistent across jurisdictions, the basic premises of anonymization law remain the same; anonymization levels may vary, and so are the obligations placed upon data handlers [72].

Whatever the approach, it seems that regulators are left with two choices: either leaving enough leeway for data handlers to determine for themselves which methods and policies would meet their expectations, or prescribing exactly which technical and organizational measures would meet their expectations. Both approaches have their merits and shortcomings. On the one hand, there is an inherent limitation on the degree of granularity that can be achieved in the law. Excessively precise regulations and guidelines may pose problems at the implementation stage and may prove to be overly restrictive, as has already been seen with the WP 29 Opinion 5/2014. The limited technical knowledge of regulators may constrain the formulation of highly detailed guidelines anyway. On the other hand, too much leeway could seriously undermine the purpose of data protection laws by increasing the likelihood that poorly anonymized data records will fall outside their scope.

> **Take-away**
>
> Anonymization laws seem to have been evolving independently, with differing requirements and definitions. Whether all the ambiguities will be fixed and whether every actor will converge around the same interpretation remains to be seen.

4 Overview and Critique of Guidelines

4.1 Contradictory Guidelines and Uncertain Standards Within the EU

Some authors consider that the EU Data Protection Law lacks a clear definition of anonymization [18]. Unlike pseudonymization, the GDPR fails to define anonymization in its Article 4 titled "definitions". The reason is that anonymization and pseudonymization are considered in a binary way[10]. Indeed, anonymized

---

[10] https://techcrunch.com/2017/10/07/how-anonymous-wifi-data-can-still-be-a-privacy-risk/.

data is excluded from the scope of the GDPR, while pseudonymized data is entirely subject to it. This is unlike some legislation (such as in Japan), which suggests a lighter regime for pseudonymized data while still imposing obligations on anonymized data. The EU approach fails to acknowledge that there is always a risk of re-identification with anonymisation, and that pseudonymized data may require lighter protection than 'classic' personal data. This is despite WP 29 acknowledging this risk. On this point, another Opinion of WP29 on the concept of personal data issued in 2007 [6] clarified the difference between anonymization and pseudonymization. Recalling ISO's previous definitions, they explained that anonymization protects privacy, while pseudonymization represents a technical, reversible process. Nevertheless, data can still be considered anonymous, even when re-identification remains possible, but complementary measures to prevent re-identification are implemented. This flexible approach was not supported in the Opinion 5/2014 on anonymization [5], which applies together with the previous Opinion on the concept of personal data. In Opinion 5/2014, WP29 required the aggregation of data (into group statistics) and the destruction of raw data (identifiers) to ensure correct anonymization. Nevertheless, the objective still remained to prove that the likelihood of re-identification was negligible. On this point, the Commission's guidelines [40] on the free flow of non-personal data suggest that it is often difficult to assess the effectiveness of an anonymization procedure. Indeed, besides many academic papers [1,3,30,31,56,74], even a study commissioned by the European Parliament's ITRE Committee has shown that it is possible to re-identify supposedly anonymized data [48].

The risk of re-identifying anonymous data stems from the technical limitations of anonymization and the lack of clear and realistic guidelines on the subject. This suggests that re-identification is not only a consequence of poor anonymization implementation.

Moreover, national DPAs disagree on how to implement anonymization. The French DPA, CNIL, adopts the WP29's approach to anonymization; other national DPAs are more flexible. For example, the UK's ICO (Information Commissioner's Office), despite UK's own data protection regulation being largely similar to that of the EU, states that [60]:

"The DPA does not require anonymization to be completely risk free— you must be able to mitigate the risk of identification until it is remote. If the risk of identification is reasonably likely, the information should be regarded as personal data— (...). Clearly, 100% anonymization is the most desirable position, and in some cases, this is possible, but it is not the test the DPA requires.",

and Ireland's DPC (Data Protection Commission) writes [34]:

"Organisations don't have to be able to prove that it is impossible for any data subject to be identified in order for an anonymization technique to be considered successful. Rather, if it can be shown that it is unlikely that a data subject will be identified given the circumstances of the individual case and the state of technology, the data can be considered anonymous."

The CNIL's guidelines on anonymization are of particular interest, as they establish a strict standard to determine whether data can be considered anonymous. They assert that data is anonymous only when it is *impossible* to re-identify the data subject. However, they recognise that when the risks of singling out, linkability, and inference are not met, data can be deemed anonymous if a subsequent analysis indicates a negligible risk of re-identification [23]. Unfortunately, the definition of what constitutes a *negligible* risk remains ambiguous, since anonymization is a context-dependent process, depending on the nature of the data and its intended use.

> **Take-away**
>
> The lack of a clear, harmonized definition of anonymization across EU legal texts and among national authorities aggravates the complexities of anonymization and favors the confusion between pseudonymization and anonymization. Although anonymization and pseudonymization rely on similar techniques, they have different aims: anonymization aims to conceal the data subject's identity, whereas pseudonymization aims to protect privacy by making re-identification more complex but not impossible. Technical documents should help practitioners assess when to opt for anonymization rather than pseudonymization. However, most of the available technical guidance does not address this issue.

4.2 Technical Documents

While non-technical guidance often lacks the precision needed for implementation, technical documentation is not always more helpful. In several cases, companies have claimed they could not find clear guidance on how to anonymize data–a claim sometimes countered by DPAs pointing to existing documents [26]. However, our review shows that most guidelines are often hard to find (not available or ignored by DPAs) or not practically useful (entry-level). We reviewed the websites of the five most active EU DPAs (France, Austria, Ireland, Germany, and Italy). Most do not provide detailed technical materials:

- CNIL (France) offers introductory guides [22,23], repeating WP29 content, and a clear (though potentially misleading) explanation of pseudonymization [24].
- Garante (Italy) provides an overview [59] to implement the GDPR, and mainly reiterates previous legal guidelines.
- BfDI (Germany) has policy papers and speeches [9,10,13,14], but limited technical depth. [17] focuses on the importance of anonymization, [11] and [12] discuss risks of other issues related to personal data.
- DSB (Austria) offers legal advice only.
- DPC (Ireland) stands out with well-structured and clear guidance [33,34] on legal questions; however, it does not offer practical advice.

Outside the EU, the UK's ICO provides excellent guidance, including on state-of-the-art methods like differential privacy and other PETs [61,62]. However, some examples are oversimplified or technically wrong[11]

The UK Anonymization Network (UKAN) also offers practical tools, such as a decision-making framework that uniquely addresses attacker modelling [37]. However, most chapters remain general (entry-level), in contrast to the referenced DIS method that requires Master's degree-level statistical knowledge.

The anonymization guide of Singapore's PDPC [80] is accessible and educative, guides the reader from data discovery to risk measures, giving informative examples; however, it is also entry-level and adds little beyond other existing material.

Some statistical agencies provide additional resources. The National Institute of Statistics and Economic Studies in France (INSEE) offers slides and working papers [63,65], but most lack practical detail. A notable exception is Bergeat's work [70] comparing and explaining experiments done by two anonymization software tools: μ-Argus and SDCMicro. It also gives plenty of citations, however, only to sources on statistics (no computer science references). It is aimed at statisticians, and it could serve as a continuation to other introductory materials, but the reader who already has at least a Bachelor's degree in mathematics or statistics. Other guides, such as [64], focus on confidentiality rules within the French statistical service rather than techniques. Statistical documents only mention statistical tools and use a different language from that of computer scientists. This could, unfortunately, result in ignoring some state-of-the-art methods, such as differential privacy. A good example is the working paper [32] that details the anonymization process applied to a large French administrative database where the authors experimented with different methods including k-anonymity, all-m anonymity, and l-diversity. They mention that they have tried to apply DP; however, they abandoned the experiment due to a lack of expertise.

Academic papers are another option, but they often assume advanced statistical or mathematical knowledge (Master's or PhD level), making them inaccessible to many practitioners. Moreover, choosing appropriate methods from the literature is difficult without deep expertise, which may explain the frequent use of outdated or misapplied techniques in practice [32,65,70,71]. Some expert-written materials aimed at non-technical readers exist [75,76,96]; however, they are rarely cited in public or institutional guidance.

Books. Books on anonymization tend to target either high-level management (e.g. [28,77,85]) or technical researchers. Some, like [15], cover a broad range of privacy topics but lack methods for evaluating anonymization quality. Jarmul's work [67] offers a more hands-on perspective, including differential privacy and privacy engineering workflows, making it useful for practitioners. Stallings' book [90] is a strong general-purpose resource, well-suited for short training programs.

---

[11] See the case study on differentially private mixed noise addition.

> **Take-away**
>
> Most technical anonymization resources are either too simplistic or too involved, offering little practical use for professionals. Practical regulatory guidance is rare and often legalistic. This leaves practitioners with a fragmented landscape, outdated methods, and an incentive to abandon anonymization altogether. Bridging these gaps requires targeted, accessible, and technically sound educational materials.

5 Inadequate Practices

EU case law lacks clarity with regard to anonymization practices. The most relevant cases focus on clarifying the concept of personal data. However, the interpretations provided help to assess what an anonymized dataset is *not*. Moreover, the Court's application of Recital 26 to real cases provides valuable insight into the question of whether data remain anonymous despite a residual risk of re-identification. The following subsections focus on relevant case law concerning the notion of personal data, the implications of which are important for anonymization, and inadequate anonymization practices, demonstrating a lack of awareness on the subject both at the institutional and organizational levels. The final subsection also addresses the inadequate practices that arise from the confusion between anonymization and pseudonymization. At least one example is given for each subsection; they refer to the most representative and recent cases, but these are not exhaustive of all the existing case law on the subject.

5.1 Case-Law on Personal Data

The General Court's SRB vs EDPS decision is a good example of a decision relating to personal data whose implications are also relevant for anonymization [54]. SRB (Single Resolution Board) carried out an insolvency procedure against Banco Popular. Within this procedure, some data were processed to assess the eligibility of the participants for compensation. Each participant was identifiable by means of an alphanumeric code generated randomly. The staff processing these data only had access to these codes and not to the key identifying them. The EDPS (European Data Protection Supervisor) considered these data pseudonymized [47], but its decision was challenged before the General Court. Using a risk-based approach, the General Court decided that the data were anonymous. Indeed, according to Breyer's Court of Justice case law [50], the additional information (the key) needed to re-identify the data subjects remained inaccessible to the processing staff. The fact that the staff could not legally access the complementary data that would allow re-identification proved enough to consider that no *reasonable means* existed to re-identify the data, which thus remained non-personal [54].

This example shows that the EU Court of justice's (EUCJ) case law on personal data builds upon its precedents rather than undergoing a radical evolution. On this point, Breyer's decision [50] was about the dynamic nature of IP addresses. These IP addresses are subject to change with each connection. The plaintiff initiated legal proceedings against the Republic of Germany for its practices concerning the storage and registration of these data. The Court of Justice had to determine whether dynamic IP addresses should be considered personal data for the service provider. The Court decided that the retention of all information by a single individual was not a prerequisite for data being considered as personal. This meant that a third party could retain such re-identifying information, and that this circumstance did not affect the qualification of the data. However, the Court acknowledged that an assessment was necessary to determine the reasonableness of combining this information, taking into account the effort, time, and cost associated with the operation, as well as the accessibility of this additional information (enabling user identification) to the service provider. Given the legal restrictions on such access in Germany, the Court determined that in the absence of legal means to obtain this information, the data in question were not deemed personal. The doctrine posits that two fundamental elements have been applied since the Breyer decision to ascertain the personal nature of data. These are: (1) the distinguishability of the data, defined as the capacity of the data points to identify an individual, and (2) the availability of additional data to "situationally relevant entities" who are capable of associating these data with a physical person [88].

The Scania decision perfectly [53] illustrates this methodology. In this case, the Court was asked to determine the legal status of a vehicle identification number (VIN), a unique alphanumeric code assigned by manufacturers to identify the proprietor of a vehicle. In its decision, the Court stated that the VIN can be personal data for independent operators and vehicle manufacturers if the former have the additional data that enable re-identification, and for the latter if they make the VIN available. The availability of data is considered in conjunction with the capacity of isolating owners of vehicles or all other people who have a title on them. Some authors have suggested an evolution in the interpretation of personal data, attributing this change to the Court's categorization of independent operators and manufacturers as "situationally relevant entities", capable of associating VIN with additional identifying information.

Take-away

The consistency of the Court's jurisprudence on the concept of personal data is paramount to contrast the phenomenon of anonymity-washing. This is particularly crucial given the occurrence of poor anonymization or privacy-protecting practices, which the EUCJ is entitled to sanction.

5.2 Case-Law on Inadequate Practices

A relevant case law that sanctioned the European Commission [51] demonstrates the importance of taking into account publicly available data to assess the risk of re-identification. The applicant received European funding as a researcher. The funds had been misappropriated, and the costs were ordered to be reimbursed. The Commission published a press release summarizing the decision, without mentioning the applicant's direct identifiers to protect their privacy. However, the researcher brought an action for the annulment of the press release, since it contained identifiable data. The General Court dismissed it, and the applicant appealed its decision to the EUCJ. The Court considered that *"information relating to the gender of a person who is the subject of a press release, that person's nationality, his or her father's occupation, the amount of the grant for a scientific project and the geographical location of the entity hosting that scientific project, taken together, contain information that may allow the person who is the subject of that press release to be identified, in particular by those working in the same scientific field and familiar with that person's professional background"* and goes on that this circumstance, *" does not allow the risk of identification of the data subject to be regarded as insignificant."*. Although the judgment focuses more on privacy protection than anonymization, it highlights the lack of understanding that simply deleting direct identifiers is insufficient to minimize the risk of re-identification. This point is also relevant to anonymization.

Confusion about anonymization practices is also widespread among companies. A good example is the IAB Europe case-law [52]. The company established a set of guidelines aimed at ensuring compliance with the GDPR concerning the collection of browsing data via a TC String (a series of characters coding the user's preferences). This string, which the company claimed to contain anonymized data, could later be used by companies for commercial purposes. The Court ruled that the TC String was a form of personal data, given its capacity to allow individuals to be identified by associating it with additional information (such as an IP address). Despite third parties retaining this additional information, IAB Europe was able to obtain it.

In this regard, the relationship between the EUCJ case-law, employing a risk-based approach to assess the reasonable means likely to be used to re-identify the data, and the WP 29 Opinion 5/2014 on anonymization appears complex [89]. On the one hand, discordance persists in the discourse of WP 29 between the zero-risk approach (re-identification must be negligible if not impossible) and the necessity for reasonableness, given that all anonymization techniques are considered imperfect [36]. On the other hand, the need to destroy raw data and to aggregate them in order to achieve anonymization, as required by WP 29, is not met by the case law of the EUCJ, which considers data to be anonymous even if the original data are not deleted, the only relevant aspect being the impossibility (legal rather than technical) to access the additional data that enable re-identification. These contradictions contribute to privacy washing practices by making it difficult to distinguish the company's bad faith from its lack of knowledge about anonymization methods, especially when data are processed for commercial purposes. In the case of IAB Europe, for example, the company assumed that, due to the unavailability of additional information, TC String contained anonymized data. This mistake is frequently observed among firms that find it difficult to distinguish anonymization from pseudonymization and anything in between. This assertion is supported by some decisions adopted by the national DPAs.

5.3 Confusions Arising from the Difference Between Pseudo and Anonymization

One of the most relevant decisions on anonymization dates to 5 September 2024, namely the CEGEDIM SANTE case [26]. It perfectly illustrates the interactions between the WP 29 guidelines on anonymization, the EUCJ's case-law, and the context-dependent nature of anonymization. Indeed, the nature of the data (health data) and their use (creation of a health data repository) are not neutral. CEGEDIM designs and sells secretarial software for the medical sector. The company collected patient health data from doctors who agreed to participate in creating a health data repository. These data were allegedly anonymized with k-anonymity techniques. The decision was based on two key factors: (1) the WP29 test[12], which determines whether the data were anonymized, and (2) EUCJ case law. However, the rapporteur isolated a 6-year-old patient with a medical condition, which would suggest pseudonymization, unless re-identification is proved to be "negligible" by "reasonable means". On this point, the CNIL concluded that the available data could be easily re-identified. However, the company contended that there were few educational materials on anonymization and that the guidelines lacked precision, rendering them unsuitable for legal certainty. Despite CNIL's rejection of the complaint, the WP 29 Guidelines on anonymization are not updated concerning the current risks associated with k-anonymity. Furthermore, the CNIL has not specified what constitutes a 'negligible risk'. This observation suggests that anonymity-washing may not be a deliberate practice.

Take-away

Despite the consistency of the EUCJ case-law relating to personal data, confusion is widespread at the institutional level and among firms as far as the distinction between personal and non-personal data. Such confusion originates from the difficulty in implementing anonymization, which is a probabilistic and context-dependent process, and in distinguishing it from pseudonymization and anything halfway between these two techniques. This issue could enable unintentional anonymity-washing.

---

6 Discussion and Overture

The gap between regulatory guidance and technical solutions gives space to anonymity-washing, whether intentional or unintentional. While frameworks

---
[12] Linkability, re-identification, and inference.

exist to support anonymization efforts, their inconsistent application, misinterpretation, and continued reliance on outdated methods – repeatedly shown to be ineffective – often create a false sense of compliance and security. Several key issues contribute to this phenomenon.

In Sect. 3 we explain the **lack of clear guidance** to apply regulations and definitions. Guidelines lack a clear definition of pseudonymization and omit a definition of anonymization. This inconsistency can be a source of confusion and anonymity-washing. Nevertheless, establishing a coherent terminology is not a straightforward task, as personal data can be strongly situation-dependent, and data can be used in numerous ways.

We have also shown that **guidelines are** often **outdated or unreliable**. It has been shown that the anonymization techniques in the WP 29 Opinion 5/2014 on anonymization are no longer reliable, and relevant questions persist, given the contradictory nature of the document. Consequently, guidelines on anonymization remain to be updated, and the information provided by the EDPB on pseudonymization and anonymization of the AI models does not address this gap.

Next, we have seen that the **differing interpretations** of the regulations among authorities compromise their uniform application, leading to legal uncertainty for businesses and organisations. For example, some authorities, like the CNIL, adopt a stringent approach, while others, like the ICO and the DPC, are more flexible.

Furthermore, in Sect. 5 we show that there is a **lack of awareness** among practitioners. They often do not recognize that their data can constitute personal data, leading to a failure to implement privacy by design principles [11]. Such misconceptions could be eliminated by adequate training and guidance that would give the right tools to practitioners and engineers to be able to competently assess their datasets and apply anonymization methods.

We believe that one crucial cause of this shortcoming is the **lack of understanding** of anonymization methods. Many practitioners, particularly those without advanced mathematical skills, struggle to understand and apply fundamental privacy principles. The complexity of privacy-enhancing technologies (PETs) creates an additional barrier, making it difficult for non-specialists to implement effective anonymization (e.g.: [12,32,52]).

Another consequence of this educational deficiency is that organizations continue to **rely on outdated anonymization methods**, such as k-anonymity and l-diversity, despite their well-documented vulnerabilities [56]. This reliance stems from a lack of awareness regarding modern privacy-preserving techniques, as well as limited resources for evaluating and adopting alternative approaches.

However, this *lag* between the state-of-the-art and the most popular, but outdated tools is neither newfound nor unparalleled. There has always been a **collaboration gap** between academia and industry that limits the transfer of theoretical advancements into practice. Without structured mechanisms to facilitate knowledge-sharing, industry professionals may not only struggle to integrate the latest research into their anonymization strategies but also completely ignore it.

6.1 Overture

To address these issues and mitigate the risks of anonymity-washing, we would like to raise awareness among privacy experts and encourage them to facilitate adoption by practitioners for practitioners. With this objective in mind, we suggest the following actions:

In order to clarify the complexity of anonymization as a probabilistic and context-dependent process we believe that one of the most important action to take is to **develop a comprehensive anonymization curriculum** that could be promoted and distributed by data protection authorities either in the form of training programs offered or thorough and up-to-date educational resources, such as books and hands-on exercises aided with structured guidance on fundamental privacy principles and their real-world applications. Key components should include: (1) A clear explanation of privacy threats and their manifestations in various datasets. (2) An overview of widely accepted privacy definitions (besides k-anonymity and l-diversity, adding differential privacy and cryptographic methods), including their advantages and drawbacks. (3) How these techniques can defend against said privacy threats. (4) Techniques for evaluating privacy technologies and applying them to real-world scenarios. (5) Strategies for auditing privacy risks and implementing mitigation measures in large-scale datasets. (6) Best practices for integrating privacy considerations into broader software engineering projects. (7) Case studies illustrating data re-identification and the consequences of inadequate privacy protections. (8) Adding hands-on learning resources, such as Jupyter notebooks and real-world datasets.

Moreover, educational resources should be **tailored to diverse audiences**. Given the varying levels of expertise among practitioners, privacy education must be designed to accommodate both technical and non-technical professionals. It is also important to emphasize the **use of state-of-the-art methods**. Practitioners should be trained to critically assess privacy techniques and understand the limitations of traditional methods in modern, large datasets. To be sufficiently critical, we should also include adequate privacy risk assessments based on attacker capabilities, data sensitivity, and intended data usage. Finally, we believe that a curriculum of this depth can not be delivered without **enhancing the collaboration between academia and industry**. We acknowledge that finding a common language between academia and industry is not always straightforward. It takes time and effort: joint initiatives, workshops, and training programs should be encouraged to bridge the gap between theoretical advancements and practical implementation. By realizing these recommendations, organizations and policymakers can move beyond superficial compliance efforts and work toward fostering a robust, meaningful approach to data privacy that will help reduce the prevalence of anonymity-washing and ensure that anonymization practices align with contemporary privacy risks, industrial demands, and capacities.

We would like to emphasize that we are not suggesting procedural safeguards or checklists, nor do we mean to imply that clear guidance alone can resolve the complexities of anonymisation. Instead, we propose addressing the underlying technical limitations and misunderstandings. Technical guidelines should not be directed at policymakers, but rather at engineers, technical personnel, or even social scientists who need to anonymise data themselves.

6.2 Future Work

As a support of the collaboration between academia and industry, we wish to create a repository of guidelines and educational materials using the accumulated knowledge that we have used to write this paper. We envision constructing a proper website aided with instructions that would help practitioners navigate and find the appropriate guideline, document, or educational resource to their needs.

Furthermore, we conjecture that there is one more potential source of many of the aforementioned problems, namely, the use of popular anonymization tools. Thus, we have already started examining these existing tools; firstly, to corroborate our conjecture, and secondly, to be able to properly include them in the aforementioned website, equipping practitioners with the necessary understanding and comparison of these products.

Acknowledgments. This work has been partly funded by Project no. 138903, implemented with the support provided by the Ministry of Innovation and Technology from the National Research, Development, and Innovation Fund, financed under the FK_21 funding scheme.

Disclosure of Interests. The authors declare no competing interests. Project funding is acknowledged in the Acknowledgments section.

References

1. Aggarwal, C,C.: On k-anonymity and the curse of dimensionality. In: VLDB. vol. 5, pp. 901–909 (2005)
2. Aliki, E., Marietjie, B., Dusty-Lee, D., Beverley, T., Carmel, S., Donrich, T.: 'Potato potahto'? Disentangling de-identification, anonymisation, and pseudonymisation for health research in Africa. J. Law Biosci. **12**(1), 1 (2025)
3. Altman, M., Aloni, C., Nissim, K.: ACM TechBrief: Data Privacy Protection. ACM TechBriefs (2024)
4. ANPD: Agenda Regulatoria 2025-2026 (2025). https://www.gov.br/anpd/pt-br/assuntos/noticias/anpd-publica-agenda-regulatoria-2025-2026
5. Article 26 Data Protection Working Party: Opinion 05/2014 on Anonymisation Techniques (2014)
6. Article 29 Data Protection Working Party: Opinion on the concept of personal data (2007)
7. Atsumi & Sakai Co.: A Guide to Data Protection in Japan (2020). https://www.aplawjapan.com/archives/pdf/data-protection-202009.pdf

8. Ayyamperumal, S.G., Ge, L.: Current state of LLM Risks and AI Guardrails (2024). https://arxiv.org/abs/2406.12934
9. BfDI: Die Anonymisierung im Datenschutzrecht (2022). https://www.bfdi.bund.de/SharedDocs/Downloads/DE/DokumenteBfDI/Reden_Gastbeitr%C3%A4ge/2022/Anonymisierung-im-DS-recht.pdf?__blob=publicationFile&v=2
10. BfDI: Aktuelle Fragestellungen des Datenschutzes (2023). https://www.bfdi.bund.de/SharedDocs/Downloads/DE/DokumenteBfDI/Reden_Gastbeitr%C3%A4ge/2023/eco-Kompetenzgruppe.pdf?__blob=publicationFile&v=2
11. BfDI: Arbeitspapier zu Telemetrie und Diagnosedaten (2023). https://www.bfdi.bund.de/SharedDocs/Downloads/DE/Berlin-Group/20230608_AP-Telemetrie-Diagnosedaten.pdf?__blob=publicationFile&v=3
12. BfDI: Arbeitspapier zum Thema "Smart Cities" (2023). https://www.bfdi.bund.de/SharedDocs/Downloads/DE/Berlin-Group/20230608_WP-Smart-Cities.pdf?__blob=publicationFile&v=2
13. BfDI: Datenschutz durch Technik – Chancen und Grenzen von Anonymisierung, Pseudonymisierung und PETs (2024). https://www.bfdi.bund.de/SharedDocs/Downloads/DE/DokumenteBfDI/Reden_Gastbeitr%C3%A4ge/2024/Datenschutz-durch-Technik-BvD.pdf?__blob=publicationFile&v=1
14. BfDI: Datennutzung vs. Datenschutz – Veranstaltung zum Europäischen Datenschutztag (2025). https://www.bfdi.bund.de/SharedDocs/Downloads/DE/DokumenteBfDI/Reden_Gastbeitr%C3%A4ge/2025/Rede-Eu-Akademie-Informationsfreiheit-Datenschutz.pdf?__blob=publicationFile&v=2
15. Bhajaria, Nishant: Data Privacy: A runbook for engineers. Simon and Schuster (2022)
16. Brazil: Lei Geral de Proteção de Dados Pessoais (Redação dada pela Lei n 13.853, de 2019) (LGPD) (2019)
17. Burkert, C., Federrath, H., Marx, M., Schwarz, M.: Positionspapier zur Anonymisierung unter der DSGVO unter Besonderer Berücksichtigung der TK-Branche. Konsultationsverfahren des BfDI 10 (2020)
18. Burt, A., Stalla-Bourdillon, S., Rossi, A.: A guide to the EU's unclear anonymization standards (2021). https://iapp.org/news/a/a-guide-to-the-eus-unclear-anonymization-standards/
19. CCPA: California Consumer Privacy Act (CCPA) (2020)
20. Chevrier, R., Foufi, V., Gaudet-Blavignac, C., Robert, A., Lovis, C.: Use and understanding of anonymization and de-identification in the biomedical literature: scoping review. J. Med. Internet Res. **21**(5), e13484 (2019)
21. Cirucci, A.M.: Oversharing the super safe stuff: "Privacy-washing" in Apple iPhone and Google Pixel commercials. First Monday (2024)
22. CNIL: L'anonymisation des données, un traitement clé pour l'open data (2019). https://www.cnil.fr/fr/lanonymisation-des-donnees-un-traitement-cle-pour-lopen-data
23. CNIL: L'anonymisation de données personnelles (2020). https://www.cnil.fr/fr/technologies/lanonymisation-de-donnees-personnelles
24. CNIL: Recherche scientifique (hors santé): enjeux et avantages de l'anonymisation et de la pseudonymisation (2022). https://www.cnil.fr/fr/recherche-scientifique-hors-sante-enjeux-et-avantages-de-lanonymisation-et-de-la-pseudonymisation
25. Cohen, A., Nissim, K.: Towards formalizing the GDPR's notion of singling out. Proc. Natl. Acad. Sci. **117**(15), 8344–8352 (2020)
26. Commission nationale de l'informatique et des libertés CNIL: Délibération SAN-2024-013 (2024)

27. Cormode, G., Srivastava, D., Li, N., Li, T.: Minimizing minimality and maximizing utility: analyzing method-based attacks on anonymized data. Proc. VLDB Endowment **3**(1–2), 1045–1056 (2010)
28. Craig, T., Ludloff, M.E.: Privacy and big data: the players, regulators, and stakeholders. O'Reilly (2011)
29. Data Security Council of India: Balancing Privacy and Innovation: Anonymisation Standards for Indian Data (2023)
30. Montjoye, Y.A., Hidalgo, C.A., Verleysen, M., Blondel, V.D.: Unique in the crowd: the privacy bounds of human mobility. Sci. Rep. **3**(1), 1376 (2013)
31. Montjoye, Y.A., Pentland, A.S.: Response to Comment on "Unique in the shopping mall: On the reidentifiability of credit card metadata". Science **351**(6279), 1274–1274 (2016)
32. Djiriguian, J., Missègue, N., Ricroch, L.: Diffuser une base anonymisée : utopie ou réalitée? Journées de méthodologie statistique de l'Insee (2022). https://journees-methodologie-statistique.insee.net/wp-content/uploads/2022/S11_4_ACTE_MISSEGUE_JMS2022.pdf
33. DPC: Data Protection: The Basics (2019). https://dataprotection.ie/sites/default/files/uploads/2019-07/190710%20Data%20Protection%20Basics.pdf
34. DPC: Guidance on Anonymisation and Pseudonymisation (2019). https://www.dataprotection.ie/sites/default/files/uploads/2022-04/Anonymisation%20and%20Pseudonymisation%20-%20latest%20April%202022.pdf
35. EDPB and AEPD: 10 misunderstandings related to anonymisation (2021)
36. Emam, K., Alvarez, C.: A critical appraisal of the Article 29 Working Party Opinion 05/2014 on data anonymization techniques. Int. Data Priv. Law **5**(1), 73–87 (2015)
37. Elliot, M., Mackey, E., O'Hara, K.: The Anonymisation Decision-Making Framework 2nd Edition: European Practitioners' Guide (2020)
38. EU-USA: Privacy Shield Framework (2016). https://eur-lex.europa.eu/eli/dec_impl/2016/1250/oj/eng
39. European Commission EC: Directive 95/46/EC of the European Parliament and of the Council on the protection of individuals with regard to the processing of personal data and on the free movement of such data, OJ L 281 (1995)
40. European Commission EC: Communication from the Commission to the European Parliament and the Council, Guidance on the Regulation on a framework for the free flow of non-personal data in the European Union, COM/2019/250 final (2019)
41. European Commission EC: Communication from the Commission to the European Parliament and the Council – two years of application of the General Data Protection Regulation, COM/2020/264 (2020)
42. European Commission EC: Communication from the Commission to the European Parliement and the CouncilL - Second Report on the application of the General Data Protection Regulation, COM/2024/357 (2024)
43. European Data Protection Board EDPB: Opinion 28/2024 on certain data protection aspects related to the processing of personal data in the context of AI models (2024)
44. European Data Protection Board EDPB: Guidelines on Pseudonymisation - version for public consultation (2025)
45. European Parliament, Council of the European Union: Regulation (EU) 2016/679 of the European Parliament and of the Council (GDPR) (2016). https://data.europa.eu/eli/reg/2016/679/oj

46. European Parliament and of the Council: Regulation (EU) 2024/1689 of the European Parliament and of the Council of 13 June 2024 laying down harmonised rules on artificial intelligence and amending Regulations (EC) No 300/2008, (EU) No 167/2013, (EU) No 168/2013, (EU) 2018/858, (EU) 2018/1139 and (EU) 2019/2144 and Directives 2014/90/EU, (EU) 2016/797 and (EU) 2020/1828 (Artificial Intelligence Act), PE/24/2024/REV/1, OJ L, 2024/1689 (2024)
47. European Parliament and of the Council: Regulation (EU) 2018/1725 on the protection of natural persons with regard to the processing of personal data by the Union institutions, bodies, offices and agencies and on the free movement of such data, and repealing Regulation (EC) No 45/2001 and Decision No 1247/2002/EC, PE/31/2018/REV/1, OJ L 295, 21.11.2018, pp. 39–98, art 15 (1) d (2018)
48. Parliament, E.: Directorate - General for Internal Policies, Policy Department Economic and Scientific Policy: Industry. Data Flows- Future Scenarios, in-depth Analysis for the ITRE Committee, Research and Energy (2017)
49. European Union Court of Justice EUCJ: Judgment of the Court (Grand Chamber): Data Protection Commissioner v Facebook Ireland Limited and Maximillian Schrems (2020)
50. European Union Court of Justice EUCJ: Breyer, Case C-582/14 (2016)
51. European Union Court of Justice EUCJ: GOC vs European Commission, Case C?479/22 P (2024)
52. European Union Court of Justice EUCJ: IAB Europe, Case C?604/22 (2024)
53. European Union Court of Justice EUCJ: Gesamtverband Autoteile-Handel (Accès aux informations sur les véhicules), case C-319/22 (2023)
54. European Union General Court EUGC: SRB vs EDPS, Case T-557/20 (2023)
55. Federal Trade Commission: Protecting Consumer Privacy in an Era of Rapid Change, Recommendations for businesses and policymakers, FTC Report (2012). https://www.ftc.gov/sites/default/files/documents/reports/federal-trade-commission-report-protecting-consumer-privacy-era-rapid-change-recommendations/120326privacyreport.pdf
56. Gadotti, A., Rocher, L., Houssiau, F., Creţu, A.M., De Montjoye, Y.A.: Anonymization: the imperfect science of using data while preserving privacy. Sci. Adv. **10**(29), eadn7053 (2024)
57. Garfinkel, S.L.: De-Identification of Personal Information. National Institute of Standard and Technology (2015)
58. GPDP: Provvedimento [10090499] (2024)
59. GPDP: GUIDA ALL'APPLICAZIONE DEL REGOLAMENTO EUROPEO IN MATERIA DI PROTEZIONE DEI DATI PERSONALI (2023). https://www.garanteprivacy.it/documents/10160/0/Guida+all+applicazione+del+Regolamento+UE+2016+679.pdf/2281f960-a7b2-4c53-a3f1-ad7578f8761d?version=2.0
60. ICO: Anonymisation: managing data protection risk code of practice (2019)
61. ICO: (Draft) Anonymisation, pseudonymisation and privacy enhancing technologies guidance (2022). https://ico.org.uk/about-the-ico/ico-and-stakeholder-consultations/ico-call-for-views-anonymisation-pseudonymisation-and-privacy-enhancing-technologies-guidance/
62. ICO: Privacy-enhancing technologies (PETs) (2023). https://ico.org.uk/for-organisations/uk-gdpr-guidance-and-resources/data-sharing/privacy-enhancing-technologies/
63. INSEE: Risque de ré-identification : deux questions pratiques relatives au critère de la l-diversité (2019). https://www.insee.fr/fr/information/4277545

64. INSEE: Guide du Secret Statistique (2024). https://www.insee.fr/fr/information/1300624
65. INSEE: Les méthodes perturbatives d'anonymisation des données individuelles (2024). https://www.insee.fr/fr/statistiques/fichier/4277545/1-SMS_secret_24_juin_2019.pdf
66. Japan: Act on the Protection of Personal Information (Act No. 57 of 2003) (Last version Act No. 37 of 2021) (2003). https://www.japaneselawtranslation.go.jp/en/laws/view/4241/en
67. Jarmul, Katharine: Practical data privacy. O'Reilly (2023)
68. Langarizadeh, M., Orooji, A., Sheikhtaheri, A.: Effectiveness of anonymization methods in preserving patients' privacy: a systematic literature review. Health Informatics Meets eHealth, pp. 80–87 (2018)
69. Mamanazarov, S.: De-identification and anonymization: legal and technical approaches. Tsul Legal Report **5**, 25 (2024)
70. Maxime Bergeat (INSEE): La question de la confidentialité des données individuelles (2016). https://www.insee.fr/fr/statistiques/2535625
71. Michael Levi-Valensin: Gestion du secret pour la diffusion grand public de cubes multidimensionnels: une expérimentation au SSM agricultiure. Journées de méthodologie statistique de l'Insee (2022)
72. Joo, M.-H., Kwon, H.-Y.: Comparison of personal information de-identification policies and laws within the EU, the US, Japan, and South Korea. Gov. Inf. Q. **40**, 101805 (2023)
73. Narayanan, A., Felten, E.W.: No silver bullet: De-identification still doesn't work. White Paper (2014)
74. Narayanan, A., Shmatikov, V.: Robust de-anonymization of large sparse datasets: a decade later. May **21**, 2019 (2019)
75. Nguyen, B.: Techniques d'anonymisation. Statistique et société **2**(4), 53–60 (2014)
76. Nguyen, B., Castelluccia, C.: Techniques d'anonymisation tabulaire: concepts et mise en oeuvre. arXiv preprint arXiv:2001.02650 (2020)
77. Nissenbaum, H.: Privacy in context: Technology, policy, and the integrity of social life. In: Privacy in context. Stanford University Press (2009)
78. OECD: Cross-border data flows, Policy sub-issue (2022). https://www.oecd.org/en/topics/cross-border-data-flows.html
79. Ohm, P.: Broken promises of privacy: responding to the surprising failure of anonymization. UCLA Law Rev. **57**, 1701 (2009)
80. PDPC: Guide to Basic Anonymisation (2022)
81. Personal Information Protection Commission Secretariat: Anonymously Processed Information - Towards Balanced Promotion of Personal Data Utilization and Consumer Trust (2017). https://www.ppc.go.jp/files/pdf/The_PPC_Secretariat_Report_on_Anonymously_Processed_Information.pdf
82. President's Council of Advisors on Science and Technology, White House: Big data and Privacy: A technological perspective (2014)
83. Québec: Regulation respecting the anonymization of personal information (2024)
84. Rubinstein, I.S., Hartzog, W.: Anonymization and risk. Wash. L. Rev. **91**, 703 (2016)
85. Sharma, S.: Data privacy and GDPR Handbook. John Wiley & Sons (2019)
86. Stadler, T., Troncoso, C.: Why the search for a privacy-preserving data sharing mechanism is failing. Nat. Comput. Sci. **2**(4), 208–210 (2022)
87. Stalla-Bourdillon, S., Burt, A.: The definition of 'anonymization' is changing in the EU: Here's what that means (2023). https://iapp.org/news/a/the-definition-of-anonymization-is-changing-in-the-eu-heres-what-that-means

88. Stalla-Bourdillon, S.: Identifiability, as a Data Risk: Is a Uniform Approach to Anonymisation About to Emerge in the EU? Available at SSRN (2025)
89. Stalla-Bourdillon, S., Knight, A.: Anonymous data v. personal data-false debate: an EU perspective on anonymization, pseudonymization and personal data. Wis. Int'l LJ **34**, 284 (2016)
90. Stallings, W.: Information privacy engineering and privacy by design: Understanding privacy threats, technology, and regulations based on standards and best practices. Addison-Wesley Professional (2019)
91. Susan, E.: Wallace: what does anonymization mean? DataSHIELD and the need for consensus on anonymization terminology. Biopreservation Biobanking **14**(3), 224 (2016)
92. Sénéchal, J.: Publication de l'avis de l'EDPB du 17 décembre 2024 sur le traitement des données personnelles dans le contexte des modèles d'IA: prémices d'une mutation profonde du RGPD? (2024). https://www.dalloz-actualite.fr/flash/publication-de-l-avis-de-l-edpb-du-17-decembre-2024-sur-traitement-des-donnees-personnelles-da
93. USA: Health Insurance Portability and Accountability Act (1996)
94. Weitzenboeck, E.M., Lison, P., Cyndecka, M., Langford, M.: The GDPR and unstructured data: is anonymization possible? Int. Data Priv. Law **12**(3), 184–206 (2022)
95. Wolff, J., Lehr, W., Yoo, C.S.: Lessons from GDPR for AI Policymaking. Va. JL Tech. **27**, 1 (2023)
96. Wood, A., et al.: Differential privacy: a primer for a non-technical audience. Vand. J. Ent. Tech. L. **21**, 209 (2018)

Open Access This chapter is licensed under the terms of the Creative Commons Attribution-NonCommercial-NoDerivatives 4.0 International License (http://creativecommons.org/licenses/by-nc-nd/4.0/), which permits any noncommercial use, sharing, distribution and reproduction in any medium or format, as long as you give appropriate credit to the original author(s) and the source, provide a link to the Creative Commons license and indicate if you modified the licensed material. You do not have permission under this license to share adapted material derived from this chapter or parts of it.

The images or other third party material in this chapter are included in the chapter's Creative Commons license, unless indicated otherwise in a credit line to the material. If material is not included in the chapter's Creative Commons license and your intended use is not permitted by statutory regulation or exceeds the permitted use, you will need to obtain permission directly from the copyright holder.

Simple Now, Complex Later: The Questionable Efficacy of Diluting GDPR Article 30(5)

Harshvardhan J. Pandit[1,2(✉)]

[1] AI Accountability Lab, Trinity College Dublin, Dublin, Ireland
me@harshp.com
[2] ADAPT Research Ireland Centre, Trinity College Dublin, Dublin, Ireland

Abstract. In mid-2025, the EU Commission proposed an amendment to the GDPR that extends the derogation to not maintain a record of processing activities under Article 30(5) to small and mid-cap organisations in addition to SMEs, with the intended goal of reducing reporting obligations and based on the Draghi report's recommendations for improving competitiveness. In this article, I systematically show how this exemption does not provide any practical benefits as the information involved must still be collected to assess whether the exemption applies and to be maintained elsewhere to fulfil other GDPR obligations. I also highlight how Article 30 records are a key requirement for oversight and accountability, and that their absence will negatively affect the organisation's data governance and compliance practices, thereby increasing risks and liability. I conclude with alternatives to mere 'simplification' based on responding to actual needs of organisations, taking advantage of RegTech/eGov technologies with known success stories, and to avoid diluting the GDPR as it risks damaging the future of EU's digital policies. While the utility of this work is focused on short-term regulatory activities, the arguments and potential solutions proposed here are informative for future rule-making efforts in the EU.

Keywords: GDPR · Rights · data governance

1 A 'Simplified' Introduction

The EU Commission has established competitiveness through "simpler, lighter, and faster regulation" as a prominent key objective in its 2024–2029 work program through the 'Better Regulation' agenda [6]. One of the measures the Commission promised for achieving this is a 25% reduction in the reporting requirements for enterprises and administrations without undermining the objectives of the relevant legislation [15], which was later increased to 35% for Small and Medium Enterprises (SMEs) as a key group involved in advancing competitiveness, with the potential of achieving €37.5 billion in business savings [9]. The Commission also published a report on "The future of EU competitiveness" [12] (also referred to as the Draghi report) that recommended the "mitigation measures" currently available to SMEs should also be applied to Small Mid-Cap enterprises (SMCs) i.e. organisations which have grown past the SME criteria. While the exact definition of SMCs is being legislatively established, the Draghi report puts great emphasis on "simplifying rules" as a series of recommendations (Part B, Section 2, Chapter 5) based on its findings that "EU regulations impose a proportionally higher burden on SMEs and SMCs than on larger enterprises". It specifically criticises the General Data Protection Regulation (GDPR) [20] as an example of a legislation that has caused "regulatory difficulties" to SMEs and SMCs in comparison to larger companies.

With the Draghi report as its justification, the Commission published a proposal on 21st May 2025 to amend the GDPR [16] with three changes: two regarding the extension of existing codes of conduct and certification criterias to include SMCs, and one extending the exception of Article 30(5), which currently covers SMEs as organisations with less than 250 employees, to also apply to SMCs as organisations with less than 750 employees. In the accompanying "legislative and financial digital statement" section, the objectives and expected outcomes outlined for the proposal include 'growth and development', (to) 'reduce administrative burdens', and 'simplified or assisted reporting'. The same section outlines there are no "lessons learned from similar experiences in the past", which implies this is a new measure with unknown effectiveness from past applications despite this being at least the third such exercise following the proposals and reviews of the Data Protection Directive and the GDPR.

Surprisingly, the section also fails to specify any "monitoring and reporting rules", despite such measures already existing for the GDPR, and the necessity for such measures to be identified ahead of time to assess the suitability of the proposal. This along with the lack of any identified risks, or an accompanying impact assessment, which in the Commission's own definition of the law-making process [6], is "carried out on initiatives expected to have significant economic, social or environmental impacts", raises questions as to whether the proposal has been rushed without taking these important steps or the details are not being shared in the interest of speeding through a political agenda. For comparison, the impact assessment on the proposal for GDPR [14] specifically lists experiences with Directive 95/46/EC (Data Protection Directive) [19] with identified risks regarding fragmentation, and an evaluation schedule for 4 years with specific instruments for the monitoring and reporting of its application. At the time of writing this article, the amendment is being discussed as part of the broader agenda under the Polish presidency of the EU Council, and the report dated 2nd June 2025 lists the outcomes of a survey to identify challenges and potential measures [1]. However, the Council, along with the Commission, also seem to favour the amendment as no criticisms or limitations associated it were identified in the report whereas the call for reducing reporting obligations and favouring SMEs continues to be present, albeit with specific measures which I have referenced in my arguments for solutions.

In this article, I therefore analyse, *prima facie*, the proposed amendments to the GDPR and whether they will indeed support the SMEs and SMCs as intended in the Commission's outlined objectives. I focus on the increased exceptions for SMEs and SMCs under GDPR Article 30(5) regarding Records of Processing Activities (ROPA), and demonstrate empirically how the exception appears beneficial as written and in conjunction with Recital 13, but is effectively redundant in practice as the effort intended to be prevented is still required to meet other GDPR obligations, and that by removing the obligation to maintain documentation the Commission is promoting an organisational culture of weakened accountability, lack of oversight, and deviating from established data governance principles risk compliance with other GDPR obligations. If the intended impact is to ease the regulatory burdens for SMEs and SMCs, then this proposal will, to put it plainly, '*cut corners now and court problems later*'.

2 Understanding GDPR Article 30

This section provides the necessary background required to understand the implications of the proposed amendments to GDPR Article 30(5) by describing its obligations and requirements on organisations and supervisory authorities, why it exists within the GDPR and its history of changes in the legislative process, and finally the current state of its adoption and implementations by organisations.

2.1 The History of Article 30 in GDPR

The Data Protection Directive [19], predecessor of the GDPR [14,20], had in its Article 18 the obligation to notify the supervisory authority regarding its (specific) processing activities. The contents of the notification were described in Article 19 and contained: controller name and contact, purposes of processing, personal data categories, categories of recipients, international data transfers, and security measures. Article 20 obliged the supervisory authority to assess this information to determine whether this processing was "likely to present specific risks to the rights and freedoms of data subjects". While these obligations were restricted to specific criteria set out by Member States (as is the structure of Directives), the onus of assessments was set out to be on the supervisory authorities.

When the proposal for the GDPR was published in 2012 [14], Article 28 revised this procedure as an obligation on the controller to maintain documentation rather than to notify the supervisory authority. The justification for this change was described in Article 22 as a shift to an accountability-based regulation where the controller would identify "policies and implement appropriate measures to ensure and be able to demonstrate that the processing of personal data is performed in compliance". Thus, the GDPR represented a paradigm change in the implementation of data protection in the EU by making the controller more responsible (and thus more accountable), and expanding the scope of processing activities which must be documented. This aligned with an introduction of new obligations and rights – such as transparency via notices, data portability, and the data protection impact assessment, which relied on the controller having an understanding of their processing and only consulting the supervisory authority in cases where such processing represented a 'high-risk' to the rights and freedoms of the data subject.

Following the revision of the GDPR draft through the trialogue negotiations, the final published version in 2016 [20] contained the obligation to maintain "records of processing activities" in Article 30, with a removal of the earlier justification in Article 22 as being redundant. The negotiation process also removed the requirement for possible delegated and implementing acts which could have seen a standardised or consistent implementation of ROPA based on Article 28 regarding "further specifying the criteria and requirements for the documentation" and that "the Commission may lay down standard forms for the documentation". While this possibility still exists as the final version of the GDPR does not prohibit these measures, there is no onus on the Commission to create such an implementing act, and so far they have not proposed any such measure either.

The negotiation process also introduced a derogation (an exemption to the requirement) regarding maintaining a ROPA for organisations with less than 250 employees as a way to ease the 'burden of obligation' on SMEs. This was clarified in Recital 13 along with a guidance note for Member States and supervisory authorities to address 'specific needs' of SMEs when implementing the GDPR. At the time, the negotiation which introduced this change emphasised the necessity to distinguish between the impact of the GDPR on SMEs as compared to larger organisations, and the intent of this derogation was to avoid 'punishing' the SMEs with additional work for which they may not have sufficient expertise or resources. The guidance to the supervisory authorities regarding specific needs also hints towards supporting the SMEs with compliance related knowledge and activities. As a result, supervisory authorities have initiated specific campaigns, guidance, and consultations targeted for the SMEs which go beyond the obligations of the GPDR as a way to support and guide them towards effective implementations [8,10] and also include targeted projects [4].

Following the publication of the GDPR in 2016, and its enforcement in 2018, the Article 30 requirements received little attention compared to other obligations such as changes in privacy notices (Article 13 and 14), consent (Article 7 and 9), and data transfers (Article 49). However, the supervisory authorities have emphasised the importance of maintaining proper documentation as a cornerstone of good data governance practices [7] and for Data Protection Officers (DPOs) as a key resource in their tasks to advice on and ensure compliance [3]. To this end, the supervisory authorities also published templates for organisations and DPOs to use, though these were done independently by each authority rather than in co-ordination [34]. These templates were commonly in the form of spreadsheets and went beyond the requirements of Article 30(1) by including additional fields such as for legal basis and specific technical, organisational, and legal measures. In prior work [34], we analysed such templates and found that though Article 30(1) refers to only 18 fields at most (see Table 1), some templates contained as many as 32 fields and that there was a large variance in the fields recommended by different authorities.

An informed explanation for this is that the authorities see the ROPA as a key document in understanding the activities of the organisation, and thus recommend keeping it as detailed as possible where the additional details come from a mixture of specific information required for other legal obligations as well as best practices and recommendations from the authority's own experience [7, 11]. In either case, the exercise showed the key role the ROPA is envisioned to play in the compliance process, and its importance as part of good data governance practices as it directly supports the oversight process. As a consequence, commercial compliance management software also provides specific features which take the ROPA as defined in GDPR Article 30(1), and build over it to support the organisation and the DPOs through specific mechanisms such as task management, request tracking for information and activities, and producing reports and documentations [34]. The Irish authority's guidance note [11] explicitly reports issues in maintaining a ROPA by some of their audited organisations, and that the ROPA is likely to be requested as part of other obligations such as " breach notification management, complaint handling, inquiries, and investigations".

2.2 Information to be Documented by Controllers and Processors

Article 30 of the GDPR is titled "Records of processing activities" (ROPA) and is placed within Chapter IV "Controller and Processor" Section 1 "General Obligations". It contains Article 30(1) that specifies information requirements for controllers and Article 30(2) that specifies them for processors. It thus forms a core obligation for controllers and processors to maintain oversight of their processing activities by documenting them as a 'record' that is then updated and maintained over time and used by stakeholders such as the legal teams, DPOs, and supervisory authorities to understand and investigate the processing activities of the organisation. Authorities have also called it a 'living document' [11] that reflects the activities of the organisation. Given that Article 30(3) requires this information be maintained in an electronic/digital form and Article 30(4) requires this information to be produced on request by a supervisory authority, authorities have acknowledged the possibility of keeping this information in a database or similar information system for larger organisations, and that a 'simple spreadsheet' could be sufficient for smaller organisations [11].

Taken together, this results in an obligation for the controller or processor to identify the necessary information and put it in a digital document as the ROPA that is then ready to be submitted to an authority at any given time. It is also possible to fulfil this obligation by having this information be present in a system where the ROPA can be exported on demand. Such use of information management systems also opens up the possibility for the ROPA information to be reused elsewhere and avoid duplication while also facilitating its collection and management – these form key points in my later arguments about the realities of the ROPA obligation and the necessity of its information. For now, it is sufficient to understand that the GDPR does not necessitate the ROPA to be a manually laborious process – only that the information specified must be maintained in a form that can be produced when needed. Here, good practice dictates identifying overlaps and repetitions between this and other compliance-related information and using this knowledge to reduce the burden of regulations.

To demonstrate this, I outline the specific information to be maintained by a controller in Table 1 where each information field is assigned an ID so it can be referenced and compared later with other information required for GDPR compliance, and the clause represents its origin clause in GDPR Article 30. For practicality, I distinguish between '*static fields*', such as the name and contact details which rarely change and can thus be specified as common information for all activities, from '*dynamic fields*' such as the purposes and personal data which will are defined for each activity. Some of the dynamic fields include conditional information dependent on whether there is an international transfer to a third country or an international organisation where the information will only be relevant when such transfers are taking place. However, it is an implied necessity and generally good practice to acknowledge that no transfers are taking place – which is reflected in field C13 to distinguish this case from situations where it is unknown whether such transfers exist as the value of the field being empty or null would be ambiguous to interpret.

The table also provides the information to be maintained by a processor, which when compared to a controller's ROPA, is an effective subset and can be considered as being strictly static as all information must be produced ahead of time to complete the data processing agreement between the controller and the processor. This information can also be part of the communicated instructions from the controller to the processor without which the processor is not authorised to process the data (Article 4(8) and Article 28(3a)). It is possible that the processor may have activities that are not explicitly mentioned in the agreement e.g., additional or specific security measures or when the recipient country changes due to the nature of cloud services – however the general category of this information is unlikely to change from the controller's perspective and due to the obligation on the processor to follow the controller's instructions (Article 28(3)).

From this, we understand two important implications of maintaining a ROPA – for processors the information is largely static, while for controllers some information is static and most of it is dynamic. The obligation to maintain and ensure the ROPA is up to date thus resides primarily on these dynamic fields and mostly on the role of the controller. While the duty to maintain the ROPA is the responsibility of the organisation as a whole, in practice this falls under the tasks of the DPO by virtue of their involvement in understanding and advising on processing activities (Article 39). However, the appointment of the DPO is only necessary in specific cases (Article 37(1)) which are based on the nature of processing activities and being public organisations rather than the classification of the organisation as a SME or on number of employees. This means not all organ-

Table 1. Information to be maintained by Controllers and Processors as per the obligation in GDPR Article 30 regarding Records of Processing Activities

ID	Clause	Information
Controller ROPA		
		Static fields – these rarely change
C1	30-1a	Controller name
C2	30-1a	Controller contact
C3	30-1a	Joint Controller name
C4	30-1a	Joint Controller contact
C5	30-1a	Controller representative name
C6	30-1a	Controller representative contact
C7	30-1a	DPO name
C8	30-1a	DPO contact
		Dynamic fields – these are per processing activity
C9	30-1b	Purposes of processing
C10	30-1c	Categories of data subject
C11	30-1c	Categories of personal data
C12	30-1d	Categories of recipients
C13	30-1e	If data is transferred to a third country or international organisation
C14	30-1e	Third Country or International Organisation as Recipient
C15	30-1e	Legal Basis for transfer
C16	30-1e	Safeguards for transfer if legal basis is from Art.49-1
C17	30-1f	Time limits for erasure of data categories
C18	30-1g	Technical and organisational safeguards (e.g., security)
Processor ROPA		
P1	A30-2a	Processor Identity & Contact
P2	A30-2a	Controller Identity & Contact
P3	A30-2b	Categories of Processing
P4	A30-2c	Third Country or International Organisation Recipient
P5	A30-2c	Legal Basis for transfer
P6	A30-2c	Safeguards for transfer if legal basis is from Art.49-1
P7	A30-2d	Technical and Organisational safeguards (e.g., security)

isations will have a DPO, and thus the duty to create and maintain a ROPA requires assigning this task to *someone* – typically alongside fulfilment of other GDPR obligations such as drafting privacy notices and managing rights.

2.3 Exemptions for SMEs

Article 30(5) of the GDPR lists exemptions, as derogations, to the obligation to maintain a ROPA for controllers based on four criteria (identifiers added to reference the exception later): E1 – Size of organisation is less than 250 people, E2 – Risk to rights and freedoms of data subjects has low likelihood[1], E3 – Processing is occasional, and E4 – Processing does not include Special categories of personal data from Article 9(1) and 10. In order to be exempted, E1 must always apply and at least one of E2, E3, or E4 must apply. In the case of E2-E4, the exemption only applies for the specific processing activity and does not extend to all other activities i.e. if one activity is occasional and another is not, the ROPA would still be required for the non-occasional activity. Further, in order to assess whether the exemption applies, E1 is not dependant on the processing activity and is unlikely to change – it is thus a 'static' exemption. In comparison, E2-E4 must be assessed for each activity and are thus 'dynamic' exemptions. Thus, though SMEs are, *per se*, intended to be exempt from the obligation to have a ROPA, they must assess and qualify each exemption individually. To assess whether a *E2-E4* dynamic exemption applies, the SME must have specific information at hand, which I illustrate through Table 2 based on information fields to be maintained in a ROPA.

Table 2. Mapping involvement of information fields in a ROPA (from Table 1) for assessing exemptions to maintain a ROPA under GDPR Article 30(5)

ID	Information	E2	E3	E4
C9	Purposes of processing	Y		
C10	Categories of data subject	Y		Y*
C11	Categories of personal data	Y		Y
C12	Categories of recipients	Y		
C13	Transfer to third country or international organisation	Y		
C14	Transfer Recipient	Y		
C15	Legal Basis for transfer	Y		
C16	Article 49(1) safeguards for transfer	Y		
C17	Time limits for data erasure	Y	Y*	
C18	Technical and organisational measures	Y		

In the table, the exemption E3 relies on the definition of processing (Article 4(2)) which includes both storage and erasure, E4 relies on assessing whether

---

[1] The wording of Article 30(5) is "unless the processing it carries out is likely to result in a risk" which I have interpreted as meaning the derogation applies when such risk is 'unlikely' i.e. has a sufficiently low likelihood, which is distinct from 'does not exist' which would have required the phrasing to be "will not result in a risk".

the category of personal data falls under Article 9(1) or Article 10 special categories and which potentially also requires knowledge about the category of data subjects as a potential source for this information e.g., as patients in hospital or as users of a health tracking app. In comparison E2 requires an assessment of whether the processing will create a risk to the rights and freedoms of data subjects. While the wording of Article 30(5) phrases this as "likely to result in a risk", I have rephrased it as "risk with low likelihood" to align with the terminology and outcome values used in typical risk/impact assessments. To ascertain whether such a risk exists, what its potential impact will be, and whether this has a low likelihood requires, *apriori*, specific information about the processing activity. Taking Article 35(1) and 35(3) regarding Data Protection Impact Assessments (DPIA) as guidelines for what information should be included, and mapping this to the information in Article 30(1), there is a large overlap between the two (also see Table 4).

To illustrate the validity of this finding, consider the following examples. If the purpose of processing is to determine access to a service or to make a decision, the outcome could qualify as a significant effect, thus making the knowledge of the purpose of processing a pre-requisite for the assessment of risk to rights and freedoms. Similarly, the category of data subjects could include vulnerabilities and power dynamics, the category of personal data could involve sensitive and special categories, the existence of recipients and international transfers requires assessments of safeguards due to change in responsibility between entities, and the existence (or lack of) technical and organisational measures can have a direct contributing effect on raising risks as well as not mitigating their impacts. These examples directly follow the reasoning in the guidelines for determining whether processing is likely to result in a high risk through a DPIA, which have been endorsed by the European Data Protection Board (EDPB) [2], and thus have a binding effect regarding the GDPR. As the assessment of 'risks' includes those that are 'high-risk', the requirements from the guidelines and the application of a DPIA necessity procedure in determination of impacts to rights and freedoms stands the test of interpreting one GDPR obligation's requirements from another. Further, case law also has an effect on reducing the scope of derogations, for example, CJEU Case 184/20 expanded the criteria for Article 9 special categories to also include the '*possibility*' to infer it from non-special categories, which requires eliminating such possibilities before the exemption in Article 30(5) can be used.

As this shows, the information required to assess the exemption in Article 30(5) is in effect closely, if not completely, overlapping with the information requirements from Article 30(1) and at least with Article 35(1), whereas the intent was to avoid having to maintain this information in the first place! In later sections, I reiterate this in the inverse i.e. where having a ROPA facilitates DPIAs and other obligations based on the information overlap between their obligations. However, it is important to note that even if the obligation to assess whether a DPIA is required as per Article 35(1) requires the same information as a ROPA, the DPIA necessity assessment is carried out before the processing activity takes place, whereas a ROPA is only an obligation for activities that are actively being carried out. This means the information will have existed before Article 30(1) or Article 30(5) would be triggered. This is surprising as the exemption to Article 30(1) was added to reduce the 'burden' of obligation, but it seems as if it is instead increasing it by requiring the information that it is trying to avoid to be documented to still be collected and used, but by not having it put in a common 'record' it must either be collected from other documentation or be re-identified – both of which are more burdensome than having it ready in the first place.

This theme of information overlap between the assessment of exemptions and the ROPA itself, as well as the existence of some, if not all, information involved before the ROPA is required to be maintained are the key issues that I highlight in my later discussions surrounding the efficacy of such exemptions and the difference between their intended and actual effects. I also revisit the information assessment to underline the importance of ROPA in ensuring the principle of accountability. These conflicting patterns between information required in some obligations, but which are then subject to derogations in others, raises the question that if this information is already known before and during determining the application of an exemption, for what good reason should an organisation not maintain it, especially when that information has uses beyond the exempted documentation? At the same time, by knowing that this information is missing or is incomplete through a ROPA provides a convenient signal for managing compliance as it can lead to potential liability through inadequacy or failure of other obligations.

3 ROPA as the Foundation of Accountability Principle

In the previous section, I discussed how the information involved in maintaining a ROPA is also relevant to other obligations, with an example of Article 35 DPIAs. In this section, I expand upon that discussion by first showing how the information in a ROPA is directly linked to the implementation of the accountability principle in GDPR Article 5(2), and then for other obligations in the GDPR regarding rights, security and data breach management, risk and impact assessments, and management of controller-processor relationships. Through these, I show that the information present in a ROPA not only forms a core part of oversight and accountability exercises, but that the only tangible effect of the Article 30(5) exemption is a specific ROPA document not being created even though the information in that document still exists as it is collected and maintained in other forms. Based on this, I argue that the lack of a ROPA is harmful to the organisations data and legal governance practices.

The ROPA acts as a key artefact for implementing and assessing the accountability principle that is mentioned but not further elaborated upon in GDPR Article 5(2), but is acknowledged as such in authoritative guidelines [1,3,7,11] and in research [25,34], where even if it is difficult to maintain it is still recommended as a key practice [11,25]. As Article 5(2) only requires that the controller "demonstrate compliance" with the other principles specified in Article

5(1), the information required to assess compliance for these Article 5(1) principles forms the pre-requisite for compliance with the accountability principle in Article 5(2). In turn, the principles outlined in Article 5(1) are connected to specific obligations and provisions in other articles of the GDPR, such as the principle of lawfulness to Article 6(1) in general and to Article 49(1) regarding international data transfers. This is supported by the statement from Article 29 Working Party Opinion 3/2010 on the principle of accountability [1] which states "procedures to ensure proper identification of all data processing operations and maintenance of an inventory of data processing operations" (pt.41), and by the EDPB endorsed Guidelines on DPOs [3] which states "In any event, the record required to be kept under Article 30 should also be seen as a tool allowing the controller and the supervisory authority, upon request, to have an overview of all the personal data processing activities an organisation is carrying out. It is thus a prerequisite for compliance, and as such, an effective accountability measure."

Table 3. Mapping involvement of information fields in a ROPA (from Table 1) for GDPR Article 5(2) for accountability principle and GDPR Articles 12–22 for rights

ID	Information	A5	A13	A14	A15	A16	A17	A18	A19	A20	A21	A22
C1–8	Controller Identity	5-1a, 5-2	13-1a, 13-1b	14-1a, 14-1b								
C9	Purposes	5-1a, 5-1b	13-1c	14-1c	15-1a	16	17-1a				21-1–3, 21-6	22-1
C10	Data Subjects	5-1a										22-1
C11	Personal Data	5-1a, 5-1c	13	14-1d	15-1b		17-1a			20-1		
C12	Recipients	5-1a	13-1e	14-1e	15-1c			18	19			
C13	Data Transfer	5-1f	13-1f	14-1f	15-2							
C14	Transfer Recipient	5-1f	13-1f	14-1f	15-2				19			
C15	Transfer Legal Basis	5-1f	13-1f	14-1f	15-2							
C16	Transfer Safeguard	5-1f	13-1f	14-1f	15-2							
C17	Erasure limits	5-1a, 5-1e	13-2a	14-2a	15-1d		17-1e	18-1b				
C18	Tech/Org safeguards	5-1d, 5-1f										22-3

Table 3 shows a mapping from the information in a ROPA (from Article 30(1)) to Article 5 as well as Articles 13–22 regarding rights. It shows how compliance with Article 5(1) involves virtually all the information fields in a ROPA. For the principle of lawfulness in 5(1a), the determination of a valid legal basis requires consideration of the purpose, personal data, and data subjects involved as these have implications regarding the use of specific legal bases in Articles 6(1) and 9(2) such as contract (e.g., for service), legitimate interests (e.g., the balancing test), and consent (e.g., for special categories). Similarly, the principle of transparency is aligned with the requirements for privacy notices outlined as rights in Article 13 and 14, and where this information must be made available proactively to the data subject as compared to the right of access outlined in Article 15.

This information overlap also exists between ROPA and other rights for rectification (Article 16), erasure (Article 17), restriction of processing (Article 18 and 19), data portability (Article 20), and objection (Article 21). For the right to not be subjected to automated decision making (Article 22), the right does not directly relate to any particular ROPA field, however, an assessment of whether this right applies requires information on whether the processing "produces legal effects ... or similarly significantly affects" for the data subject, which in turn requires an assessment of at least the purposes and data subjects involved. Additionally, the implementation of derogations described in Article 22(4) requires information regarding the technical and organisational measures used to safeguard the rights and freedoms of the data subjects.

GDPR requires controllers to implement these rights via specific procedures for communicating about their existence to the data subject (Article 12(1)), and for facilitating their exercise (Article 12(2)), where these procedures and the accompanying information must be prepared ahead of time rather than upon request. For example, Article 13 and 14 are commonly implemented as privacy notices posted on a website, and for the implementation of Articles 15–21, the existence of an information management system that keeps track of exercised requests and can accurately find associated data is a key requirement. In order to implement these rights, therefore, the associated information is required before they can be actively deployed, and as Table 3 shows, this information has a high overlap with ROPA fields from Article 30(1). Thus, the ROPA also forms an essential foundational document for preparing the exercise of rights, and can act as the input and as a '*litmus test*' for their implementations.

Table 4. Mapping involvement of information fields in a ROPA (from Table 1) for GDPR Articles 25–35 regarding controller obligations

ID	Information	A25	A26	A32	A33	A34	A35
C1–8	Controller Identity		A26-1		A33-1b	A34-2	A35-1, A35-7a, A35-7b
C9	Purposes	A25-1, A25-2	A26-1	A32-1			A35-1, A35-7a
C10	Data Subjects	A25-1	A26-1	A32-1	A33-1a	A34-2	A35-1, A35-7a
C11	Personal Data	A25-1, A25-2	A26-1	A32-1	A33-1a	A34-2	A35-1
C12	Recipients		A26-1	A32-1			A35-1
C13	Data Transfer			A32-1			A35-1
C14	Transfer Recipient			A32-1			A35-1
C15	Transfer Legal Basis			A32-1			A35-1
C16	Transfer Safeguard			A32-1			A35-1
C17	Erasure limits	A25-2	A26-1				
C18	Tech/Org safeguards	A25-1, A25-2	A26-1		A33-1d, A33-5	A34-2, A34-3a	A35-7d

The information maintained in a ROPA is also a foundation for other key obligations associated with the role of the controller. Table 4 shows how the ROPA has a large overlap with obligations regarding data protection by design and by default (Article 25), security (Article 32), data breach management (Articles 33 and 34), and conducting a DPIA (Article 35). In the case of a DPIA, the ROPA information is required in both stages where first the necessity to conduct a DPIA is assessed (Article 35(1)) and then a DPIA is conducted to identify risks and impacts. And in the case of joint-controllers as outlined in Article 26, the information in a ROPA has an overlap in the determination of the allocation of responsibilities as it requires that all parties first understand the context and nature of processing.

4 Debating the Utility of Proposed Article 30(5) Dilution

These findings that show the ROPA information is involved in most other obligations should not come as a surprise as the ROPA is effectively a core summary of the processing activities undertaken under the responsibilities of the controller. This aspect has been acknowledged and further emphasised in the guidances issued by supervisory authorities, and is also further elaborated upon in the context of the ROPA being an essential companion to the tasks of the DPO. From this, it is an inescapable conclusion that the ROPA, and its obligation in Article 30, is a key mechanism in the intent of the GDPR to foster accountability as a foundational principle, and that the oversight of processing activities through their documentation is a key first step in this process.

Though the GDPR already contains an exemption for SMEs, the realities of the ROPA dictate that this information is already required to be identified, and that the only 'relief' given to SMEs is from *maintaining* it. However, by not maintaining it, the organisations are also now not prepared to implement the other obligations where the same information applies, and thus risk additional work later as the information is not readily documented, and so the resulting lack of oversight could lead to liabilities and courting problems later. I term this the *Catch-30* problem where the exemption intended to reduce the workload of SMEs in theory instead risks resulting increasing work in this manner. Since it is not possible to determine whether a derogation applies without analysing its requirements, and since it is also not advisable to have information involved in other obligations to not be maintained due to derogations in Article 30(5), I highlight the futility of the exemption as thus only being useful in marginally small amounts by comparison. By proposing the GDPR Article 30(5) derogation be extended to even more organisations, the benefits remain small, but the risk of organisations not being prepared grows larger without any real benefit.

The fallout from this will also extend beyond the organisations themselves as supervisory authorities rely on the organisations to provide them information on their processing activities. Currently, they rely on ROPA as the first step in understanding the activities of the organisation, and a badly maintained ROPA is an immediate symptom of bad governance practices within the organisation or an intentional misdirection from the organisation, either of which raise alarms regarding their GDPR compliance [29]. By removing the requirement for ROPA from more organisations, the investigating process is likely to take more time as authorities have to request information and organisations have to expend time and effort to prepare it, and there is likely to be a back-and-forth exchange of information in this process which further expends time and resources. Additionally, the existing decisions and case law regarding GDPR also underscore how the Article 30 obligations are inherently tied to compliance issues with other Articles [5].

To date, there is only one instance (as far as I could find) where a fine was issued solely for a violation involving a ROPA[2], and where other decisions referencing the Article 30 provisions are accompanied by violations of other articles – which as I have highlighted earlier share information with the ROPA requirements. Article 30(1) and 30(2) issues and violations are thus not the cause, but are symptoms of other underlying and manifested problems, and that by identifying information as being missing, incorrect, or incomplete, the ROPA is a key indicator that it is highly likely there is also something wrong with the other obligations.

Still somewhat surprisingly, GDPR authorities have seemingly assented to the Commissions's proposed 'simplification' measure, at least in the form of "preliminary support" through their collective response under the EDPB and as a joint letter with the European Data Protection Supervisor (EDPS) [13,17]. In this, the EDPS notes that the proposal does not affect the core principles of the GDPR, whereas the findings of this article show that the simplification does affect the accountability principle by significantly reducing the ability of the organisation to understand its own processing activities due to the absence of a well-maintained record. In its statement, the EDPB Chair acknowledges the importance of ROPA, that the existing derogation "did not always achieve its goal", and that the proposed simplification provides flexibility to SMEs and SMCs. However, they have also highlighted the gaps in assessment of this proposal's intended impacts by asking the Commission "to better evaluate the impact on the organisation subject to this change, to assess whether the draft proposal ensure a proportionate and fair balance between the protection of personal data and the interests of organisations". I make particular note of this phrasing in their argument: "that this would not affect the obligation of controllers and processors to comply with other GDPR obligations", as my argument in this article is that this does affect other compliance activities based on the analysis and evidence of information and effort involved in maintaining a ROPA being not an isolated obligation, but a common foundation for other obligations in the GDPR. Instead, by opting not to maintain a ROPA, the organisation will also be opting to disregard good data governance practices, and will likely create risks and liabilities in implementation of other obligations. Thus, both the EDPS and the EDPB should also revise their positions on the validity of the proposal.

To conclude, the Commission's current proposal should be revised due to its lack of practical usefulness and the high probability that it encourages practices that risk liability and compliance for the organisations it intends to support and promote. It is in effect a limited dilution of the GDPR as it reduces the obligations for a specific group of organisations. The justification for this is absent from the proposal, there has been no impact assessment conducted regarding

---

[2] Case EXP20220092 by the AEPD (Spain) regarding non-provision of ROPA under Article 30(4).

validity of measures, and further – and most importantly – I question whether it will actually lead to the intended outcomes.

5 Potential Alternatives

In the previous sections, my emphasis was on highlighting that the current proposal to increase the dilution of ROPA maintaining obligations to include both SMEs and SMCs will not have the intended effect. However, it is important to acknowledge the context of the Commission's proposal as being grounded in the findings of the Draghi report with the objective to ensure the competitiveness of the EU economy by supporting the SMEs and SMCs as key stakeholders. I therefore explore potential avenues where such support can be materialised and the intended effects can be achieved without damaging the legacy of the GDPR or risk its further domino effect into dilution of other regulations.

5.1 Distinguish Personal Data Processing as a Business Model

The GDPR applies indiscriminately to all organisations that process personal data. However, some of these organisations operate within existing highly regulated environments (e.g., pharmacies) where the requirements of the GDPR are miniscule in comparison to the sectorial requirements and documentation involved. Here, the personal data involved is not as an end to itself, but a part of their operations and service provision. It is only when this personal data is used beyond these core activities in a direct way, such as for profiling and advertising, that it becomes an issue and requires more scrutiny.

The Commission's proposal to expand the scope of codes of conducts and certifications to SMCs should also take into account these sectorial 'patterns of commonalities' and develop effective frameworks through which SMEs and SMCs can be assured of their GDPR compliance practices. In this manner, the focus will always be on the irregularities and the activities that fall outside the 'known' spheres of compliance, and thus promote regulatory learnings and requirements for further regulations like the AI Act [27]. Taking such a measure will provide support and assurance to the many SMEs and SMCs who are subjected to the GDPR because they involve personal data in the course of activities such as HR or typical customer and marketing activities, for which common resources can be collectively developed and provided at the EU rather than Member State levels both as a way to pool resources and to avoid fragmentation.

5.2 Ensuring Compliance Solutions Are Compliant

The GDPR led to the practice of organisations utilising external platforms and services to manage their compliance (referred to as Compliance Management Platforms or CMPs), where such CMPs promise fully compliant solutions that the SMEs and SMCs perceive as being a quick way to meet their obligations. However, such organisations often do not act in the best interests of their clients and act like liabilities in disguise. For example, 'common market practices' adopted based on compliance claims have been shown to be severely problematic regarding consent management and other functionalities [28,35]. By not addressing these issues of real-world power dynamics, and instead focusing on simplification, organisations will continue to pretend they are compliant under a mistaken or a wilfully ignorant perspective. To remedy this, the Commission's proposals to revitalise the use of codes of conduct as per GDPR Article 40 and certifications as per Article 42 should also focus on the tools and vendors used by SMEs and SMCs to achieve compliance and to avoid misleading and bad compliance practices. In essence, SMEs and SMCs should be able to 'trust' compliance solutions and their providers.

5.3 Harmonise Compliance Measures

The Draghi report also makes a case for the competitiveness of the EU being reliant on the advent of AI technologies, and for which SMEs and SMCs require regulatory support rather then obstructions. This is not a call for deregulation as the goal of regulations should be to balance the economic needs with the social well-being founded through rights and freedoms. Instead, the current process of drafting individual regulations with unique compliance mechanisms, which then requires SMEs and SMCs to discover how and where they might be subject to each specific regulation and how to comply with them in different and overlapping forms. This is a key cause of concern as SMEs and SMCs do not have adequate resources that larger organisations do, but also because lawmaking and standards processes rarely focus on SMEs and SMCs beyond derogations like the GDPR does. In addition, established larger organisations have a stronger economic position to risk compliance violations whereas SMEs and SMCs may prefer to be cautious rather than risk getting fined due to their economic constraints.

Take the example of a newly formed SME/SMC that focuses on AI technologies using personal data – it must not only take in to account the GDPR, but also now the AI Act, and where these are not designed to be 'complied with' together despite being 'authored' by the same governance system. Though the AI Act references GDPR as being applicable regarding processing of personal data, it does not go beyond this 'simple' acknowledgement. This means organisations and authorities face a common burden of figuring out how to comply with the AI Act and how to reuse GDPR compliance to avoid duplication of efforts. The drafting of the laws does not facilitate this process, and the fragmentation of rules across EU/EEA Member States further complicates it. Our prior work [33] shows how DPIA requirements are so fragmented across Member States that there is no clarity or certainty on its complementary status with the FRIA in AI Act Article 27(4), and that the GDPR's roles of controller and processor are not accounted for in the AI Act despite there being a significant scope of AI systems processing personal data somewhere along their lifecycle and high-risk AI systems dominantly involving such processing.

It is highly expected that organisations that already address the GDPR are also interested in using AI technologies and will thus have to consider the AI Act. If instead, the AI Act was written in a way that would offer such organisations a natural progression from their existing processes and obligations to include AI, it would have been more useful than the current duplication of individual and national efforts on this topic. In particular, GDPR authorities must now expend considerable time and resources to understand and provide guidance and resources based on combining the GDPR with the AI Act. This interpretation is supported by the current Council agenda under the Polish presidency as concerning multiple reporting obligations across different regulations, fragmentation in implementations and enforcements across Member States, and suggested making interoperability a part of the impact assessment in the lawmaking process [9].

Another example of streamlining – the ISO JTC1/SC27 group recently initiated a project to revise the existing ISO/IEC TS 27560:2023 standard for consent records and receipts [23] to cover all legal bases [24] as the information involved in processing based on consent and other legal bases under the GDPR has a large effective overlap based on GDPR Article 30 (a point also emphasised earlier in this article). Our previous work also shows how this approach allows integrated solutions for GDPR and Data Governance Act [32]. This means organisations should prioritise identifying the core information regardless of the legal basis or regulation used, and that the further specific legal or sectorial requirements should then be implemented additionally. This provides a single consistent set of information for organisations to manage, and is much easier and convenient than having to maintain several different records for different legal basis. This is directly based on the findings of the GDPR's Article 30 implementations in Member States and the recommendations of the supervisory authorities through their guidelines and templates [34]. We have also included an appendix in the 27560 draft that provides guidance on how AI technologies can be recorded in a manner that then aligns with and simplifies process such as impact assessments and determination of roles based on the utility of Article 30 for GDPR.

If the AI Act had been published in such a manner where it specifically and directly updated the requirements of the GDPR where AI systems utilise personal data, SMEs and SMCs would have received a consistent and harmonised set of requirements to maintain records in the same document and format with some information coming from the GDPR and some from the AI Act. At the same time, the GDPR would have benefitted from the AI Act's comprehensive coverage of 'automated' systems, particularly in context of Article 22 and the right to object to decision-making, while also paving the way to regulate development of recent rapid developments such as generative AI models and AI agents, which also heavily involve personal data, by reusing the established Article 6 legal bases and the transparency, access, and objection rights outlined in Articles 12–23. Such harmonisations are necessary to reduce the 'friction' between regulations as GDPR's purpose limitations is intended to limit processing whereas the AI Act's also wants to stimulate AI development [9].

5.4 Utilise RegTech and eGov Technologies

The Data Protection Directive required the supervisory authorities to have a system in place that would have accepted notifications from controllers containing information which corresponded to the ROPA in GDPR. This system was removed due to a perceived burden on the authorities to implement and maintain this system, and to instead have organisations take on more responsibilities and involve authorities only when concerned. I propose that this notification system be re-introduced, especially for SMEs and SMCs. A common 'compliance platform' is an excellent way to support maintaining documentation where the system utilises advances in information management to avoid manual laborious processes for both the organisation and the authority. Its feasibility, especially within economic constraints, can be studied from success stories like the Jamaican Data Protection Act in 2020 [21,30] which required the assigned Commissioner to develop such a notification system for organisations to register their activities. Since organisations under the GDPR are effectively required to publicly publish information due to Articles 13 and 14, this is not an additional burden as the same system can also assist in the creation of privacy notices for these articles. Notably, the Jamaican implementation utilises common 'patterns' or 'use-cases', such as HR, marketing, and account creation, identified through a detailed consultation process. These allow the organisation to express its intended activity with a guided and controlled vocabulary that is backed by a machine-readable interoperable format (see below) to produce documentation on both ends, thus benefiting the organisation and providing authorities with audit-ready information without duplication of efforts.

Without such a 'technologically effective' solution, sustaining and succeeding is difficult for the increasing amount of regulations and organisational processes, especially for future visions such as Data Spaces. For this, I point to our efforts in producing the Data Privacy Vocabulary (DPV) [31] which provides such a resource in a way that takes into account the legislative and organisational 'separations' while still providing a consolidated and harmonised mechanism for information representation and exchange. We engaged with the stakeholders of the Jamaican Data Protection Act in this context, where the DPV's taxonomies were key to the implementation of the system, and where I believe the EU with its vastly greater capacity for innovation and resource allocation can implement this in an even more efficient manner. Such approaches are already used in the eProcurement system[3] for EU public procurement, and are thus not out of place in the EU's legal toolkit. The recent call for tenders to support the AI Office also explicitly involves producing software to aid the enforcement of the AI Act[4]. And the EU Council also agrees with this approach by noting measures such as a centralised glossary, harmonised and pre-filled templates, and targeted open source 'kits' and 'forms' for SMEs [9].

---

[3] https://docs.ted.europa.eu/epo-home/.
[4] AI Act: Technical Assistance for AI Safety https://ted.europa.eu/en/notice/-/detail/272332-2025.

Bringing this to GDPR would allow benefits not just to the organisation, but also to the enforcer. The submission of a ROPA to the authority via an eGov or electronic information management system also allows the authority to identify areas of concern and produce targeted guidance in response to the specific needs of SMEs and SMCs, and to proactively carry out impact assessments at scale across sectors or for specific organisations based on a common methodology. For SMEs and SMCs, this would be a boon as most of their current GDPR implementations would thus be offloaded to automated software that is backed by the authority, thereby reducing the effective reporting requirements and also providing them with legal clarity and support as needed. The effort required to produce such a system is not disproportionate to the benefits it will provide, and can be offset by developing a common system across EU (which incidentally will also help the one-stop-shop system), with registration fees as done in Jamaica and in the UK, and through the fines collected under the GDPR. It will also help streamline the rights exercise requests, assist in breach reporting, and allow authorities to provide targeted support to struggling organisations at scale. Sitra, which is an innovation fund based in Finland, recently published an op-ed supporting such use of RegTech and emphasising its necessity in the evolving technological landscape [26].

However, while these approaches promise efficiency and speed, they must be explored with a critical perspective so to avoid mere compliance theatre as the Commission and the authorities would still be relying on organisations to be responsible, especially where high-risk applications do not incorporate the underlying principles and intended effects [36]. These approaches also require substantial effort in context of the limited budgets that the authorities have had to work with since the onset of GDPR enforcement. Recent analysis into the budgets and decision-making ability of GDPR authorities, however, shows that budgetary conditions have improved [22]. The potential of this approach also aligns well the Commission's Horizon research programme, particularly under Cluster 4 for use of data and AI technologies for compliance. This gives another possibility for the feasibility of proposed approaches through fiscal co-ordination, e.g., between the research programs and between authorities.

6 Concluding Remarks

The European Digital Rights group, comprised of NGOs, civil society organisations, and experts recently published an open letter titled "Reopening the GDPR is a threat to rights, accountability, and the future of EU digital policy" [18]. As a signatory to this letter, I agree that the current proposal represents an 'opening' of diluting amendments to the GDPR, despite the Commission arguing otherwise, as it effectively demonstrates that: 1) the GDPR is open to be changed; 2) the way to do this is through economic coercion focused on the plight of the SMEs and SMCs; and that 3) this is how to weaken future regulations. The GDPR represented a long, lengthy, and perilous process which was subject to intense lobbying and derailment campaigns, but which ultimately prevailed, even if in a comparatively diluted form. Any change to this therefore should be accompanied with a robust and thorough impact assessment, which is entirely lacking in the current proposal. Instead, this work shows its questionable efficacy and that the exemption seems alluring on paper but has no merit. If accepted, the proposal will not reduce any of the actual work or information involved, and thus provide no sustainable benefit to the SMEs and SMCs as it only removes the requirement to maintain information in a specific document but still requires that information be maintained elsewhere. Based on this, the Commission should therefore revise the current proposal and for good measure also carry out an assessment that shows the empirical validity of this and future proposed measures. In this, it should also strive to identify other avenues to meet its intended objectives that will assist in harmonising rather than undermining the role and usefulness of GDPR compliance measures for other regulations such as the AI Act.

During the period when this article was being finalised, the Danish presidency also took over the presidency of the EU Council, and has authored a non-public 'non-paper' which includes the this and other GDPR 'simplification' measures, and which is confirmed by the agenda for associated events[5]. While it is difficult to predict the future of these measures, it is clear that there is significant political manoeuvring around simplification at both national and EU levels with planned meetings and proposals being expected for the rest of this year. As such, the utility of the analysis and arguments presented in this paper may seem limited in scope as they may not hold for future measures. However, the approach taken in this paper to analyse the practical efficacy of measures based on information involved and the arguments presented in favour of considering other promising and broader solutions would still be valuable. In particular, future regulatory activities such as the Data Union Strategy[6] will benefit from the arguments regarding the harmonisation of compliance measures, utilising common machine-readable information formats, and learning from success stories around the world.

Acknowledgements. The AI Accountability Lab is funded under the AI Collaborative, an Initiative of the Omidyar Group; the Bestseller Foundation; and the John D. and Catherine T. MacArthur Foundation. The ADAPT SFI Centre for Digital Media Technology is funded by Science Foundation Ireland through the SFI Research Centres Programme and is co-funded under the European Regional Development Fund (ERDF) through Grant#13/RC/2106 P2. This work has been funded by the EU's Horizon programme under grant agreement No.101168490 (RECITALS project).

Disclosure of Interests. Harshvardhan J. Pandit is the current chair of the W3C Data Privacy Vocabularies and Controls Community Group (DPVCG) and the editor/maintainer of Data Privacy Vocabulary (DPV), and is a part of the ISO/IEC JTC1/SC27 committee and editor of the 27560 revision project.

---

[5] https://danish-presidency.consilium.europa.eu/en/events/informal-meeting-of-justice-and-home-affairs-ministers/.
[6] https://digital-strategy.ec.europa.eu/en/policies/strategy-data.

References

1. Article 29 Working Party: Opinion 3/2010 on the principle of accountability (2010). https://ec.europa.eu/justice/article-29/documentation/opinion-recommendation/files/2010/wp173_en.pdf, wP 173
2. Article 29 Working Party: Guidelines on data protection impact assessment (dpia) and determining whether processing is "likely to result in a high risk" for the purposes of regulation 2016/679 (2017). https://www.edpb.europa.eu/our-work-tools/general-guidance/endorsed-wp29-guidelines_en, wP248 rev.01, endorsed by the EDPB
3. Article 29 Working Party: Guidelines on data protection officers ('dpos') (2017). https://ec.europa.eu/newsroom/article29/items/612048, wP243 rev.01, endorsed by the EDPB
4. byRisk consortium: byrisk project grant agreement no. 101193352 (2024). https://byrisk-project.eu/
5. CMS Legal Services EEIG: GDPR enforcement tracker (2025). https://www.enforcementtracker.com/. Accessed 2 June 2025
6. Commission, E.: Better regulation (2024). https://commission.europa.eu/law/law-making-process/better-regulation_en
7. Commission Nationale de l'Informatique et des Libertés (CNIL): Record of processing activities (2019). https://www.cnil.fr/en/gdpr-toolkit/record-processing-activities, guidance on maintaining records of processing activities under Article 30 GDPR
8. Commission Nationale de l'Informatique et des Libertés (CNIL): Tpe-pme: le cepd publie un guide rgpd disponible en français (2019). https://www.cnil.fr/fr/tpe-pme-le-cepd-publie-un-guide-rgpd
9. Council of the European Union: 9383/25 outcomes of the discussions on simplification activities in the digital field and balancing regulation and innovation in the technology-driven economy (2025). https://data.consilium.europa.eu/doc/document/ST-9383-2025-INIT/en/pdf, report by the Polish presidency
10. Data Protection Commission: Guidance for smes (2019). https://www.dataprotection.ie/en/dpc-guidance/guidance-smes
11. Data Protection Commission: Records of processing activities (article 30) guidance (2023). https://www.dataprotection.ie/en/dpc-guidance/records-of-processing-article-30-guidance
12. Draghi, M.: The future of European competitiveness – a competitiveness strategy for europe. Tech. rep., European Commission (2024). https://commission.europa.eu/topics/eu-competitiveness/draghi-report_en
13. EDPB-EDPS: Edpb-edps joint opinion 01/2025 on the proposal for a regulation on simplification measures for smes and smcs, in particular the record-keeping obligation under art. 30(5) gdpr. https://www.edpb.europa.eu/our-work-tools/our-documents/edpbedps-joint-opinion/edpb-edps-joint-opinion-012025-proposal_en
14. European Commission: Proposal for a regulation of the european parliament and of the council on the protection of individuals with regard to the processing of personal data and on the free movement of such data (general data protection regulation) (2012). https://eur-lex.europa.eu/legal-content/EN/TXT/?uri=CELEX:52012PC0010, cOM(2012) 10 final
15. European Commission: Long-term competitiveness of the eu: looking beyond 2030 (2023). https://eur-lex.europa.eu/legal-content/EN/TXT/?uri=CELEX:52023DC0168, cOM(2023) 168 final

16. European Commission: Proposal for a regulation of the european parliament and of the council amending regulations (eu) 2016/679, (eu) 2016/1036, (eu) 2016/1037, (eu) 2017/1129, (eu) 2023/1542 and (eu) 2024/573 as regards the extension of certain mitigating measures available for small and medium-sized enterprises to small mid-cap enterprises and further simplification measures (2025). https://eur-lex.europa.eu/legal-content/EN/TXT/?uri=CELEX:52025PC0501, cOM(2025) 501 final/2
17. European Data Protection Board, European Data Protection Supervisor: Edpb-edps letter on european commission draft proposal on simplification of record-keeping under the gdpr (2025). https://www.edps.europa.eu/data-protection/our-work/publications/edps-edpb-joint-opinions/2025-05-08-edpb-edps-letter-european-commission-simplification-record-keeping-under-gdpr
18. European Digital Rights (EDRi): Reopening the gdpr is a threat to rights, accountability, and the future of eu digital policy (2025). https://edri.org/wp-content/uploads/2025/05/Final-EDRI-letter-against-GDPR-simplification.pdf, open letter signed by 121 organisations and individuals
19. European Parliament and Council: Directive 95/46/ec of the european parliament and of the council of 24 october 1995 on the protection of individuals with regard to the processing of personal data and on the free movement of such data (1995). https://eur-lex.europa.eu/eli/dir/1995/46/oj, oJ L 281, 23.11.1995, pp. 31–50
20. European Parliament and Council: Regulation (eu) 2016/679 of the european parliament and of the council of 27 april 2016 on the protection of natural persons with regard to the processing of personal data and on the free movement of such data, and repealing directive 95/46/ec (general data protection regulation) (2016). https://eur-lex.europa.eu/eli/reg/2016/679/oj, oJ L 119, 4.5.2016, pp. 1–88
21. Government of Jamaica: The data protection act (2020). https://japarliament.gov.jm/attachments/article/339/The%20Data%20Protection%20Act%2C%202020.pdf
22. Irish Council for Civil Liberties (ICCL): 5 years: GDPR's crisis point - ICCL report on EEA data protection authorities (2023)
23. ISO/IEC JTC 1/SC 27: Ts 27560:2023 privacy technologies – consent record information structure. Tech. Rep. ISO/IEC TS 27560:2023, International Organization for Standardization (2023). https://www.iso.org/standard/80392.html
24. ISO/IEC JTC 1/SC 27: Wd 27560 privacy technologies – consent record information structure. Tech. Rep. ISO/IEC TS 27560:2023, International Organization for Standardization (2023). https://www.iso.org/standard/80392.html
25. Labadie, C., Legner, C.: Building data management capabilities to address data protection regulations: learnings from EU-GDPR. J. Inf. Technol. **38**(1), 16–44 (2023)
26. Lehtonen, K., Toivanen, M.: Why technologies are the missing piece in the eu's simplification efforts (2025). https://www.euractiv.com/section/tech/opinion/why-technologies-are-the-missing-piece-in-the-eus-simplification-efforts/, euractiv Opinion sponsored by Sitra, published May 30, 2025
27. Lewis, D., Lasek-Markey, M., Golpayegani, D., Pandit, H.J.: Mapping the regulatory learning space for the eu ai act (2025). https://arxiv.org/abs/2503.05787
28. Mertens, G., Bielova, N., Roca, V., Santos, C.: You can't trust your tag neither: privacy leaks and potential legal violations within the google tag manager. In: EuroS&P 2025-10th IEEE European Symposium on Security and Privacy (2025)
29. noyb – European Center for Digital Rights: Third noyb "advent reading" from facebook/dpc documents (2021). https://noyb.eu/en/third-noyb-advent-reading-facebookdpc-documents, published December 12, 2021

30. Office of the Information Commissioner, Jamaica: Guidance on data controller registration under the data protection act (2024). https://oic.gov.jm/page/information-note-registration
31. Pandit, H.J., Esteves, B., Krog, G.P., Ryan, P., Golpayegani, D., Flake, J.: Data privacy vocabulary (DPV) – version 2.0. In: The Semantic Web – ISWC 2024, pp. 171–193. Springer, Cham (2025). https://doi.org/10.1007/978-3-031-77847-6_10
32. Pandit, H.J., Lindquist, J., Krog, G.P.: Implementing ISO/IEC TS 27560:2023 consent records and receipts for GDPR and DGA. In: Privacy Technologies and Policy, pp. 228–251. Springer, Cham (2024). https://doi.org/10.1007/978-3-031-68024-3_12
33. Rintamäki, T., Golpayegani, D., Lewis, D., Celeste, E., Pandit, H.J.: Impact assessment requirements in the GDPR vs the AI act: overlaps, divergence, and implications (2025). https://doi.org/10.31219/osf.io/6qhzj, oSF Preprints
34. Ryan, P., Brennan, R., Pandit, H.J.: DPCAT: specification for an interoperable and machine-readable data processing catalogue based on GDPR. Information **13**(5), 244 (2022). https://doi.org/10.3390/info13050244
35. Santos, C., Nouwens, M., Toth, M., Bielova, N., Roca, V.: Consent management platforms under the GDPR: processors and/or controllers? In: Annual Privacy Forum, pp. 47–69. Springer, Cham (2021)
36. Terzis, P., Veale, M., Gaumann, N.: Law and the emerging political economy of algorithmic audits. In: Proceedings of the 2024 ACM Conference on Fairness, Accountability, and Transparency, pp. 1255–1267 (2024)

Open Access This chapter is licensed under the terms of the Creative Commons Attribution-NonCommercial-NoDerivatives 4.0 International License (http://creativecommons.org/licenses/by-nc-nd/4.0/), which permits any noncommercial use, sharing, distribution and reproduction in any medium or format, as long as you give appropriate credit to the original author(s) and the source, provide a link to the Creative Commons license and indicate if you modified the licensed material. You do not have permission under this license to share adapted material derived from this chapter or parts of it.

The images or other third party material in this chapter are included in the chapter's Creative Commons license, unless indicated otherwise in a credit line to the material. If material is not included in the chapter's Creative Commons license and your intended use is not permitted by statutory regulation or exceeds the permitted use, you will need to obtain permission directly from the copyright holder.

Professional Methods & Tools for Analysis and Decision Making

Turning to Online Forums for Legal Information: A Case Study of GDPR's Legitimate Interests

Lin Kyi[1](✉), Cristiana Santos[2], Sushil Ammanaghatta Shivakumar[1], Franziska Roesner[3], and Asia Biega[1]

[1] Max Planck Institute for Security and Privacy, Bochum, Germany
lin.kyi@mpi-sp.org
[2] Utrecht University, Utrecht, The Netherlands
[3] University of Washington, Seattle, USA

Abstract. Practitioners building online services and tools often turn to online forums such as Reddit, Law Stack Exchange, and Stack Overflow for legal guidance to ensure compliance with the GDPR. The legal information presented in these forums directly impacts present-day industry practitioner's decisions. Online forums can serve as gateways that, depending on the accuracy and quality of the answers provided, may either support or undermine the protection of privacy and data protection fundamental rights. However, there is a need for deeper investigation into practitioners' decision-making processes and their understanding of legal compliance when seeking for legal information online. Using GDPR's "legitimate interests" legal ground for processing personal data as a case study, we investigate how practitioners use online forums to identify common areas of confusion in applying legitimate interests in practice, and evaluate how legally sound online forum responses are. Our analysis found that applying the legal basis of legitimate interest is complex for practitioners, with important implications for how the GDPR is implemented in practice. The legal analysis showed that crowdsourced legal information tends to be legally sound, though sometimes incomplete. We outline recommendations to improve the quality of online forums by ensuring that responses are more legally sound and comprehensive, enabling practitioners to apply legitimate interests effectively in practice and uphold the GDPR.

Keywords: GDPR · Legitimate Interest · Online Forums · Legal Information · Compliance

1 Introduction

The General Data Protection Regulation (GDPR) came into effect in May 2018 to protect EU users' personal data [31]. However, it also brought challenges for organizations who must translate abstract legal principles into specific technical requirements to assure compliance [20,42,48,51,79].

© The Author(s) 2026
N. Arastouei et al. (Eds.): APF 2025, LNCS 16183, pp. 153–177, 2026.
https://doi.org/10.1007/978-3-032-07574-1_7

How then, do practitioners (anyone involved in applying the GDPR for their respective organization, including developers, designers, business owners, and others), particularly those without in-house legal support, navigate GDPR obligations? While some official compliance guidance by regulatory authorities exists, some practitioners, also referred to as posters in this paper[1], may turn to online forums to seek legal information. We use the term "legal information"[2] to signify the legal case-related recommendations in a given post. Online forums can provide scenario-specific, cost-free, and quick access to answers, and their use by industry practitioners has been documented in other contexts [43,84,92]. Online forums can serve as gateways that, depending on the accuracy and quality of the answers provided, may either support or undermine the protection of privacy and data rights through adherence to data protection regulations.

In this paper, we investigate online forums in the context of GDPR compliance. We look at how practitioners seek legal information using the following online forums – Reddit, Law Stack Exchange, and Stack Overflow – to be compliant with the GDPR.

We explore online forums for the following reasons. First, developers tend to primarily use online forums to support their privacy-related decisions [69,85]. Developers often struggle to meet legal requirements as they often lack privacy and legal expertise [48,49]. Second, other tools to support their decision-making processes, such as official and reliable guidance for developers, are largely lacking [23,36]. These guides are not contextually-sensitive for developer's projects, thus they are left with industry-based sources [86] which, while might be practical, are typically unofficial, potentially biased, and not subject to rigorous legal or regulatory review. Consequently, the legal information presented in these forums directly impacts present-day industry practitioner's decisions, given the prevalence of forums to aid developers [85]. With the development of Large-Language Models (LLMs), a novel source to access online legal information has been introduced into the software development process. This shift is reflected in trends, such as Stack Overflow reporting a decline in user activity, which they attributed to the rise of AI systems [25]. Third, more practitioners and users have started using LLMs and other AI assistants for legal information seeking and use [7,25] which are trained on online forum data [47]. Incorrect information present in these forums will thus have even bigger consequences with the usage of these new technologies [15]. Therefore, it is important that online forums provide correct legal information for current and potential future uses of legal information.

---

[1] Here, *posters* refer to the practitioners who are posting questions in online forums. We also use the term *practitioners* when referring to the same users posting questions too.

[2] There is a difference between "legal information" and "legal advice." When posters refer to their concrete cases on Stack Overflow, they are provided with legal information tuned to their context. Legal advice is instead given by a legal professional and establishes an attorney-client relationship, which is not the case in online forums. In this paper, we use the term "information" to signify the legal case-related recommendations about a given post.

The GDPR offers an extensive data protection regime that yields thousands of posts and responses when searched for in online forums. To make data analysis more feasible, we decided to focus our investigation specifically on the questions and responses that practitioners posed relating to "legitimate interests," one of the GDPR's six legal grounds for collecting data. We focused on legitimate interest because of its vague nature, yet is highly important due to its flexibility and breadth, covering legal bases for data collection not currently mentioned by the GDPR [41].

Legitimate interest is defined in Art. 6(1)(f) of the GDPR as the processing that is necessary for the legitimate interests pursued by data controllers [77] or third parties [31,34]. While consent is generally well-established and recognized due to the proliferation of cookie banners, legitimate interest is not [55]. In this paper, we analyze online forum discussions relating to legitimate interests to understand what confusions practitioners may have in applying it, and assumptions practitioners have about this legal basis.

The vague nature of legitimate interests has led to documented examples of its misuse and non-compliance [41,55]. We hypothesize that one potential reason for legitimate interest misuse lies in the difficulty of understanding it.

Contributions. Our paper presents two main contributions. First, through a qualitative analysis of the questions in the online forums, we identified the main challenges practitioners may face when applying the legitimate interest legal basis "in the wild" by studying online forum posts. Second, our analysis of forum answers offering legal information indicates that while information may seem legally sound, there are precautions practitioners must take before relying on these forums. In our paper, we offer recommendations for how online legal forum posts could be formulated to ensure legally sound answers, therefore helping to better protect users' fundamental rights to privacy and data protection.

2 Background

2.1 Empirical Studies on the Legitimate Interest Legal Basis

Court cases have shown that many uses of legitimate interests are illegal when used for targeted advertising purposes [22], supplemented by empirical studies that have investigated the use of this legal basis. Matte et al. [60] found that hundreds of advertisers relied on legitimate interests for purposes that should instead rely on consent [60]. Kyi et al. found that in the context of cookie banners, the use of legitimate interests are not transparent to users: very few websites mentioned that they relied on legitimate interests, and of those which did, not all allowed users to object thereto. Their user study revealed that users are not fond of most legitimate interest-based purposes, such as personalized advertising, and preferred sharing data for purposes which did not benefit companies and advertisers [55].

2.2 Importance of Online Forums for Software Development

Online forums are an important source of information for software developers [10,12,68]. Previous research has shown that Stack Overflow influences developers' practices, such as code reuse from Stack Overflow posts [92], and impacts developers' productivity on GitHub [88]. However, they may also promote poor practices such as reusing code, which has negative impacts on the security and privacy of systems [43].

The number of GDPR-related Stack Overflow posts in recent years has been increasing [85], which suggests that privacy and data protection are becoming more important for developers [82]. The knowledge shared in online forums can impact how developers abide to security and data protection obligations [5,43,57,85]. Privacy-related discussions on Stack Overflow seem to be connected to external events relevant to privacy, such as new privacy restrictions [57,82]. When such an event happens, developers often felt privacy restrictions required more efforts from them without many benefits [57].

Online Legal Compliance Information. The most common privacy-related information that developers suggested on Stack Overflow refers to legal compliance, as 38.7% of answers related to GDPR and California Consumer Privacy Act (CCPA) compliance according to a study conducted by Tahaei et al. [84]. Developers found it difficult to translate legal requirements, which some saw as full of "legalese," into technical terms [14,45,78,80,83]. Developers frequently asked about how to adhere to legal requirements that are imposed by various platforms, such as different app stores. It was commonly advised for developers to check that their company's privacy policy was compliant, and to ask for user consent [84].

Several online resources have emerged, aimed at helping industry practitioners, often developers, apply the GDPR. Some are from Data Protection Authorities (DPAs), such as the French DPA's "GDPR Developer's Guide" [23] and European Data Protection Board's "Data Protection Guide for Small Business" [36]. Other sources of online information derive from developers aimed at helping fellow developers [4], and GDPR compliance guides from Consent Management Platforms (CMPs), such as OneTrust [86].

3 Methods

As the topic of our analysis spans questions at the intersection of technology and law, we collected data from three popular online forums that technology practitioners may turn to for advice: Reddit, Law Stack Exchange, and Stack Overflow. Our general approach was to collect and analyze this data to understand the struggles and discussions practitioners are having online when it comes to GDPR compliance, and to evaluate the legal soundness of the answers.

We split our qualitative analysis into two sections to investigate i) the possible elements of confusion about GDPR compliance, specifically focusing on legitimate interests (Sect. 4), and ii) the legal soundness of online forum answers (Sect. 5).

3.1 Data Collection

Reddit. We searched for posts and comments from industry practitioners containing the phrase "legitimate interest(s)" on September 27, 2024. We made requests to the Reddit API to collect relevant data for our analysis, filtered results based on the subreddit, and stored this data in a CSV file. Our scrape collected the title of the post, URL (in case further analysis was needed), comments, the post's body text, subreddit name, upvotes for the post, age of the post, and word count. We manually removed some posts from our dataset which were out of the scope of this study (e.g., describing legitimate interests in offline contexts). Most of our posts came from the r/GDPR and r/privacy subreddit due to the relevance of these posts for our analysis.

Law Stack Exchange and Stack Overflow. Similar to Reddit, we searched for posts and comments containing "legitimate interest(s)" on Stack Overflow and Law Stack Exchange and used data from Stack Exchange's public data dump from May 2024. We paired the posts with their comments and answers, and cleaned the data. We collected the title of the post, body text, URL, number of views, upvotes, comments, age of the post, and word count of the post.

3.2 Dataset

In total, we collected 319 posts (not including comments and answers); 10 posts were from Stack Overflow, 203 posts from Law Stack Exchange, and 106 from Reddit, a sample size on par with previous qualitative papers analyzing online forums in privacy-specific contexts [82,84] and those used in qualitative legal research [58,90]. For the legal soundness analysis, we collected the answers to questions from Law Stack Exchange which were marked by posters as "Accepted," which yielded 94 answers. We discuss the data analysis methods for our two-part analysis in each respective section.

Ethical Considerations of Using Online Forum Data. Social media data can be rich and allow researchers to understand social phenomena, but also presents several ethical challenges [13]. A study using social media data was preferred over other research methods, such as interviewing or surveying industry practitioners, because: i) it would be difficult to gather industry participants who would be willing to discuss their company's data practices in a research context, ii) this data is readily available for analysis, and iii) online forums allow researchers to view how practitioners might navigate legal compliance "in the wild". A social media analysis would ensure a more targeted and scalable study of what industry practitioners are discussing for technical implementations of legitimate interest. Reddit and Stack Exchange (including Stack Overflow) are two commonly-used sources of data for academic research [40,74].

Due to the potential legal and ethical implications of these posts (such as an employee or company getting into legal troubles), when quoting participants, we did not mention usernames, and took precautions to paraphrase the posts. Sometimes we engaged in *ethical fabrication* to maintain user anonymity when posters mentioned specific scenarios that could possibly be identifiable [11,28,59]. Although Stack Exchange prefers that researchers attribute posts [8], due to the potential legal and ethical implications, we paraphrased quotes and did not link them to protect user identities.

4 Analysis 1: Practitioner Discussions and Inquiries

In this section we report on the qualitative analysis of the *posts* we collected from the three forums. We investigated the practitioner roles seeking legal information, and common points of discussion (or confusion) about applying legitimate interests in practice.

Qualitative Analysis. We analyzed the content from the three forums and conducted a *thematic analysis* to find underlying patterns within the dataset by labeling important parts in the data (*codes*), and grouping these codes to form *themes* [19]. To investigate what practitioners discuss in online forums, we had two annotators analyse the collected posts. They first annotated a random set of 15 posts together to discuss what to focus the analysis upon. They decided to keep track of: i) the (perceived) role or industry of the poster, ii) the general topic they were seeking information about, and iii) codes related to the poster's query. After this was established, the annotators coded the same random set of 15 posts to calculate the interrater reliability. The agreement rate was 85%, with a Cohen's $\kappa = 0.66$, which indicates substantial agreement [61]. Due to the high agreement, the annotators split the dataset, and annotated the remaining half (107 posts) on their own. In total, 135 codes were identified from the dataset, which fit into nine major themes. When describing our results only paraphrased quotes are included, sometimes with ethically fabricated information to maintain anonymity [59].

4.1 Results: Practitioner Discussions and Inquiries

Due to the qualitative nature of this analysis, we do not provide quantified numbers of how many posts came from which role, and instead use terminology that has been used in previous qualitative research to describe relative frequencies (see Fig. 1) [30,46,55].

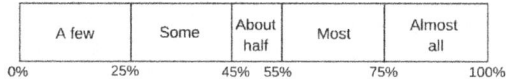

Fig. 1. The terminology used to represent the frequency of themes in qualitative research, related to inferred practitioner roles. This graphic was taken from [55]. Note: This figure represents terminology used to describe the frequency of themes in qualitative research. 'A few' refers to approximately 0 to 25%, 'Some' refers to approximately 25 to 45%, 'About half' refers to approximately 45 to 55%, 'Most' refers to approximately 55 to 75%, and 'Almost all' refers to 75 to 100%.

Several Practitioner Roles Are Involved in GDPR Compliance. Applying legitimate interests, and more broadly, the GDPR, is challenging for various types of practitioners. Often, posters explicitly indicated their role. However, other times we were able to infer their role based on the nature of the question. For example, we assumed that technical questions were posed by a developer, and client communication questions came from someone working within the marketing domain. The majority of online GDPR compliance information tends to target developers, but our analysis showed that other roles are involved, or have an interest, in the application of legitimate interests, in line with recent work [81].

About half of the posts asked technical questions, therefore leading us to believe these posters might be *developers*. There were some posts related to *marketing* and some which seemed to come from *business owners*. Additionally, a few posts were from other roles related to *research, human resources, business customers* (employees of a business that posed questions about how their business partner handles data), and other *miscellaneous industries* (e.g., event planning, education, content creation, etc.).

GDPR Accountability is Difficult to Determine. Deciding on the roles responsible for GDPR compliance is important for the concrete application of legitimate interests, since the lawful application of this legal basis has been doubted in previous research [41,55], therefore impacting the GDPR compliance for that company. We found that practitioners often queried about who in their company is responsible for GDPR compliance. Oftentimes, posters assumed it was the role of the developer to be the "de facto" data protection officer for their company, and some others believed it was the role of the owner of a given service. The following quote reveals why developers are often given the responsibility: *"I'm a developer, not a lawyer, who is trying to comply with the GDPR and ePD as best as I can for my company. If we had more money, I would hire a lawyer to handle this for me, but we don't so I'm in charge of this."* Discerning this role clearly is crucial since compliance obligations and liability depend on their accurate characterization (Recital 79 GDPR) [33,50]. Given the broad and flexible nature of legitimate interest as a legal basis [41,52], it is especially important to decide who is accountable for GDPR compliance within a team for ensuring the proper application of this legal basis.

Determining Accountability with Third Parties Involved is Challenging. In some cases, a poster mentioned that their service was not collecting any data, but third parties were, and therefore were confused about whether they (the first party service provider) would be accountable for GDPR data processing across their whole data supply chain. As discussed in previous literature [53], this problem reveals that practitioners are uncertain about who the data controller and processors were, who is accountable for compliance, and about the implications for joint controllership arrangements (as per Art. 26 GDPR).

GDPR Compliance Relies on the Compliance of Others. Posts referred to scenarios where services relied on third party functionalities to function, therefore becoming difficult for practitioners to keep track of what data is collected and handled by each outsourced service. Some practitioners mentioned using non-compliant tools which impacted the compliance of their own service. Whether practitioners work alone, are part of a team, manage a development team, or are a service provider carrying out development services for third parties, it is essential to ensure that personal data processing are sufficiently protected throughout the life-cycle of the project (according to the data protection by design principle (Art. 25 GDPR)). For example, a developer relied on WordPress to run their website; this same website used Google Fonts, which was considered non-compliant by a German Regional Court [56], and therefore the developer was held accountable for a third party tool's processing and got fined. Such decisions echo recent case law on data controllership between a first and third party providers [64–66].

Choosing a Legal Basis for Data Processing Can Be Confusing. Several posts aimed to clarify which legal basis practitioners should rely upon in their particular scenario. Often, legitimate interest was compared with consent (6(1)(a) GDPR), or contract necessity (6(1)(b)). In some cases, practitioners wondered if they could rely on both legitimate interest and consent, using legitimate interest as a fallback for users who could reject consent. This strategy might explain the prevalence of illegal cookie banners that use both consent and legitimate interest for the same processing purposes, a practice observed in a previous study [55] and commented on by the European Data Protection Board (EDPB) [35].

The Legitimate Interest Legal Ground is Sometimes Preferred over Other Legal Grounds. Our analysis revealed that applying legitimate interest is an appealing legal ground for four many reasons.

First, this legal ground can be invoked as a last resource, such as when companies are unable to obtain prior consent, or in situations where they believed users would not consent, such as requesting users to consent to email marketing. The following quote shows how this legal ground may be abused to collect more data from users who did not consent: *"Users who don't consent to advertising are a problem because my app relies on ads, therefore I'll lose revenue if ads aren't displayed. Is there a way to make it required for users to consent? Otherwise I won't be able to offer my service anymore.*" This observation supports legal speculation that legitimate interests could potentially be abused as a loophole to collect more data [41,52].

Second, legitimate interests might be used for the mere convenience of the practitioner. For example, when a system is already collecting user data before consent can be given, or when a user does not have access to a system to give consent, applying the legitimate interest legal ground is more convenient compared to asking for retroactive consent.

Third, legitimate interest may be used because other legal grounds for data collection do not apply to their scenario. Our analysis revealed that there were a variety of potential legitimate interest use cases practitioners posted about which reveals the benefits of having a broad and flexible legal ground.

Fourth, many posts held the assumption that legitimate interest may be applied to retain data in a scenario where users exercise the *"Right to be Forgotten"* (Art. 17 GDPR). This has practical implications because controllers can lose money if data is deleted, and some companies may face challenges locating the user's data upon an account deletion request, according to our analysis.

Questions from Practitioners Indicate Knowledge, but Also Misunderstandings of the GDPR. Some practitioners mentioned some legal arguments in their questions, and other cases revealed that practitioners already had previous experience with the GDPR, but could not get concrete granular information needed for their particular situation. Various examples in our dataset demonstrate that practitioners have a sincere intention to process personal data in a compliant manner: *"I've read the entire GDPR but I'm still confused."*

Trying to comply with the GDPR is made more difficult when it comes to the legitimate interest legal ground, as these are more broad and flexible in their application, with little guidance on how they should be used. While other legal bases such as consent are well-established with the advent of cookie banners and the general understanding that companies need to request user consent in order to collect and process data, there is less knowledge about the legitimate interest legal ground [55]. However, we find that developers (and those applying the GDPR) were often confused by their *own* service's data processing. The examples below illustrate commons points of confusion.

Practitioners are Confused About Data Collection and Tracking. Some practitioners were unsure of what data was being tracked, what data was stored in which cookie(s), what happens to user data after it is collected, and what data third parties have access to: *"I'm using a third-party tool for the app I've developed, but I don't know which server users will be routed to, or what country the server is in."*

Some practitioners were unsure about data collection implications in other scenarios, such as the data collected if a user was registered or not, and what to do if they receive a user account deletion request. There was also some confusion about what practitioners and organizations should do with user data, and whether they could rely on legitimate interest to keep user data. This highlights the difficulty of determining which legal basis and purpose should be applied to certain data.

There are Some Misunderstandings Around Consent. Practitioners were sometimes unable to tell if a user consented to data processing or not, and mentioned that the law does not explain how to *use* consent, only how to *get* consent. In fact, the most viewed posts in our sample referred to questions about whether the purposes of certain tracking technologies were *strictly necessary* for a service to work, and hence, whether they could be exempted from consent (as per Art. 5(3) ePrivacy Directive).

However, the European Data Protection Board (EDPB) and DPA guidelines explain with detail when trackers are to be considered essential for services to function, and as such, exempted from consent [35,67,71]. Some posters faced doubts about how consent impacts their data practices, such as what services can be offered and what data should then be collected if users reject consent.

Previous work has shown that the legitimate interest ground is commonly seen in cookie banners, being treated similarly to consent [55,60]. Therefore, the challenges practitioners face in distinguishing whether users have provided valid consent indicate that companies may struggle to manage and categorize the data collected from users and align it with the appropriate legal basis.

Anonymization and Pseudonymization are Misunderstood. Oftentimes, it was mentioned that true anonymization is difficult, and just because data is hashed, it does not mean it can evade GDPR requirements. However, there was discussion about whether anonymization and pseudonymization would be sufficient to protect user's personal data, and whether the GDPR applies to anonymized and pseudonymized data: *"I believe the GDPR wouldn't apply if I properly anonymize the data because it wouldn't count as personal information."*

What Counts as Personal Data is Misunderstood. We found that most held conflicting beliefs of what counted as personal data. Some believed that data is not personal if it only identifies a device instead of an individual person, while others correctly understood that the GDPR has a broad concept of what counts as *personal data* and what is an *identifiable person*.

A few practitioners mentioned personal data as being anything from nicknames and usernames, any demographic data, photos and videos of others, and user emails. Data gathered from users, such as medical data and Google searches could also count as personal data, according to some posts. These disagreements and misunderstandings highlight how opaque and complex industry data practices can be for developers and service owners, and the potential consequences for GDPR compliance that might occur when even those building the services are unsure of data processing requirements.

Turning to Online Forums for Legal Information   163

5   Analysis 2: Legal Assessment of GDPR Compliance Information in Online Forums

In this section we analyzed 94 *accepted answers* to the posts collected from Law Stack Exchange. We use the term "poster" to refer to the practitioner who originally posted a query, and "commentator" to the one providing an answer.

Dataset. We filtered our Law Stack Exchange dataset used in the first round of analysis to include only posts that were marked by the original poster as "Accepted" [39]. "Accepted answers" are answers where the original poster of a question marked a certain answer as the one which most solved their problem [39]. We deliberately focused on these answers because other forum users with similar use cases might assume they contain "correct" information to solve their problems [82], and might act according to the answer(s) received. This yielded 94 answers.

Annotation. One co-author, a legal scholar specialized in EU data protection law and with over five years of experience, analyzed the answers.

The evaluation of the *Accepted* forum answers consisted upon the following criteria: i) *Legal soundness*: whether answers gave *sound, partly sound,* or *not sound* legal information to the post's question(s); and ii) *Completeness*: whether answers gave *complete* or *incomplete* legal information to the question posted.

To analyze the legal soundness of the answers, it was necessary to resort to legislation, judicial and regulatory decisions, and guidelines from the EDPB or from DPAs to confirm whether the provenance of some arguments in the given answers hold. As some questions included technical terminology, it was necessary to further understand the background technical scenario to fully assess the content of the answers.

5.1   Results: Legal Soundness

In our analysis, based on the information provided in the post, we found that the majority (73.4%) out of 94 accepted answers were deemed to be legally sound; 20.2% were partly legally sound, and only 6.4% were not legally sound. Out of these 69 legally sound answers, 8.9% were incomplete, meaning they were missing information that would be useful for practitioners to know when applying legitimate interests.

We note that the majority of answers appeared legally sound due to the low complexity of the questions, e.g., *"Should the session end if users reject cookies?", "Do low-effort cookie banners comply with the GDPR?", "Does tracking IP addresses count as processing personal data?",* or *"Will opting in users into phone push notifications count as a GDPR violation?".* In these situations, legal soundness would apply regardless of the poster's jurisdiction or the type of organization they work at due to the general nature of these questions.

Completeness. The *Completeness* of forum answers is due to the posts and answers to these posts. Some posts contained several sub-questions or were very broad, and some answers involved mentioning other legal sources and legal terminology, which contributed to the legal *Completeness* of an answer.

It is Difficult to Comprehensively Answer Several Questions. Some posters included several sub-questions in a single post, similar to: *"Is this legal? Do I have any say in it? Can I refuse to use this service? What other data could they have access to?"* In such cases, we observed that, even if the answer appeared to be sound, some subquestions tended to remain unanswered.

General Questions Trigger General Answers. In response to very general questions (*"Do GDPR rules apply to my case?"*), often several hypotheses were raised, especially when the concrete purpose for processing personal data was unclear: *"It's not likely I can provide a correct answer because it depends on what you're trying to achieve."* The answers then remained general even if a question was edited several times with more factual information added by the poster. The presence of such general answers might lead to poor compliance practices because it is important to discern which GDPR rules the poster is concerned about in order to avoid a catch-all response.

Answers Sometimes Include Citations of Legal Sources and National Laws. GDPR legal provisions and even Recitals were convened in the answers. Notably, excerpts from case law of the Court of Justice of the EU were used (e.g., [2,3,64,65]), as well as guidelines from the EDPB (mostly on consent [35,38,71] and behavioural targeting [70]), and several UK DPA guidelines. When some posts questioned the applicability of certain national laws, answers provided excerpts of the consulted legal provisions supporting their explanations.

However, in our sample, no regulatory decisions from DPAs were cited (which include concrete cases that could inform several questions and answers closely related to the posts), even if there exists a publicly available online repository with relevant DPA decisions and more general GDPR insights that can be shared across Europe [63].

The ePrivacy Directive is Rarely Cited. Some posters asked whether consent was required for tracking technologies such as browser fingerprinting, third party website resources (e.g., Google Fonts, embedding GitHub Gists, etc.), and analytics. Answers mostly ignored the applicability of the ePD [87] to such cases, potentially because of the incorrect conviction that only the presence of cookies triggers the application of this directive [29]. The ePD was furthermore mentioned neither when some commentators said that Google Analytics could count as a legitimate interest, nor in answers concerning assigning a unique ID to a device for tracking location data.

Answers Use Imprecise Legal Terminology. While most answers were generally legally sound, we noted imprecision in the adopted terminology. Examples include the use of the term "personal identifiable information (PII)" from American data protection law instead of "personal data" used in the EU, references to "permission to use the data" instead of "consent", stating that "permission must be clear and positive" to indicate unambiguous consent, or even inaccurate explanations of the three-tiered balancing test [34] of the legitimate interest legal basis.

Soundness. Here, we discuss common areas where commentators did not give legally sound information.

Incorrect Legitimate Interest-Based Purposes are Sometimes Suggested. Several commentators asserted that posters could use the legitimate interest legal ground for purposes such as the use of Google Ads, online exam proctoring, or personalized advertising.

While the legal basis of legitimate interest is open-ended (with a broad and unspecific scope), several regulatory decisions and EDPB guidelines determined that personalized advertising purposes cannot rely on legitimate interest grounds [1,6,32,34,60]. Moreover, some legal scholars argued that legitimate interests should not be used as a ground to collect data by higher education institutions for proctoring [44]. This reveals that there is a mismatch between the legal field and some commentators' conceptions of legitimate interests, which may result in this legal ground being misused if posters were to follow this legal information.

Legitimate Interests are Incorrectly Invoked under the *"Right to be Forgotten"*. Several posters wanted to know if they could deny a request for account deletion from their users under legitimate interests. They moreover wondered whether they could keep data based on legitimate interests in cases where relevant data records could not be located. Answers related to these posts mentioned the right to erasure, but did not account for all the legal grounds for this right to be exercised (under Article 17(1)), or its exceptions (prescribed in Article 17(3) and Recital 65) that could be potentially applicable to override the deletion request. We argue that incomplete answers about erasure obligations are mostly due to the difficulty of operationalizing such grounds and exceptions in practice [9].

Legitimate Interests are Invoked Without Considering a Balancing Test. Several answers suggested that posters could deny data deletion requests on the ground of "overriding legitimate grounds for the processing" (Article 17(1)(c)) and provided several concrete examples, such as keeping a revision history in the interest of security, or storing a certificate after an account is deleted. However, these suggestions did not duly indicate that the data controller bears the burden of proof, meaning to demonstrate whether those recommended *overriding* legitimate grounds do indeed exist [18,54,72]. If a controller fails to demonstrate the existence of overriding legitimate grounds, the data subject is entitled to have their data deletion request executed.

Sound answers regarding this issue of the balancing test ought to account for several factors [62]. Such factors include how compelling the legitimate interest of the controller is; the nature and source of the legitimate interests; the degree of impact on the interests, rights and freedoms of the data subjects; the nature of the data; the way that data are being processed; the source and accessibility of the data; the reasonable expectations of the data subject; the status of the data controller and data subject as well as what safeguards are in place beyond the minimum required by the GDPR.

Legitimate Interests are Incorrectly Invoked in the Context of Publicly Available Data. In response to posts asking about whether they can use publicly available data for their commercial purposes, some commentators asserted that scraping data publicly available on the web could be based on legitimate interests and it would suffice to disclose the practice in a privacy policy on a relevant website, as per Article 14 GDPR. The reuse of publicly available online data for commercial purposes requires user consent in most data processing scenarios [21,24,26,37]. The legitimate interest basis can only in theory justify reuse of this data if the the three-tier test is fulfilled and most importantly, considers large-scale data collection, user's reasonable expectations of their data being reused , and inclusion of sensitive data, requirements that ultimately impede the use of this legal grounding.

The answers also did not account for potential sensitive categories of data, nor the obligation to directly and *actively* inform the involved data subjects about their rights (e.g., to object to legitimate interests), the source of the scraped data, as well as the mandatory information required by Article 14(1–3) GDPR [27,38]. Yet, some answers acknowledged that the public nature of the scraped data might be factored in the legitimate interest test: *"The data subject making this info public is a factor in the legitimate interest balancing test, but it depends on how you use the data and if they can expect their data to be used this way."*

Consent Requirements are Interpreted Incorrectly. Some answers did not regard the legal requirements for consent requests [35], in particular the *prior, unambiguous* and *revocable* requirements. One commentator assured that *"An email with an opt-out function should be compliant"* as it offers a way to withdraw consent that is as easy as it is to give consent (as per Article 7(3), Recital 42 GDPR). The legal requirement for an *unambiguous consent request* was not always clearly explained, despite several EDPB guidelines clarifying that consent should be given by a clear affirmative action from users (Article 4(11), Recital 32) [76] and as such, silence, inactivity, or other assumptions of related passive actions are illegal. Lastly, it is not always understood what the "strict necessity exemption" of Article 5(3) ePD entails and which purposes should be considered essential and necessary to provide a service explicitly requested by a user.

The *Contract Necessity* Legal Basis is Generally not Mentioned. As mentioned in Sect. 2, contract necessity is a lawful basis for processing personal data "necessary for the performance of a contract" in which the data subject is involved in (Article 6(1)(b), (Recital 65)) [17]. However, even if an implicit contractual relationship was mentioned in the main question of the post, this legal basis was mostly not discussed in the answers, and instead posters were encouraged to rely on consent or legitimate interest as a legal basis.

The Concept of Personal Data is Not Always Properly Understood. Understanding the concepts of "personal data" and "processing" is essential for the compliant development of any application reliant upon user data, and the GDPR applies to any data that is identifiable. Therefore, misunderstanding what personal data is can result in incorrect applications of the GDPR. However, we observed that some answers provided an incorrect definition or erroneous examples of applications of the concept of personal data, as per Article 4(1). For instance, some answers did not consider online identifiers, like IP addresses, as potentially identifiable data [2, 16]: *"It's personal data if they're a registered user and you can identify the data subject, but if they aren't registered and you only collect their IP address, it's not personal data"*.

6 Discussion

We analyzed 319 online forum posts from practitioners who asked questions relating to the legitimate interest legal basis, along with 94 *accepted* answers. We discuss the implications of our results regarding the application of the legal ground of legitimate interests and GDPR compliance.

Posters are Motivated to Comply but Still Need Guidance in Applying Legitimate Interests in Practical Settings. Those who do not care about compliance or are malicious in their compliance are unlikely to seek legal information in the first place. However, of those who did post a question, it does not seem like *most* posters are actively trying to circumvent the law based on the amount of posts seeking legal information, and the amount of views posts had. Rather, our analysis suggests there is a wide range of potential areas of confusion and doubt amongst practitioners, therefore showing that practitioners require more guidance when applying legitimate interests and the GDPR in practice.

Several Factors Increase the Chances of Non-compliance. Our findings suggest that non-compliance is often due to various factors. First, practitioners may misunderstand the complex legal language and open-textured concepts (like *strict necessity* or *balancing test*, and the multitude of stipulations in the GDPR and the ePD). Second, there is a lack of legal training amongst practitioners in charge of developing services that require GDPR compliance. Third, the reliance on third-party tools which are not always GDPR-compliant creates a domino effect of non-compliance for services using these tools. Lastly, it is difficult to find reliable information online; some posters mentioned seeing contradicting information, or not finding information specific to their scenario. All combined, these issues make GDPR compliance a difficult feat, thereby potentially resulting in privacy implications for end-users of a service.

Legal Compliance is a Multi-stakeholder Issue. Our study shows that posters asking about the GDPR potentially come from a variety of roles, such as developers, marketers, business owners, human resources, etc. We consider it to be important that DPAs, the EDPB, and other relevant organizations provide more concrete guidelines and recommendations tailored to practitioners, while considering different roles. It should be more clear when one is a data controller, processor or within a joint controller relationship.

There are Several Potential Legitimate Interest Use Cases. Our analysis showed the breadth of potential cases under which legitimate interest may apply, but also highlighted how legitimate interests can potentially be misused and abused by practitioners, especially in situations where consent is difficult to obtain. Often, legitimate interests were shown to be a preferred legal ground, and commentators did not often mention other legal bases posters could use, nor did they mention the proper provisions needed to invoke legitimate interests.

Time and Investment from Commentators Might give Credibility. In our analysis, most *Accepted* answers were considered as legally sound based on the information provided. Comprehensive answers (with case law notes, excerpts of guidelines, and references to national laws) denote time and attention from commentators. Unlike Stack Overflow, which can be used in job applications to display one's technical knowledge and abilities [91], those answering Law Stack Exchange questions did not generally specify if they had a legal background, nor was it clear what the incentive is for commentators to participate and give thorough answers for free.

Dedicated Resources Exist but are Not Referred to in Forums. Online forums may be preferred by practitioners to find legal information because of the granularity of questions and answers which relate to applying the GDPR for a specific scenario. The legal sources that were cited in the answers do not mention already-available online resources for developers mentioned in Sect. 2.2, but instead referred to DPA guidelines. The granularity of concrete scenarios that developers face seem to have inspired the creation of the French Data Protection Authority's (CNIL) developer guide [23], which is an example of how the law can be operationalized to more concrete settings. Interestingly, this resource was not mentioned in posts or comments we analyzed.

6.1 Implications for Legal Compliance

Online Forums have an Implicit Role in Data Protection. Based on the number of posts relating to GDPR questions, and the number of views and comments under these posts, it suggests that some practitioners are turning to these forums to find information that is most applicable to their specific scenario to better comply with the GDPR. Therefore, this indicates that there is a strong case for considering the role of online forums for GDPR compliance. Therefore, DPAs could provide more applicable scenario-based guidance and specific technical requirements so that practitioners can better understand how to properly apply the GDPR in practical contexts.

Resorting to these forums may indicate a lack of legal resources for smaller and medium-sized companies who in turn might not have in-house legal department at their disposal to discuss GDPR compliance issues. We posit that the status and the social responsibility of online legal forums merit attention, and call for discussions on the features that should be added or removed to make the sourced information more helpful, accurate, complete, and shaped to the practitioners' needs.

Based on our findings, we present several suggestions for how to better design online legal forums to help practitioners apply and understand the GDPR correctly. Forums could include, for example: i) practical resources to assist practitioners in setting up law-abiding services according to their sector of activity, especially addressing scenarios where GDPR legal provisions are vague and use open textured concepts, ii) frequently asked questions (FAQs) on the legal bases and purposes used, iii) a large typology of examples of data that could be considered personal, and iv) implementable scenarios (per sector), v) reconcile contradictions between posts on the same topic vi) regular check ups of answers to consider possible updates of legislation and new DPA guidelines.

Disclaimers of Incomplete or Incorrect Answers. It is difficult to establish the legal expertise of those answering the posts; some mentioned having legal expertise in their profile pages (sometimes with a link to their personal webpage, or using a nickname which is also used on other social media), while the majority did not refer to their profession. Even though some more straightforward answers were sound (to the point of citing legal sources) and recommended examples of best practices, commentators usually included disclaimers that posters should get legal information from a lawyer for a rigorous determination of their case.

Even if a given answer is not correct, a practitioner is not in a position to hold a commentator liable when incorporating such legal information into their services/products. Law Stack Exchange itself states that it "is for educational purposes only and is not a substitute for individualized information from a qualified legal practitioner. Communications on Law Stack Exchange are not privileged communications and do not create an attorney-client relationship" [73]. Such a disclaimer might exonerate the forum and commentators from any legal responsibility regarding the answers given, though this might not be sufficiently understandable nor visible for users seeking legal information and receiving detailed feedback. Therefore, these forums may act as a filter to help posters discern the level of legal complexity and whether there is a need to get help from a lawyer, and the level of risk they are taking if they do not consult with one.

6.2 Guidelines Towards Writing Forum Posts for Legally-Sound Answers

GDPR compliance relies on the efforts of several stakeholders. As such, those involved in GDPR compliance for an organization are in charge of a large and important task that requires not only understanding legal documents and the requirements for compliance, but also applying the law into practice.

Our results suggest that there are several areas of confusion practitioners may have about applying legitimate interests into practice, and there are several ways that legal compliance can go wrong if given incorrect advice on a forum. It is also possible that in the near future, more practitioners and users may start turning to AI chatbots for legal information [7], which are also trained on online forum data [47, 75].

Therefore, it is important that online forums provide correct legal information for current and future uses of this information for legal compliance. Our analysis found that most commentators take time and care in crafting their responses, but legal soundness is also reliant on other factors, such as a poster's jurisdiction, practices and industry. In this section, we present three recommendations to ensure that posters can receive responses that are as legally sound as possible, which online legal forums could include in their rules and guidelines for posters.

First, posters should include the jurisdiction of their organization, and the jurisdiction of their user base. The jurisdiction should specify the country at stake, since different European Member States may have different national law specifications. Second, posters should also mention i) the industry their organization is involved in, especially if it deals with sensitive data, such as health information, so that posters know of special safeguards they need to adopt with users' data, ii) processing purposes, and iii) their concrete role within data processing activities. Third, commentators should provide a disclaimer about the limitations of the concrete answer and add the fact that the dedicated legal information should neither bind the poster nor be construed or interpreted as legal advice.

6.3 Limitations

Doubts of Generalizable Results to Other Forums and Legal Bases. The first limitation is that of generalizability. Since we only checked the accepted answers on Law Stack Exchange relating to the legitimate interest legal basis, we are not sure how generalizable our results are to other forums or legal bases. Additionally, we have a sample bias as we only analyzed online forums, therefore it is possible that compliance with GDPR's legitimate interests might be more straightforward for more practitioners.

Our Legal Analysis of Answers is Limited to Information Provided. The legal analysis in Sect. 5 was merely confined to the facts and bounded to the scenarios described by the poster, and to the interpretation sustained by the commentator. Accordingly, legal ambiguities within these answers were observed due to the limited knowledge and context circumscribed by each post, such as the type of organization posters work at, whether posters were actually data controllers (processors, sub-processors, or none), the accuracy of the processing purposes mentioned, the nature and sensitivity of the data collected, the exact way data is processed, the source and accessibility of the data, or the concrete jurisdiction or national law the poster refers to, among other circumstances.

As such, our analysis on the correctness and completeness of the answers is thus limited and constrained to the reported posted facts and interpretations given by the commentators. Therefore, we acknowledge that there is a margin of doubt while labeling answers as "legally sound", "not legally sound" or "incomplete". We emphasize that only a judicial assessment that requires more specific fact-finding of each respective question and answer could render a final appraisal of such analysis and provide definitive certainty.

Due to these limitations, we therefore proposed guidelines in Sect. 6.2 for framing legal compliance questions in our Discussion section to ensure more legally sound responses to posters' questions in the future.

Future Directions. Based on the observed usage of online forums for legal information in our study, we can foresee LLMs being used in the future for quick legal compliance information. Using crowdsourced data for legal compliance information, whether from online forums or LLMs, can have a wide range of legal and ethical implications which are yet to be explored [89]. To mitigate the risks that come with using crowdsourced data for legal compliance information, more measures must be taken to ensure that high-quality, legally-sound information is being shared in online forums and LLMs. As such, we believe future work in this space could investigate how practitioners use LLMs for legal information, and further discuss the ethical and legal challenges and protections available for users of these services.

As GDPR compliance involved several stakeholders not only limited to those in law, but also those in tech, we suggest more collaborations between human-computer interaction researchers and the legal community to better understand the human factors of legal compliance and create solutions for practitioners involved.

7 Conclusion

In this paper, we investigated the practical challenges of legal compliance for practitioners by analyzing posts and answers from online forums (Reddit, Stack Overflow, and Law Stack Exchange), using legitimate interest as a case study. Our two-part analysis indicated that: i) finding out how to be compliant is difficult mostly for small and medium-sized companies, ii) practitioners seek information for their specific scenarios, and iii) legal compliance information from *Accepted* Law Stack Exchange answers are generally legally sound, but sometimes incomplete, with the mentioned limitations of our analysis.

We believe that legitimate interests are prone to being misused due to the broad and flexible nature, leading practitioners to misunderstand their concrete applications. In light of this, the human-computer interaction and legal communities should consider the role of online forums in the data protection landscape, and pay more attention to the human factors of legal compliance to give more actionable and scenario-specific guidelines to foster data protection by design and by default.

References

1. Opinion 2/2010 on online behavioural advertising (2010). https://ec.europa.eu/justice/article-29/documentation/opinion-recommendation/files/2010/wp171_en.pdf
2. Case 582/14 – Patrick Breyer v Germany. Court of Justice of the European Union ECLI:EU:C:2016:779 (2016)
3. Case C-434/16 - Peter Nowak v Data Protection Commissioner. Court of Justice of the European Union ECLI:EU:C:2017:994 (2017)
4. GDPR for Developers (2025). https://gdpr4devs.com/
5. Acar, Y., Backes, M., Fahl, S., Kim, D., Mazurek, M.L., Stransky, C.: You get where you're looking for: the impact of information sources on code security. In: 2016 IEEE Symposium on Security and Privacy (SP), pp. 289–305. IEEE (2016)
6. Decision on the merits 21/2022 of 2 February 2022 Complaint relating to Transparency & Consent Framework (2022)
7. Armstrong, K.: Chatgpt: Us lawyer admits using ai for case research (2023)
8. Atwood, J.: Attribution required (2009)
9. Ausloos, J.: The Right to Erasure in EU Data Protection Law. Oxford University Press, Oxford (2020)
10. Bacchelli, A., Ponzanelli, L., Lanza, M.: Harnessing stack overflow for the ide. In: 2012 Third International Workshop on Recommendation Systems for Software Engineering (RSSE), pp. 26–30. IEEE (2012)
11. Barakat, H., Redmiles, E.M.: Community under surveillance: impacts of marginalization on an online labor forum. In: Proceedings of the International AAAI Conference on Web and Social Media, vol. 16, pp. 12–21 (2022)
12. Barua, A., Thomas, S.W., Hassan, A.E.: What are developers talking about? an analysis of topics and trends in stack overflow. Empir. Softw. Eng. **19**(3), 619–654 (2014)

13. Beadle, K., et al.: SoK: a privacy framework for security research using social media data. In: 2025 IEEE Symposium on Security and Privacy (SP), pp. 1178–1196. IEEE (2025)
14. Bednar, K., Spiekermann, S., Langheinrich, M.: Engineering privacy by design: are engineers ready to live up to the challenge? Inf. Soc. **35**(3), 122–142 (2019)
15. Belanger, A.: Air canada has to honor a refund policy its chatbot made up (2024). https://www.wired.com/story/air-canada-chatbot-refund-policy/
16. European Data Protection Board. Opinion 4/2007 on the concept of personal data (WP 136), adopted on 20.06.2007 (2007)
17. European Data Protection Board. Guidelines 2/2019 on the processing of personal data under Article 6(1)(b) GDPR in the context of the provision of online services to data subjects (2019)
18. European Data Protection Board. Guidelines 5/2019 on the criteria of the Right to be Forgotten in the search engines cases under the GDPR (part 1) (2020)
19. Braun, V., Clarke, V.: Using thematic analysis in psychology. Qual. Res. Psychol. **3**(2), 77–101 (2006)
20. Bygrave, L.A.: Data protection by design and by default: deciphering the EU's legislative requirements. Oslo Law Rev. **4**(2), 105–120 (2017)
21. CNIL. Délibération san-2020-018 (2020)
22. Data Protection Commission. Data protection commission announces conclusion of two inquiries into meta Ireland (2023)
23. Commission Nationale de l'Informatique et des Libertés (CNIL). GDPR Developer's Guide (2020). https://www.cnil.fr/en/gdpr-developers-guide
24. Commission Nationale de l'Informatique et des Libertés (CNIL). Ouverture et réutilisation de données personnelles sur Internet: la CNIL publie ses recommandations (2024). https://www.cnil.fr/fr/ouverture-et-reutilisation-de-donnees-personnelles-sur-internet-la-cnil-publie-ses-recommandations
25. Silva, L., Samhi, J., Khomh, F.: LLMs and stack overflow discussions: reliability, impact, and challenges. J. Syst. Softw. **230**, 112541 (2025)
26. Irish DPA. Data protection commission reference: In-21-4-2 in the matter of meta platforms ireland ltd. (formerly facebook ireland ltd.) (2022)
27. Polish DPA. Decision zspr.421.3.2018 (2019)
28. Dym, B., Fiesler, C.: Ethical and privacy considerations for research using online fandom data. Transformat. Works Cult. **33**, 1–19 (2020)
29. European Data Protection Board (EDPB). Opinion 5/2019 on the interplay between the eprivacy directive and the gdpr, in particular regarding the competence, tasks and powers of data protection authorities (2019)
30. Emami-Naeini, P., Dixon, H., Agarwal, Y., Cranor, L.F.: Exploring how privacy and security factor into iot device purchase behavior. In: Proceedings of the 2019 CHI Conference on Human Factors in Computing Systems, CHI '19, pp. 1–12. Association for Computing Machinery, New York (2019)
31. European Commission. 2018 Reform of EU data protection rules (2018). https://ec.europa.eu/commission/sites/beta-political/files/data-protection-factsheet-changes_en.pdf
32. European Court of Justice. Case C-252/21: Request for a preliminary ruling from the Oberlandesgericht Düsseldorf (Germany) lodged on 22 April 2021 – Facebook Inc. and Others v Bundeskartellamt (2023)
33. European Data Protection Board. Guidelines 07/2020 on the concepts of controller and processor in the GDPR Version 1.0 (2020). https://edpb.europa.eu/our-work-tools/public-consultations-art-704/2020/guidelines-072020-concepts-controller-and-processor_en

34. European Data Protection Board (EDPB). Opinion 06/2014 on the notion of legitimate interests of the data controller under article 7 of directive 95/46/ec (wp 217) (2014)
35. European Data Protection Board (EDPB). Guidelines 05/2020 on consent under regulation 2016/679 (2020)
36. European Data Protection Board (EDPB). SME Data Protection Guide (2023). https://www.edpb.europa.eu/sme-data-protection-guide/home_en
37. European Data Protection Board (EDPB). Guidelines 1/2024 on processing of personal data based on Article 6(1)(f) GDPR (2024). https://www.edpb.europa.eu/system/files/2024-10/edpb_guidelines_202401_legitimateinterest_en.pdf
38. Law Stack Exchange. General disclaimer (2023)
39. Stack Exchange. How does accepting an answer work? (2019)
40. Stack Exchange. Academic papers using stack exchange data (2022)
41. Ferretti, F.: Data protection and the legitimate interest of data controllers: much ado about nothing or the winter of rights? Common Mark. Law Rev. **51**(3), 843–868 (2014)
42. Finck, M., Biega, A.J.: Reviving purpose limitation and data minimisation in data-driven systems. Technol. Regulat. **44–61**, 2021 (2021)
43. Fischer, F., et al.: Stack overflow considered harmful? the impact of copy&paste on android application security. In: 2017 IEEE Symposium on Security and Privacy (SP), pp. 121–136. IEEE (2017)
44. Fouad, Y, Lodder, A., Hurdey, J., et al.: A lawful basis for online proctoring (2018)
45. Greene, D., Shilton, K.: Platform privacies: governance, collaboration, and the different meanings of "privacy" in iOS and Android development. New Media Soc. **20**(4), 1640–1657 (2018)
46. Habib, H., et al.: "It's a Scavenger Hunt": usability of websites' opt-out and data deletion choices. In: Proceedings of the 2020 CHI Conference on Human Factors in Computing Systems, CHI '20, pp. 1–12. Association for Computing Machinery, New York (2020)
47. Hämäläinen, P., Tavast, M., Kunnari, A.: Evaluating large language models in generating synthetic hci research data: a case study. In: Proceedings of the 2023 CHI Conference on Human Factors in Computing Systems, pp. 1–19 (2023)
48. Horstmann, S.A., Domiks, S., Gutfleisch, M., Tran, M., Acar, Y., Moonsamy, V., Naiakshina, A.: Those things are written by lawyers, and programmers are reading that. Mapping the communication gap between software developers and privacy experts. Proc. Priv. Enhan. Technol. (2024)
49. Horstmann, S.A., et al.: "Sorry for Bugging you so much." Exploring developers' behavior towards privacy-compliant implementation. In: 2025 IEEE Symposium on Security and Privacy (SP), pp. 1215–1233 (2025)
50. Information Commissioner's Office. Data controllers and data processors: what the difference is and what the governance implications are (2018). https://ico.org.uk/for-organisations/guide-to-data-protection/guide-to-the-general-data-protection-regulation-gdpr/controllers-and-processors/
51. Jasmontaite, L., Kamara, I., Zanfir-Fortuna, G., Leucci, S.: Data protection by design and by default: framing guiding principles into legal obligations in the GDPR. Eur. Data Prot. L. Rev. **4**, 168 (2018)
52. Kamara, I., Hert, P.: Understanding the balancing act behind the legitimate interest of the controller ground: a pragmatic approach. Brussels Priv. Hub **4**(12), 35 (2018)

53. Kollnig, K., et al.: A fait accompli? an empirical study into the absence of consent to third-party tracking in android apps. In: Seventeenth Symposium on Usable Privacy and Security (SOUPS 2021), pp. 181–196 (2021)
54. Kuner, C., Bygrave, L.A., Docksey, C., Drechsler, L., Tosoni, L.: The eu general data protection regulation: a commentary/update of selected articles. Update of Selected Articles (May 4, 2021) (2021)
55. Kyi, L., et al.: Investigating deceptive design in GDPR's legitimate interest. In: Proceedings of the 2023 CHI Conference on Human Factors in Computing Systems, pp. 1–15 (2023)
56. LG München I (Regional Court Munich I). Verletzung des Persönlichkeitsrechts durch Datenschutzverstoß (Violation of the right of personality due to data protection infringement) (2022). https://www.gesetze-bayern.de/Content/Document/Y-300-Z-BECKRS-B-2022-N-612?hl=true
57. Li, T., Louie, E., Dabbish, L., Hong, J.I.: How developers talk about personal data and what it means for user privacy: a case study of a developer forum on reddit. Proc. ACM Hum.-Comput. Interact. **4**(CSCW3), 1–28 (2021)
58. Liepina, R., et al.: Gdpr privacy policies in claudette: challenges of omission, context and multilingualism. In: ASAIL@ICAIL (2019)
59. Markham, A.: Fabrication as ethical practice: qualitative inquiry in ambiguous internet contexts. Inf. Commun. Soc. **15**(3), 334–353 (2012)
60. Matte, C., Santos, C., Bielova, N.: Purposes in IAB Europe's TCF: which legal basis and how are they used by advertisers? In: Antunes, L., Naldi, M., Italiano, G.F., Rannenberg, K., Drogkaris, P. (eds.) APF 2020. LNCS, vol. 12121, pp. 163–185. Springer, Cham (2020). https://doi.org/10.1007/978-3-030-55196-4_10
61. McHugh, M.L.: Interrater reliability: the kappa statistic. Biochemia medica **22**(3), 276–282 (2012)
62. Norwegian DPA against Meta Platfroms Case 21/03530-16 (2023)
63. noyb.eu. GDPRhub (2025). https://gdprhub.eu/
64. European Court of Justice. Case câĂŚ210/16 wirtschaftsakademie schleswig-holstein, ecli:eu:c:2018:388 (2018)
65. European Court of Justice. Case c-40/17 fashion id gmbh & co.kg v verbraucherzentrale nrw ev, ecli:eu:c:2019:629 (2019)
66. European Court of Justice. Case c-673/17 verbraucherzentrale bundesverband v. planet49, ecli:eu:c:2019:801 (2019)
67. Information Commissioner's Office. Guidance on the use of cookies and similar technologies (2019). https://ico.org.uk/media/for-organisations/guide-to-pecr/guidance-on-the-use-of-cookies-and-similar-technologies-1-0.pdf
68. Parnin, C., Treude, C., Grammel, L., Storey, M.A.: Crowd documentation: exploring the coverage and the dynamics of API discussions on stack overflow. Georgia Institute of Technology, Tech. Rep. **11** (2012)
69. Parsons, J., Schrider, M., Ogunlela, O., Ghanavati, S.: Understanding developers privacy concerns through reddit thread analysis. In: Joint Proceedings of REFSQ-2023 Workshops (2023)
70. Article 29 Working Party. Opinion 2/2010 on online behavioural advertising (2010)
71. Article 29 Working Party. Opinion 04/2012 on cookie consent exemption (WP 194) (2012)
72. Article 29 Working Party. Google Spain SL and Google Inc. v Agencia Española de Protección de Datos (AEPD) and Mario Costeja González (2014)
73. Article 29 Working Party. Guidelines on transparency under Regulation 2016/679, WP260 rev.01 (2016)

74. Proferes, N., Jones, N., Gilbert, S., Fiesler, C., Zimmer, M.: Studying reddit: a systematic overview of disciplines, approaches, methods, and ethics. Social Media + Society **7**(2), 20563051211019004 (2021)
75. Sanh, V., et al.: Multitask prompted training enables zero-shot task generalization. In: International Conference on Learning Representations (2022)
76. Santos, C., Bielova, N., Matte, C.: Are cookie banners indeed compliant with the law? Deciphering EU legal requirements on consent and technical means to verify compliance of cookie banners. Technol. Regul. 91–135 (2020)
77. Santos, C., Nouwens, M., Toth, M., Bielova, N., Roca, V.: Consent management platforms under the GDPR: processors and/or controllers? In: Gruschka, N., Antunes, L.F.C., Rannenberg, K., Drogkaris, P. (eds.) APF 2021. LNCS, vol. 12703, pp. 47–69. Springer, Cham (2021). https://doi.org/10.1007/978-3-030-76663-4_3
78. Senarath, A., Arachchilage, N.A.G.: Why developers cannot embed privacy into software systems? An empirical investigation. In: Proceedings of the 22nd International Conference on Evaluation and Assessment in Software Engineering 2018, pp. 211–216 (2018)
79. Shanmugam, D., Diaz, F., Shabanian, S., Finck, M., Biega, A.: Learning to limit data collection via scaling laws: A computational interpretation for the legal principle of data minimization. In: 2022 ACM Conference on Fairness, Accountability, and Transparency, pp. 839–849 (2022)
80. Spiekermann, S.: The challenges of privacy by design. Commun. ACM **55**(7), 38–40 (2012)
81. Stöver, A., et al.: How website owners face privacy issues: thematic analysis of responses from a covert notification study reveals diverse circumstances and challenges. Proc. Priv. Enhan. Technol. (2023)
82. Tahaei, M., Bernd, J., Rashid, A.: Privacy, permissions, and the health app ecosystem: a stack overflow exploration. In: Proceedings of the 2022 European Symposium on Usable Security, pp. 117–130 (2022)
83. Tahaei, M., Frik, A., Vaniea, K.: Privacy champions in software teams: understanding their motivations, strategies, and challenges. In: Proceedings of the 2021 CHI Conference on Human Factors in Computing Systems, pp. 1–15 (2021)
84. Tahaei, M., Li, T., Vaniea, K.: Understanding privacy-related advice on stack overflow. Proc. Priv. Enhan. Technol. **2022**(2), 114–131 (2022)
85. Tahaei, M., Vaniea, K., Saphra, N.: Understanding privacy-related questions on stack overflow. In: Proceedings of the 2020 CHI Conference on Human Factors in Computing Systems, pp. 1–14 (2020)
86. Taylor-Hiscock, R.: Your complete guide to General Data Protection Regulation (GDPR) compliance. OneTrust Blog (2021)
87. European Union. Directive 2009/136/EC of the European Parliament and of the Council (2009)
88. Vasilescu, B., Filkov, V., Serebrenik, A.: Stack overflow and github: associations between software development and crowdsourced knowledge. In: 2013 International Conference on Social Computing, pp. 188–195. IEEE (2013)
89. Veale, M., Binns, R., Edwards, L.: Algorithms that remember: model inversion attacks and data protection law. Phil. Trans. R. Soc. A: Math. Phys. Eng. Sci. **376**(2133), 20180083 (2018)
90. Webley, L.: Qualitative approaches to empirical legal research, pp. 926–948. Oxford Handbooks. Oxford University Press, Cambridge (2010)

91. Winter, T.: How to source developers from Stack Overflow (2021)
92. Yuhao, W., Wang, S., Bezemer, C.-P., Inoue, K.: How do developers utilize source code from stack overflow? Empir. Softw. Eng. **24**(2), 637–673 (2019)

Open Access This chapter is licensed under the terms of the Creative Commons Attribution-NonCommercial-NoDerivatives 4.0 International License (http://creativecommons.org/licenses/by-nc-nd/4.0/), which permits any noncommercial use, sharing, distribution and reproduction in any medium or format, as long as you give appropriate credit to the original author(s) and the source, provide a link to the Creative Commons license and indicate if you modified the licensed material. You do not have permission under this license to share adapted material derived from this chapter or parts of it.

The images or other third party material in this chapter are included in the chapter's Creative Commons license, unless indicated otherwise in a credit line to the material. If material is not included in the chapter's Creative Commons license and your intended use is not permitted by statutory regulation or exceeds the permitted use, you will need to obtain permission directly from the copyright holder.

Illuminating the DPIA Blackbox – A Survey of Data Protection Impact Assessment Practices in Organisations

Malte Hansen[1(✉)], Greta Runge[2], Nils Gruschka[1], and Meiko Jensen[3]

[1] Department of Informatics, University of Oslo, Oslo, Norway
{maltehan,nilsgrus}@ifi.uio.no
[2] Fraunhofer Institute for Systems and Innovation Research, Berlin, Germany
greta.runge@isi.fraunhofer.de
[3] Karlstad University, Karlstad, Sweden
meiko.jensen@kau.se

Abstract. According to the European General Data Protection Regulation (GDPR), a Data Protection Impact Assessment (DPIA) is mandatory for all ongoing and planned processing of personal data if said processing is likely to affect the privacy and data protection rights and freedoms of the data subjects. However, upon examining the real-world implementation of this requirement, various approaches emerged, resulting in a heterogeneous landscape of DPIA processes.

In this paper, we present the results of a survey that investigated the state of adoption of DPIA process methodologies in real-world organisations. Our survey reveals that handwritten DPIA reports and ad-hoc methods continue to dominate the DPIA landscape in Europe. Moreover, according to our data, processes involving multiple stakeholders are often not adequately assessed in terms of DPIA-related risks.

Keywords: DPIA · data protection impact assessment · privacy impact assessment · GDPR

1 Introduction

New digital technologies are emerging at an increasing rate, and data processing is becoming increasingly important for their effectiveness. To manage resources for these processes, data sharing and the utilisation of external services, such as cloud services, are also expanding. This introduces various data protection risks that have to be addressed. An essential tool in assessing these challenges is a data protection impact assessment (DPIA), introduced as a mandatory requirement by the General Data Protection Regulation (GDPR) [1].

But how are DPIA processes implemented in practice? Published DPIA results are hard to find, and the available results are mostly limited to the DPIA report, which does not provide detailed insights into how the DPIA was conducted. To gain information about the DPIA process itself, several guidelines, templates, and DPIA tools are available online. However, they are often very generic and do not adequately address an organisation's specific issues. This applies particularly to organisations engaged in data sharing or that are part of a large data ecosystem.

ENISA identified the risks stemming from the specific constellations of actors, such as unknowingly sharing sub-processors, in a data space as a major challenge [2]. The Big Data Value Association also recognised a lack of frameworks for addressing legal issues and proper risk evaluation in data sharing within data spaces [3]. Similarly, the Spanish supervisory authority AEPD stated that *"the DPIA and the solutions that manage the limitations and risks to rights and freedoms must emerge from a common effort"* [4, p. 69]. Recital 95 of the GDPR [1] further clarifies that processors should assist the controller during a DPIA. DPIA procedures, therefore, require special attention to address these challenges adequately. However, *"the task of supporting a holistic DPIA with multiple data controllers and data intermediaries is a non-trivial one"* [2, p. 13], and the aspect of a joint DPIA involving several different stakeholders with shared responsibility has not been explored yet by existing models [5]. This leads to the following research questions:

- **RQ1:** What are the current practices of the DPIA process in general?
- **RQ2:** What are the current challenges of the DPIA process?
- **RQ3:** How do current DPIA processes address external influences?

To answer these questions, we conducted an anonymous user survey asking about DPIA practices in organisations. The results of this survey are presented and discussed below in the following structure: We introduce the concept of DPIA in Sect. 2, followed by a review of related work in the field in Sect. 3. Afterwards, we introduce the methodology used for the survey in Sect. 4, followed by the presentation of the results in Sect. 5. The results are analysed and discussed in the context of different perspectives in Sect. 6 before summarising our findings and giving an outlook on future work in Sect. 7.

2 Background

The GDPR introduced DPIAs as a mandatory requirement for Data Controllers (DC) before implementing or updating IT systems and processes under certain conditions. To be precise, the GDPR states that a DPIA must be carried out *"where a type of processing in particular using new technologies, and taking into account the nature, scope, context and purposes of the processing, is likely to result in a high risk to the rights and freedoms of natural persons"* [1, Art. 35(1)]. To address these risks, a DPIA aims to cover the data flows and consequences of data processing as thoroughly as possible and to evaluate them objectively according to uniform criteria so that typical sources of risk can be countered with adequate technical and organisational measures. A short paper of the *Datenschutzkonferenz* of the German data protection authorities defines the DPIA as *"a specific tool for describing, assessing and mitigating risks to the rights and freedoms of natural persons in relation to the processing of personal data"* [6, p. 1]. The French data protection authority, the Commission Nationale de l'Informatique et des Libertés (CNIL), describes the DPIA as a tool for a DC to *"build and demonstrate the implementation of privacy protection principles so that data subjects retain control over their personal data"* [7, p. 4]. Furthermore, a DPIA aims to provide transparency to the public and policymakers, enabling an informed discussion about risks [8].

A key characteristic of the DPIA is its cyclic nature. The GDPR requires that the DPIA process be reviewed after a change to the risks of the processing (Art. 35(11), GDPR). The GDPR does not define an inherent methodology or process flow. However, researchers and data protection authorities have proposed various DPIA methodologies and models (see Sect. 3). A fundamental resource for these models is the guidelines on conducting a DPIA [9] released by the Article 29 Working Party, the predecessor of the European Data Protection Board (EDPB). These guidelines clarify basic principles, such as the execution threshold at which a DPIA becomes mandatory, also known as DPIA screening or threshold analysis, and the involvement of stakeholders. While they do not provide a methodology for these steps, they introduce a generic, iterative process for the execution of the DPIA following the threshold analysis, consisting of seven steps:

1. Description of the envisaged processing
2. Assessment of the necessity and proportionality
3. Measures already envisaged
4. Assessment of the risks to the rights and freedoms
5. Measures envisaged to address the risks
6. Documentation
7. Monitoring and review

Another approach to structuring the DPIA is to divide it into different phases. Martin et al. [10] structure the DPIA in five stages. Phase I, initiation of the DPIA, covers the threshold analysis. Next, the DPIA will be prepared in Phase II. This includes the process description, identification of Data Subjects (DSs) and stakeholders, and forming the DPIA team. Phase III describes the execution of the DPIA, beginning with the risk assessment and concluding with the documentation of the results in the DPIA report. Afterwards, Phase IV will implement the DPIA by testing the mitigation measures and demonstrating compliance, before the process enters the final Phase V, the periodic review of the DPIA.

While both approaches mostly follow the same procedure, they emphasise different steps. The procedure and overlap of the two approaches are illustrated in Fig. 1.

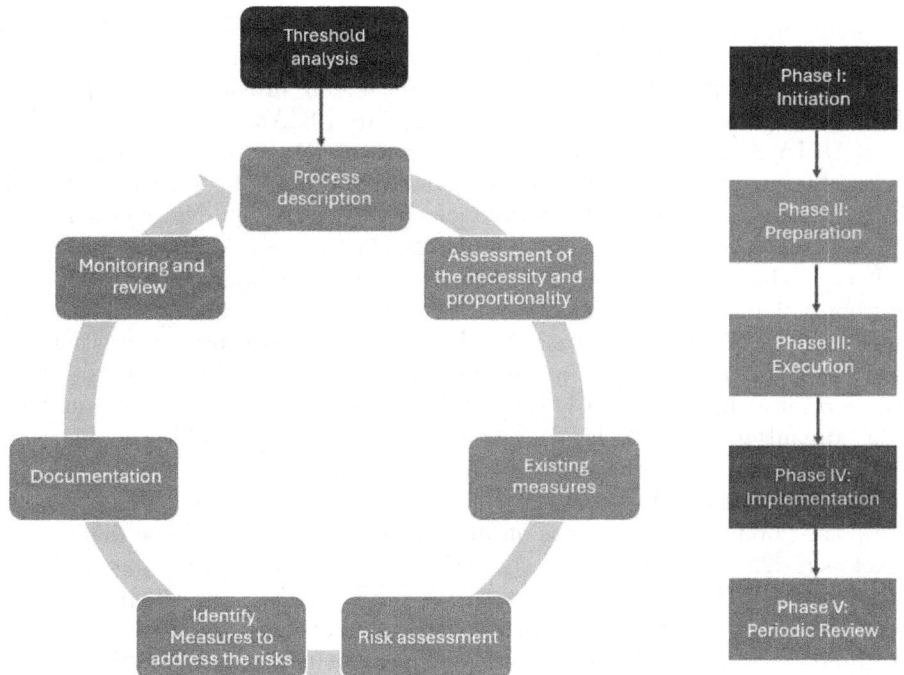

Fig. 1. Overlap of DPIA methodologies as defined by the EDPB/Article 29 Working Party [9] (left) and Martin et al. [10] (right)

3 Related Work

Following the introduction of the GDPR, various European data protection authorities, including the UK's Information Commissioner's Office (ICO) [11], the Spanish AEPD [12], and the French CNIL [13], developed text-based DPIA templates for quick adaptation by data controllers (DCs). Notably, CNIL also released a software tool and knowledge base [14], which explains essential notions of a DPIA to increase its ease of use. While not designed for DPIAs, the second version of the ISO/IEC 29134:2023 guidelines for privacy impact assessment [15] is a common reference.

In one of the first models for a DPIA, Bieker et al. introduced a three-phase process consisting of a *preparation*, *evaluation*, and *report and safeguards* stage [16]. A cornerstone of the evaluation stage in this approach is the identification of privacy protection goals, first introduced by Hansen et al. [17]. These protection goals expand the traditional information security goals of confidentiality, integrity, and availability with the privacy-focused goals of unlinkability, transparency, and intervenability. The privacy protection goals served as a fundamental resource in the approach introduced by Martin et al. [10] in Sect. 2 as well.

Later, Gonscherowski et al. did an exemplary execution of a DPIA in a mobility use case, utilising the principle introduced by Bieker et al. [18]. Haag et al. focused on explaining the process to medical staff, providing examples and a checklist while not including a concrete template [19]. An example of a template for a DPIA report can be found in the work of Kloza et al., which includes detailed input fields for legal, practical, and organisational considerations [20].

A review of common DPIA methodologies in practice by Nagele et al. highlights the improper application of DPIAs, lacklustre execution of the process, as well as a lack of common standards and guidelines [5]. Demetzou argues that the concept of 'high risk' is not legally qualified under the GDPR, leading to deficiencies during the threshold analysis [21]. A study assessing the implementation process of a DPIA in twelve companies further highlights the substantial resources required for a thorough DPIA. It identifies communication issues between technical, organisational, and legal professionals, as well as possible complications arising from an individual's role within the company [22]. A case study based on the approach by Martin et al. [10], running twelve tests in SMEs, acknowledges the potential of DPIAs as an instrument to support decision-makers and developers [22]. However, the tests also highlighted challenges in communication between DPIA team members, the resources required by the process, and potential conflicts with the business's interests. Further, a literature review by Wairimu et al. found that PIA methodologies, including DPIA methodologies, often lack evaluation and validation [23].

Georgiadis and Poels [24] conducted a literature review to develop a DPIA methodology tailored toward big data analytics. They conclude that, currently, no methodology exists that addresses all the requirements and privacy risks in the big data analytics sector. According to them, an ample list of provided privacy controls in a PIA process might be a bigger risk than an aid, highlighting the need for section-specific solutions [25]. This can also be seen in the differences in the methodology for healthcare information systems developed by Todde et al. [26], the guidelines for federated identity management models [27] and digital identity management in general [28], or the domain-specific refinements added to the LINDDUN privacy threat framework [29]. A different perspective on DPIAs is to see it as a tool to protect the interests of weak and underrepresented groups of individuals, for which current DPIA practices do not meet the norm [30].

As demonstrated by the approaches presented above, there is no uniform method for conducting a DPIA. While some small-scale case studies and insights into the DPIA procedures employed by organisations exist, an overview of best practices and common challenges with the DPIA process is hard to obtain.

The issue of a *compositional DPIA* involving data processing operations spanning multiple stakeholders has not been studied extensively. Horák et al. explored a DPIA for a cybersecurity data-sharing platform but have not looked at the joint execution of a DPIA. De and Le Métayer developed a privacy risk assessment methodology focusing on reusability [31]. A semantic specification for DPIAs by Pandit [32] is a crucial step towards creating machine-readable and shared DPIAs. However, the expression of principles and controls remains challenging.

Overall, existing DPIA approaches still lack several important properties required in collaborative processing scenarios: a formalised vocabulary to standardise results, means for accurate threshold analysis, a lack of reusability, procedures for risk assessment and measure selection, and means for multiple actors to work on the same DPIA process.

4 Methodology

As outlined in the research questions, this paper aims to gain a deeper understanding of organisations' current DPIA practices and the challenges they face, particularly regarding the federated constellations of actors within the regulatory European data ecosystem.

Section 3 highlights that there currently is no established standard process for DPIAs. Instead, various guidelines exist for both general and sector-specific use cases. Furthermore, these guidelines offer guidance and a sequence for the process, but do not provide detailed instructions on how to implement the components of the DPIA. As an internal process, there is no way to gain insight into these details except through the DPIA report, which is rarely made publicly available. The first step to understand the current state of DPIAs is therefore to learn about the general trends common in DPIA processes. For this reason, we conducted an anonymous, quantitative survey targeting professionals from diverse backgrounds who participated in a DPIA to learn about the structure of their DPIAs.

Responses were collected between March 6 and April 1, 2025, via *Nettskjema*, a web-based survey tool developed by the University of Oslo[1]. Potential respondents were contacted via email and social media platforms, including LinkedIn, to solicit their responses. The email invitations leveraged professional associations and the network of experts in the field. The survey was conducted per the ethical guidelines of the University of Oslo and assessed by the Norwegian Agency for Shared Services in Education and Research[2] for compliant use of personal data. In total, 30 responses were submitted, with one submission discarded because it provided contradictory answers.

The survey questions were primarily designed to learn about the structure and resources common in DPIA processes, while considering the deficiencies outlined in Sect. 3. The questions were primarily multiple-choice, with options for 'I don't know' and 'Other' to allow respondents to add more or less detail as needed. As the survey was anonymous, it first collected general information about the respondents' experience with DPIAs, the organisation in which they conducted the DPIA, and the regularity with which DPIAs occurred. These questions aimed to gauge the respondents' perspective and their familiarity with the DPIA as a process. The following questions then address the contents of the DPIA in the respondents' organisation. The goal was to determine if an unofficial standard could be identified by inquiring about the methods used in different

---

[1] https://nettskjema.no.
[2] https://sikt.no/.

phases of the DPIA. For this purpose, questions regarding the composition of the DPIA team, the tools used, threshold analysis, risk assessment, and identification of measures to mitigate the risk were included. The next section of questions focused on the compositional aspects, addressing the inclusion of third parties during different stages of the DPIA. The final questions requested details about the DPIA report and its overall result, including the quality and challenges faced during the entire process. For the challenges, only three answers were allowed to assert that a priority can be derived.

The complete questionnaire and results are available on github[3].

5 Results

In the following section, we present the aggregated results of the survey responses. To increase readability, the percentages will be rounded to the next integer. The total number of responses considered in the results is 29. The results are grouped into seven different categories: (1) general information about the respondent and their organisation, (2) general structure of the DPIA, (3) threshold analysis, (4) risk assessment and identification of measures, (5) third-party cooperation, (6) DPIA result, and (7) challenges in the DPIA process.

5.1 General Information

While the survey was anonymous, some basic information about the participant and their organisation was collected to provide some context to the answers.

Concerning information about the respondents, they were asked about the roles they typically fulfil during a DPIA and their experience with the process. The majority of respondents, 38%, are Data Protection Officers (DPOs). The next largest group are legal advisors with 14%, followed by project leaders, specialists in relation to the use case of the process to be assessed by the DPIA, IT experts, and external DPIA experts with 10% each. Further, a manager and chief privacy officer participated. The relevance of DPIAs, even before the GDPR came into force, is evident in the respondents' experiences. 38% work with DPIAs for seven to nine years already, with 7% having ten or more years of experience. 38% of participants started working with DPIAs shortly after the GDPR entered into force, having three to six years of experience. There were also some newcomers, with 14% having one to two years of experience and one respondent working with DPIAs for less than a year.

Regarding the organisations the respondents are part of, 45% of organisations work in commercial services, such as e-commerce, banking, or software development, while 34% work in public services and 21% in education and research. Roughly a third of these organisations are SMEs, with 21% having between 50 and 250 employees, 10% having ten to 50, and one organisation employing less than ten persons. Consequently, the rest are large organisations with 62% having 1000 or more employees and one organisation having between 251 and 999.

---

[3] https://github.com/Hinnaaak/DPIA_User_Survey.

Conducting a DPIA does not appear to be a one-time thing for most organisations, with only one having conducted a single DPIA in the last five years. 7% conducted two to four, 24% five to ten, 28% eleven to 25, and 34% more than that. One respondent did not know how many DPIAs their organisation had done in the last 5 years. If we take a look at only the last year instead, we get 14% with one DPIA, 34% with two to four, 31% with five to ten, 7% with eleven to 25, and 14% with more than that.

5.2 General Structure of DPIAs

The first step in understanding the structure of DPIA processes in organisations is to know who carries out the DPIA. To provide an example of the composition of a DPIA team, we can take a look at the UK's ICO. They recommend including the business area or project leader, DPO, information security staff, data processors, and legal advisors, as well as other relevant experts [33]. Furthermore, the views of the affected individuals or their representatives should also be consulted.

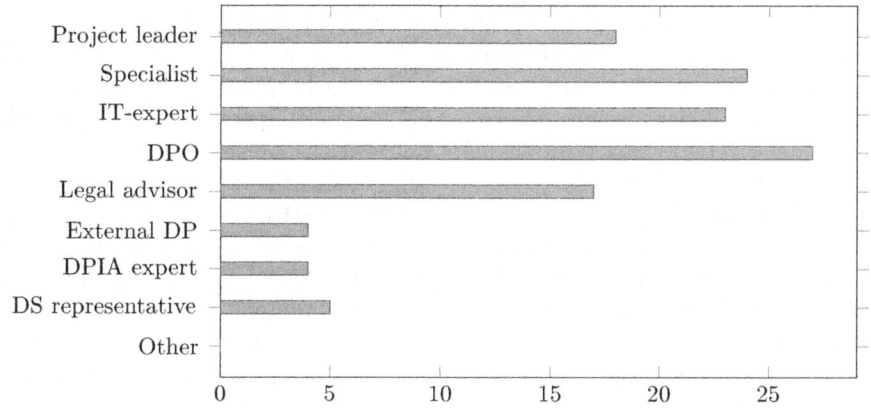

Fig. 2. Roles included in the DPIA process (n = 29)

The answers received do not necessarily follow these recommendations by the British supervisory authority, as 45% responded that their DPIA team consists of only two to four people. 34% reported a size of five to seven, roughly matching the ICO's recommendation. 14% invest more human resources, reporting teams of size eight to ten, while 7% go even bigger, working with ten or more people. Regarding the distinct types of people involved in the DPIA process, as illustrated in Fig. 2, we observe that the responses align with the recommendations in some areas, while deviating in others. Specialists for the use case, IT-experts, and DPOs are found in more than four-fifths of DPIA teams, and the project leaders and legal experts participate in roughly 60%. However, the roles often located outside the organisation are not represented with the same frequency. Representatives of individuals and external processors are only included in 17% and 14% of the responses. External DPIA experts are also reported in only 14% of cases, indicating a low usage of external DPIA services.

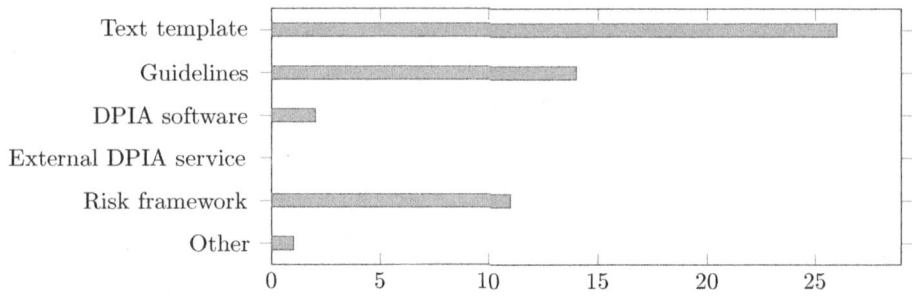

Fig. 3. Tools and aids used for a DPIA (n = 29)

Figure 3 illustrates the tools and aids utilised during the DPIA process, thereby confirming this assumption. No respondent stated that they use an external DPIA service in their organisation. Do keep in mind, however, that 10% reported themself as an external DPIA expert. Instead of external DPIA services, 90% rely on text templates for their DPIA. Additionally, organisations rely on official guidelines (48%) and risk management frameworks (38%) to conduct their DPIAs. While a variety of commercial DPIA software can be found online, only two respondents reported using DPIA software, and one stated they use AI. When asked for the specific tools they use, the majority responded with a self-developed solution (55%) or a self-developed template derived from a template or guideline (10%). 17% instead use a provided template directly. These templates originate from various sources, including governments and municipalities, supervisory authorities, and sector-specific shared resources, such as templates for hospitals.

5.3 Threshold Analysis

Nägele et al. critiqued that DPIAs are often conducted for processes that do not require a complete DPIA [5]. The question arises how the threshold analysis for DPIA looks in practice. According to the answers we received, 45% of respondents follow up with a complete DPIA on roughly a quarter of processes screened. 24% each report half and three-thirds of processes respectively, while 7% conduct a complete DPIA for every process.

The factors used to arrive at the conclusion are shown in Fig. 4. The 7% that follow up on every screening can be seen here as well. The most prominent factor, however, is the checklist with 86%. Following a checklist for processing activities that are likely to result in a high risk to individuals during the threshold analysis can also be found in many guidelines, such as those released by the EDPB [9]. Guidelines in general impact the outcome of the screening for 76% of organisations. Going away from tools used in the threshold analysis, discussion within the DPIA teams is the most frequent factor with 55%, while the decision is left to the DPO in 45% of cases. Rarely (10%), external consultants are brought in to provide an additional perspective.

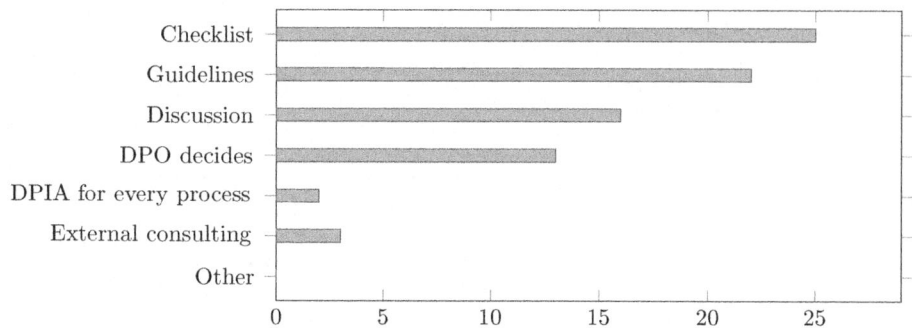

Fig. 4. Factors used to decide if a complete DPIA is mandatory (n = 29)

5.4 Risk Assessment and Measures

Risk assessments can be highly complex and are therefore hard to accurately gauge with a quantitative survey approach. Instead, we asked for the tools and aids used to identify both risks and measures. The most prominent methods to identify risks (see Fig. 5) are risk management frameworks, internal lists of risks, and internal consulting, which are utilised by roughly two-thirds of respondents each. Further, internally utilised methods include discussions (55%) and threat modelling (38%). Further, 31% use other DPIAs as reference. While it is not clear if these DPIAs are internal or external, based on the responses in Sect. 5.6, we can assume that these are more often internal. External risk guidelines are used in approximately one-third of cases, with the 'Other' response being similar to an external guideline. Online searches (21%) and external consulting (17%) are other sparsely used examples of getting information from outside.

If we compare the methods to identify measures for the risks (see Fig. 6) to these numbers, established technical and organisational measures and an internal list of measures are prominent as well, with 72% each. Discussions were stated the same number of times, increasing their relevance by 17% in comparison to the risk identification. Organisations from the public sector and research and education are especially fond of discussions, with three-thirds using them for risk and 94% for measure identification. Guidelines (48%) and other DPIAs (41%) increase in relevance as well, while online searches (14%) get used slightly less. Internal consulting, on the other hand, is used only 38% instead, while external consulting received the same number of responses as before.

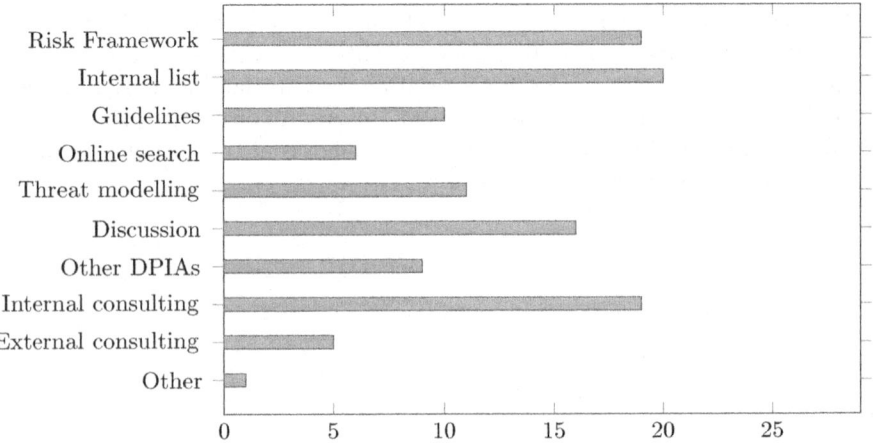

Fig. 5. Tools and aids used to identify risks (n = 29)

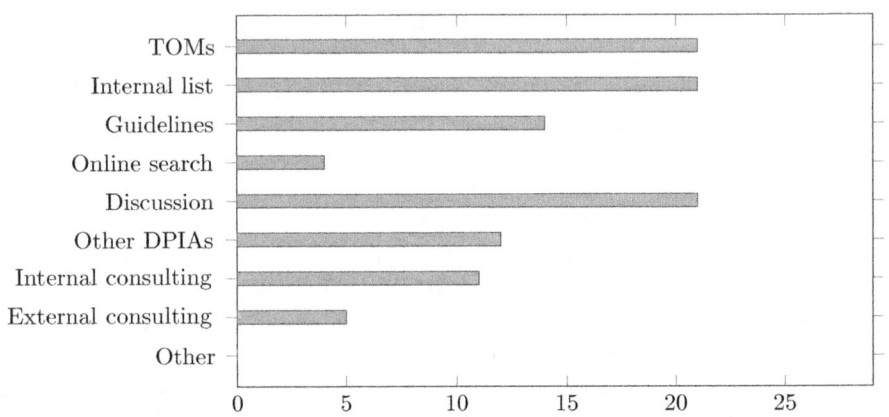

Fig. 6. Tools and aids used to identify measures (n = 29)

5.5 Third-Party Cooperation

The answers in Sect. 5.2 have shown that DPs are rarely included in the DPIA teams. That does not mean they are not considered during the DPIA. 86% stated that they request information from external DPs where they are involved in the processing activities, and 69% further request a list of risks and measures from them. To provide some additional information, Fig. 7 illustrates the parts of the DPIA where the third party is involved. The organisations do the screening exclusively by themselves, and only receive external input for the DPIA report in 10% of cases. Rougly a third of the time, third parties are involved during the process description (38%) and evaluation (31%). The aspects where organisations communicate with their collaborators the most are the risk assessment (48%) and identification of measures (45%). While 34% of respondents stated they do not include third parties during any stage of the DPIA, 60% of them still request information from them where they are involved in the processing.

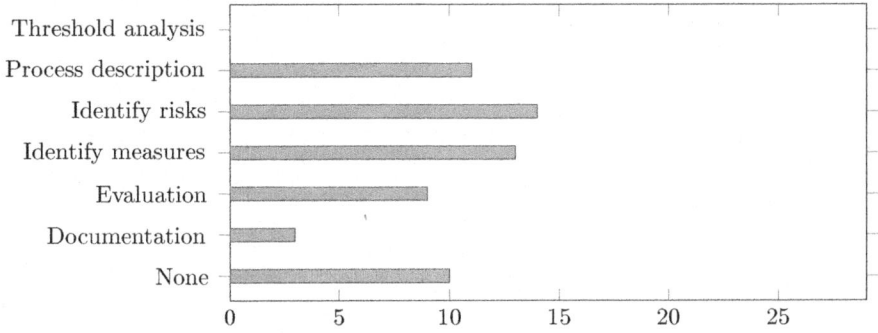

Fig. 7. Where representatives from third parties are involved (n = 29)

Besides DPs there is also the case of joint controllership, which can be tricky to address in a DPIA as it is not clear how the shared responsibility impacts the requirements for the DPIA process. From the 38% of respondents that were involved in a DPIA for processing activities with joint controllership, 40% stated they have agreements in place to distribute the responsibility between the parties, while 20% hold discussions between the two parties to address this issue. Another 20% decide depending on the circumstances, giving the main responsibility to the controller with more control over the processing or the one with more resources and expertise. One respondent's organisation resolves the shared responsibility by allowing each controller to conduct their own DPIA.

5.6 DPIA Results

While the GPDR demands a report to document the results of the DPIA, the format is not strictly defined. 69% of respondents document the DPIA result in text form only, while the rest additionally provide it in a structured data format.

As shown in Sect. 5.4, other DPIA results can be a valuable resource during the identification of risks and measures in a DPIA. The existence of a DPIA for a comparable processing activity might further relieve an organisation from the requirement to conduct a DPIA. Hence, sharing DPIA results can be advantageous. However, only 7% make their DPIA results publicly available and 41% share them with external stakeholders on request. Sharing results is more popular in larger organisations. 11% of respondents from organisations with 1000 or more employees reported about publishing their results, and 56% share results on request.

Another important aspect of the DPIA is its cyclical nature, requiring regular review and reevaluation of the DPIA results. Figure 8 shows when respondents review a DPIA. One common trigger for a review is the time passed. 55% report they review a DPIA after a specified time frame of once per year or more often, while 17% have a time frame of less than once per year. Another trigger is changes to either the process (59%) or the information system (52%). A security breach leads to a review of DPIAs in 24% of cases, while 7% report that they do not review their DPIAs at all.

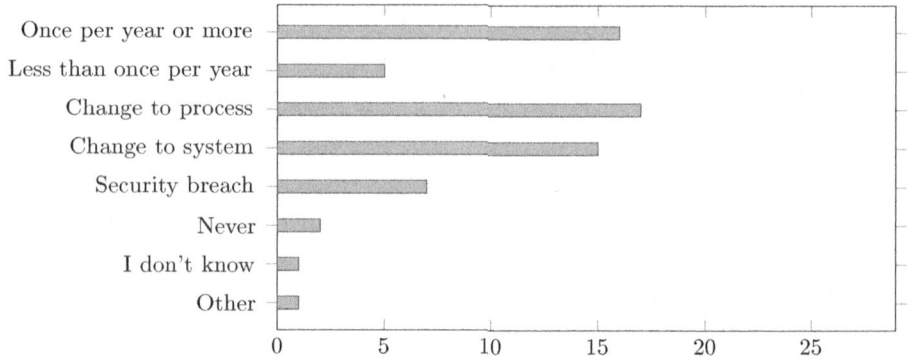

Fig. 8. When DPIAs are reviewed (n = 29)

Finally, the respondents were asked about their confidence in the DPIA result (see Fig. 9). Overall, participants appear to think that their DPIA process yields a somewhat satisfactory result, with no one reporting an inferior outcome and only one respondent categorising their DPIAs as poor. 38% report their results as acceptable, and the majority thinks their work is good (34%) or very good (24%).

5.7 Challenges

While the questions above primarily aimed to identify common patterns during the DPIA process, we were also interested in what the respondents identified as

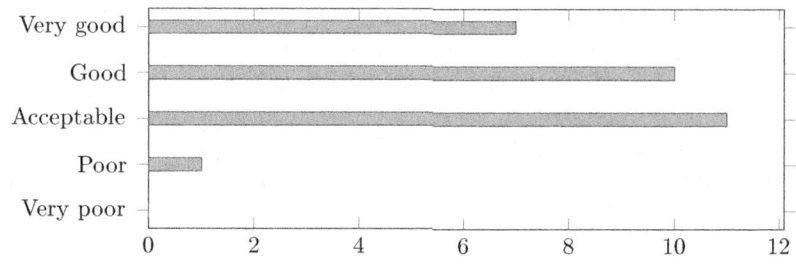

Fig. 9. Confidence in the result of the DPIA (n = 29)

the most significant challenges they faced during the DPIA process. Up to three challenges could be given. The responses are displayed in Fig. 10.

The two biggest challenges stated were the complexity of data processing activities (79%) and lack of time (59%). Overall, organisations struggle with different types of deficiencies, with a lack of budget (14%), expertise (24%), and adequate DPIA tools (24%) all receiving some attention. The identification of risks and measures was also highlighted as problem areas in 17% and 28% of responses, respectively. Unclear legal requirements are seen as a major issue by 14% of participants. Finally, one respondent complained about a lack of knowledge from third parties, and another one criticised the overall culture surrounding DPIAs, leading to a tedious and conservative DPIA process.

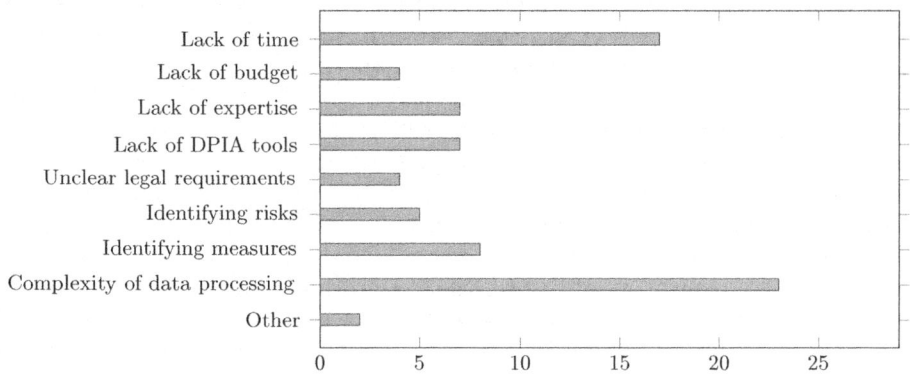

Fig. 10. Biggest challenges during a DPIA (n = 29)

6 Analysis and Discussion

6.1 Reusability of DPIAs

Given the substantial resources invested in the DPIA process, reusing the results or parts of them is desirable. When a process is sufficiently similar, a previous DPIA can even completely exempt the DC from the requirement for a DPIA.

Almost all respondents report that their organisation conducts multiple DPIAs per year. While using other DPIAs to identify both risks (31%) and measures (42%) is common, it is not a standard procedure. Apart from internal sources, the DPIA results of other organisations can also be used as a reference. This is especially important for types of processing that the organisation has no previous experience with. With only 7% of respondents sharing their DPIA results publicly and 41% sharing them on request only, which requires information about the existence of this DPIA, obtaining external references is challenging.

The specific combinations of types of processing and data used, an organisation's information system, and other relevant criteria influence the risks, measures, and general outcomes of a DPIA. Considering the size of the European data ecosystem, the correlations between these criteria are most likely not unique. Other DPIA results can therefore be a valuable tool for improving the quality of results and alleviating a lack of time and expertise. Further research should examine how DPIA results can be made publicly available, e.g., in the form of an open repository, without creating more risks or disclosing confidential information of the organisations.

6.2 Cooperation and Compositional Aspects

While external processors become involved at various stages of the DPIA process (see Fig. 7), Fig. 2 illustrates that they are rarely part of the DPIA team. As most organisations request information from involved processors, an organisation judging the external party's contributions to the DPIA as irrelevant or unimportant is unlikely. However, with a lack of time and budget being prevalent challenges, and the DC having full responsibility for the DPIA, getting people not contracted to your organisation permanently involved can be difficult.

With external parties only sparsely getting involved, if at all, during the actual DPIA process, the question arises as to what information is being requested from them, especially in terms of completeness and comprehensibility. An issue that has recently been raised by ENISA [2] is risks stemming from the composition of actors involved in a processing activity. Addressing these risks requires communication and insights into the information systems from all parties involved. Whether the level of collaboration that is expressed by the respondents' answers is sufficient to meet these criteria is doubtful.

The biggest challenge during DPIAs, according to the participants, is the complexity of processing activities. The most effective approach for a DPIA process to handle this complexity is likely an improvement of the process description. The hardest parts of a process to describe for a DPIA team are probably those that are not located within their own information system. However, only 38% of respondents involve third parties during the process description.

Overall, more information is needed about the exact forms and contents of communication between collaborating parties during a DPIA. The impact of other existing legal mechanisms between the parties, such as data processing agreements, also warrants attention. Additionally, the inconsistent involvement of third parties warrants an investigation into how DPIA processes can be designed to facilitate external participation more effectively.

6.3 Review of DPIAs

As shown in Fig. 8, there are various triggers for a DPIA review. With changes to the process at 59% being the most prominent reason, a consistent pattern for when a DPIA gets reviewed is hard to spot across organisations. The GDPR demands a review of the DPIA *"at least when there is a change of the risk represented by processing operations"* [1, Art. 35(11)]. Complementary, the guidelines by the EDPB [9] recommend reviewing periodically, after a change to the legislation, or a change to the processing operations. Especially changes to the process might incur changes to the risks, as consequences are hard to estimate beforehand. This strict interpretation would make a revision of the DPIA mandatory after a change to the process, and thus 41% of respondents would be non-compliant. You can argue the same way for organisations that do not engage in periodic reviews. The question arises, why does the review process appear to be lacklustre? This issue requires further investigation into the approach taken by organisations. It can be assumed that stricter guidelines and a clearer definition of when a change to the risks occurs are needed. For which changes to the processes do changes to the risk apply as well, and how do other triggers, such as changes to the system or a security breach, correlate with it?

Data spaces, as an emerging data ecosystem, face additional challenges regarding a DPIA review due to changes in the process. The external parties involved in data sharing for a process can change dynamically within a data space. These dynamically changing third parties all have their own local risks and might introduce new compositional risks. These risks would need to be shared and assessed each time, highlighting the need for automating the review of these changes to the process.

6.4 Experience with DPIAs

The majority of respondents have multiple years of experience with DPIA processes. Their familiarity with the procedure might diminish the impact of some challenges and issues on the process. The respondents stated that the complexity of processing activities is the biggest challenge. This leads to the assumption that this issue might be systematic rather than stemming from a lack of expertise. The four respondents with 1 to 2 years of DPIA experience all stated a lack of time as a major challenge. Three of them also criticised the existing DPIA tools. Although the sample size is small, a learning curve can be assumed, as familiarity with the process and tools is expected to improve efficiency and consequently reduce the time required for a DPIA. However, the reason for stating a lack of tools as a challenge can also stem from an insufficient quality of the tools. Interestingly, the one respondent with less than a year of experience did not provide either a lack of time or tools as one of the three biggest challenges, further warranting additional research in the influence of experience on the DPIA process.

6.5 DPIA Culture

At the level of organisation conducting DPIA Processes, awareness of privacy and security issues related to the handling of large amounts of data is crucial for data protection practices [34]. The potential of DPIA, therefore, lies not only in its use as a technical or legal instrument but also in its ability to foster a culture of data protection within organisations. The data protection culture addressed here encompasses internal awareness and sensitivity to data handling, as well as the development and implementation of principles, rules, and roles within the organisation [35,36]. The involvement of third parties, particularly in identifying risks, can be considered supportive, but there is also a risk of compromising internal sensitivity to organisation-centred risks (see Fig. 7). It is also important for an organisation to be aware of the specific types of data involved in the DPIA and what their materiality means for the handling of that data. At the individual level within organisations, skills in handling data appear to be crucial for the DPIA process.

A culture of data protection can be seen as a significant factor in the effectiveness of the DPIA, as it creates a framework within organisations in which the responsible handling of data is embedded as a value in data protection practice, thereby going beyond the fulfilment of legal requirements. This culture becomes visible when data protection is understood in practice as an integral part of corporate strategy, supported by organisational measures, and prioritised. As Fig. 5 shows, the organisational framework for a DPIA appears to be uncertain at present. In addition to procedural challenges such as the complexity of data processing, the factors of time, expertise, budget, and a systemic approach are considered particularly challenging organisational parameters.

6.6 Interaction Between the DPIA and Other Legislation

A relevant aspect outside the survey's scope is the interaction between the DPIA and legislation other than the GDPR. The impact of other current and potentially future legislation must be considered in the design of DPIA processes.

Kelemen and Hohmann [37] have demonstrated similarities between the DPIA and the obligations for risk assessment related to services and systems used by very large online platforms under the Digital Services Act [38]. Another novel piece of legislation is the AI Act [39], which introduces the Fundamental Rights Impact Assessment (FRIA) for high-risk artificial intelligence systems. The requirements for FRIA and DPIA overlap on multiple occasions, and the automation and reusability aspects of the DPIA could serve as an extension to the FRIA [40]. Initial approaches to a framework for identifying synergies between DPIAs and FRIAs have already been discussed [41]. Further, a tool that reuses DPIA results in FRIAs has been introduced [42]. While these approaches focus on how DPIAs can be used to supplement a FRIA, the question of how the FRIA and other legislation might impact the DPIA process remains.

As we advance, interactions with the risk assessment obligations under other legislation must be examined more closely. Matching requirements and procedures between the different risk assessment frameworks is potentially symbiotic. This can simplify the complexity stemming from the various legal requirements and complement both results.

6.7 Limitations

This research is subject to some limitations. First, the design of questions can introduce some bias. Most questions were either single or multiple-choice questions with pre-defined options. While we attempted to make these options as comprehensive as possible and included an *Other* option, it cannot be ruled out that respondents may have omitted some niche practices because they were not included in these options.

Since the survey was anonymous, the possibility of malicious answers or multiple submissions exists. We decided to accept this risk because there is no real incentive to manipulate the results.

Another issue is the sample size and difficulties in reaching possible respondents. The target audience is specific, and while many people may have been consulted for a DPIA in the past, they don't necessarily feel sufficiently involved with DPIAs to respond to the call for participation. Additionally, we did not find any DPIA-specific communities. This increased the reliance on networks and communities related to the broader field of privacy, data protection, and GDPR compliance. This might have introduced another bias in the results, as these participants are likely more involved with the topic than the average member of an organisation. Further, the small sample size made it challenging to identify correlations between the group of respondents.

Lastly, the survey's quantitative design means that the insights into the respondents' DPIA process are rather superficial. While we can draw meaningful conclusions about general trends and challenges regarding DPIA procedures in organisations, we did not obtain information about how a specific step of the DPIA is executed or what DPIA results look like. Further research is needed to address this gap and enable us to develop improvements for the DPIA process. Expert interviews, participating in a DPIA process, and collecting DPIA results from various sources may be reasonable next steps to address this issue.

7 Conclusions and Future Research Directions

As can be seen from our survey results, the implementation of data protection impact assessments remains somewhat heterogeneous in the European landscape, with a tendency to implement ad-hoc rather than formalised DPIA processes. Most survey respondents confirmed the utilisation of non-standardised DPIA methodologies, or the use of existing methods at the level of guidelines rather than a formal approach or tool. Individual, hand-written text documents make up the majority of DPIA reports, inspired by templates published by data protection authorities or domain-specific organisations.

Our survey also revealed that while third parties (external processors) are often requested to provide information about their data processing approaches and DPIA risk inputs, they are typically not actively involved in the DPIA process itself. The biggest challenge here lies in the complexity of data processing, which often renders a comprehensive DPIA process—covering all stakeholders and risk sources—unfeasible in terms of time and resources.

Based on our analysis of the survey results, it would be worthwhile to analyse different approaches to standardisation, formalisation, and (semi-)automation of the DPIA process to reduce efforts and improve quality, comparability and interoperability. We further plan to identify different DPIA cultures and the sociotechnical factors that determine the DPIA process. Finally, we will develop a generic DPIA process repository that can serve as a template library for ongoing DPIA processes.

Disclosure of Interests. The authors have no competing interests to declare that are relevant to the content of this article.

Appendix

Questions and answer options of the survey:

1. How many years of experience do you have in DPIAs or privacy impact assessments in general? None; Less than a year; 1–2 years; 3–6 years; 7–9 years; 10 or more years

2. Which role do you primarily have during a DPIA? Project leader; Specialist (In relation to the use case of the process the DPIA is conducted for); IT-Expert (e.g. cybersecurity or sys-admin); Data Protection Officer; Legal advisor; External Data Processor representative; External DPIA expert; Representative of the affected individuals (e.g. works council); Other

3. Which sector does your organisation belong to? Commercial Services (e.g. e-commerce, banking, insurance, software development or consulting); Public Services (e.g. healthcare, public transport, law enforcement); Manufacturing; Agriculture, Food, Forestry, and Mining; Education and Research (commercial or public); Other

4. How many employees does your organisation have? 1–9; 10–50; 50–250; 251–999; 1000 or more

5. How many DPIAs did your organisation conduct in the last 5 years? 0; 1; 2–4; 5–10; 11–25; 25 or more; I don't know

6. How many DPIAs does your organisation on average conduct in a year? 0; 1; 2–4; 5–10; 11–25; More than 25; I don't know

7. How many people are on average involved in the DPIA Team in your organisation, including externals? 1; 2–4; 5–7; 8–10; More than 10; I don't know

8. Which roles are included in the DPIA process? Project leader; Specialist (In relation to the use case of the process the DPIA is conducted for); IT-Expert (e.g. cybersecurity or sys-admin); Data Protection Officer; Legal advisor; External Data Processor representative; External DPIA expert; Representative of the affected individuals (e.g. works council); Other

9. Which tools or aids do you typically use for a DPIA? Text template; (Official) guidelines; DPIA software; External DPIA service; Risk management framework; I don't know; Other

10. Please give the name of the tools or aids you use (free text response)

11. After conducting the threshold analysis, which fraction of processes require a complete DPIA? None; Roughly 50

12. How do you decide a complete DPIA is mandatory when evaluating processing activities? Checklist; (Official) guidelines; Discussion with the DPIA team; The DPO decides; We do a DPIA for every process; External consulting; I don't know; Other

13. Which methods do you use to identify possible risks? Risk Frameworks; Internal list of risks; External list of risks/guidelines; Online search; Threat modeling; Discussion; Other DPIAs; Internal consulting; External consulting; I don't know; Other

14. Which methods do you use to identify measures to address the risks? Established technical organisational measures; Internal list of measures; External list of measures/guidelines; Online search; Discussion; Other DPIAs; Internal consulting; External consulting; I don't know; Other

15. In which parts of the DPIA process do you typically involve representatives from third parties? Threshold analysis; Process description; Identify and assess risks; Identify measures to mitigate risks; Evaluation of the DPIA; Documentation of results; I don't know; None

16. Do you request information from external Data Processors where they are involved in the Processing Activities? Yes; No; I don't know

17. Do you request a list of risks and measures or a DPIA from external Data Processors where they are involved in the Processing Activities? Yes; No; I don't know

18. Did you ever conduct a DPIA for processing activities with joint controllership? Yes; No; I don't know

19. In which form do you document the result of your DPIA? Text only (e.g. PDF); Structured data format only (e.g. JSON or XML); Text and structured data format; I don't know; Other

20. Are DPIA results shared with external stakeholders? Yes, publicly available; Yes, shared upon request; No, internal use only; I don't know

21. When do you review a completed DPIA? After a fixed period of time (1x per year or more often); After a fixed period of time (Less than 1x per year); After a change to the process; After a change to the information system (IT architecture); After a security breach; Never; I don't know; Other

22. How confident are you in the accuracy of the DPIA result on average? Very Poor; Acceptable; Very Good

23. What are the biggest challenges you and your organisation face during a DPIA? Lack of time; Lack of budget; Lack of expertise; Lack of adequate tools for DPIAs; Unclear legal requirements; Difficulties identifying data protection risks concerning the individual; Difficulties identifying adequate data protection measures; Complexity of data processing activities; Other

References

1. European Parliament and Council: Regulation (EU) 2016/679 of the European Parliament and of the Council of 27 April 2016 on the protection of natural persons with regard to the processing of personal data and on the free movement of such data, and repealing Directive 95/46/EC (General Data Protection Regulation) (2016). https://eur-lex.europa.eu/legal-content/EN/TXT/PDF/?uri=CELEX:32016R0679&from=EN. Visited 25 Jan 2024
2. Drogkaris, P., Prieto, J.G. (eds.): European Union Agency for Cybersecurity: Engineering Personal Data Protection in EU Data Spaces (2024)
3. Curry, E., et al.: Data sharing spaces: the BDVA perspective. In: Otto, B., ten Hompel, M., Wrobel, S. (eds.) Designing Data Spaces: The Ecosystem Approach to Competitive Advantage, pp. 365–382. Springer, Cham (2022). https://doi.org/10.1007/978-3-030-93975-5_22
4. Agencia Española de Protección de Datos: APPROACH TO DATA SPACES FROM GDPR PERSPECTIVE (2022). https://www.aepd.es/documento/approach-to-data-spaces-from-gdpr-perspective.pdf. Visited 27 June 2024
5. Nägele, P., Petrlic, R., Schemmel, F.: Die Datenschutz-Folgenabschätzung in der Praxis. Datenschutz und Datensicherheit - DuD **44**(11), 719–728 (2020). ISSN: 1614-0702, 1862-2607. https://doi.org/10.1007/s11623-020-1356-3. http://link.springer.com/10.1007/s11623-020-1356-3. Visited 29 Apr 2024
6. Datenschutzkonferenz. Datenschutz-Folgenabschätzung nach Art. 35 DS-GVO (2018)
7. Commission Nationale Informatique & Libertés: PIA, methodology (2018)
8. Friedewald, M.: Datenschutz-Folgenabschätzung: Chancen, Grenzen, Umsetzung. In: TATuP-Zeitschrift für Technikfolgenabschätzung in Theorie und Praxis/J. Technol. Assess. Theory Pract. **26**(1-2), 66–71 (2017). https://www.ssoar.info/ssoar/handle/document/68742. Visited 24 Jan 2024
9. Article 29 Working Party: Guidelines on Data Protection Impact Assessment (DPIA) and determining whether processing is "likely to result in a high risk" for the purposes of Regulation 2016/679 (2017)
10. Martin, N., et al.: The data protection impact assessment according to article 35 GDPR. In: Fraunhofer Institute for Systems and Innovation Research ISI (2020)
11. Information Commissioner's Office: Sample DPIA template. v0.3, February 2019. https://ico.org.uk/media/2258461/dpia-template-v04-post-comms-review-20180308.pdf. Visited 14 Mar 2024
12. Agencia Española de Protección de Datos: Template for data protection impact assessment report (DPIA) for private sector (2022)
13. Commission Nationale Informatique & Libertés: PIA, templates (2018)
14. Commission Nationale Informatique & Libertés: PIA, knowledge bases (2018)
15. International Organization for Standardization: Information technology — Security techniques — Guidelines for privacy impact assessment. Standard. International Organization for Standardization, Geneva, CH (2023)
16. Bieker, F., Friedewald, M., Hansen, M., Obersteller, H., Rost, M.: A process for data protection impact assessment under the European general data protection regulation. In: Schiffner, S., Serna, J., Ikonomou, D., Rannenberg, K. (eds.) APF 2016. LNCS, vol. 9857, pp. 21–37. Springer, Cham (2016). https://doi.org/10.1007/978-3-319-44760-5_2
17. Hansen, M., Jensen, M., Rost, M.: Protection goals for privacy engineering. In: IEEE Security and Privacy Workshops, pp. 159–166. IEEE (2015)

18. Gonscherowski, S., et al.: Durchführung einer Datenschutz-Folgenabschätzung gem. Art. 35 DSGVO auf der methodischen Grundlage eines stan- dardisierten Prozessablaufes mit Rückgriff auf das SDM am Beispiel eines "Pay as you drive"-Verfahrens (V 0.10) (2017)
19. Haag, I., et al.: Datenschutz-Folgenabschätzung gemäßszlig; Art. 35 DS-GVO (2019). https://opusihandbuch.kronsoft.de/documents/DSFA-B3S-Gesundheitsversorgung-Art.35-DSGVO.pdf. Visited 24 Jan 2024
20. Kloza, D., et al.: Data protection impact assessment in the European Union: developing a template for a report from the assessment process. LawArXiv, October 2020. https://doi.org/10.31228/osf.io/7qrfp. https://osf.io/7qrfp. Visited 13 Dec 2023
21. Demetzou, K.: Data protection impact assessment: a tool for accountability and the unclarified concept of 'high risk' in the general data protection regulation. Comput. Law Secur. Rev. **35**(6), 105342 (2019)
22. Friedewald, M., et al.: Data protection impact assessments in practice: experiences from case studies. In: Katsikas, S., et al. (eds.) Computer Security. ESORICS 2021 International Workshops. LNCS, vol. 13106, pp. 424–443. Springer, Cham (2022). ISBN: 978-3-030-95483-3 978-3-030-95484-0. https://doi.org/10.1007/978-3-030-95484-0_25. https://link.springer.com/10.1007/978-3-030-95484-0_25. Visited 29 May 2024
23. Wairimu, S., et al.: On the evaluation of privacy impact assessment and privacy risk assessment methodologies: a systematic literature review. IEEE Access (2024). https://ieeexplore.ieee.org/abstract/document/10418587/. Visited 28 May 2024
24. Georgiadis, G., Poels, G.: Towards a privacy impact assessment methodology to support the requirements of the general data protection regulation in a big data analytics context: a systematic literature review. Comput. Law Secur. Rev. **44**, 105640 (2022). https://www.sciencedirect.com/science/article/pii/S0267364921001138. Visited 29 May 2024
25. Vemou, K., Karyda, M.: Evaluating privacy impact assessment methods: guidelines and best practice. Inf. Comput. Secur. **28**(1), 35–53 (2019). https://www.emerald.com/insight/content/doi/10.1108/ICS-04-2019-0047/full/. Visited 29 May 2024
26. Todde, M., et al.: Methodology and workflow to perform the data protection impact assessment in healthcare information systems. Inf. Med. Unlocked **19**, 100361 (2020). https://www.sciencedirect.com/science/article/pii/S2352914820301477. Visited 29 May 2024
27. Stevanovic, U., et al.: Data Protection Impact Assessment - An Initial Guide for Communities (2018)
28. López, C.T., Domingo, I.A., Torrijos, J.V.: Approaching the data protection impact assessment as a legal methodology to evaluate the degree of privacy by design achieved in technological proposals. A special reference to Identity Management systems. In: Proceedings of the 16th International Conference on Availability, Reliability and Security, pp. 1–9. ACM, Vienna, Austria, August 2021. isbn: 978-1-4503-9051-4. https://doi.org/10.1145/3465481.3469207. https://dl.acm.org/doi/10.1145/3465481.3469207. Visited 29 May 2024
29. Wuyts, K., et al.: Effective and efficient privacy threat modeling through domain refinements. In: Proceedings of the 33rd Annual ACM Symposium on Applied Computing, pp. 1175–1178 (2018). https://dl.acm.org/doi/abs/10.1145/3167132.3167414. Visited 29 May 2024
30. Calvi, A.: Gender, data protection & the smart city: exploring the role of DPIA in achieving equality goals. Eur. J. Spat. Dev. **19**(3) (2022)

31. De, S.J., Métayer, D.L.: A refinement approach for the reuse of privacy risk analysis results. In: Schweighofer, E., Leitold, H., Mitrakas, A., Rannenberg, K. (eds.) Privacy Technologies and Policy. LNCS, vol. 10518, pp. 52–83. Springer, Cham (2017). isbn: 978-3-319-67279-3 978-3-319-67280-9. https://doi.org/10.1007/978-3-319-67280-9_4. http://link.springer.com/10.1007/978-3-319-67280-9_4. Visited 29 May 2024
32. Pandit, H.J.: A semantic specification for data protection impact assessments (DPIA). In: Towards a Knowledge-Aware AI, pp. 36–50. IOS Press (2022)
33. Information Commissioner's Office: How do we do a DPIA? ICO, 17 November 2024. https://ico.org.uk/for-organisations/uk-gdpr-guidance-and-resources/accountability-and-governance/data-protection-impact-assessments-dpias/how-do-we-do-a-dpia/. Visited 28 May 2025
34. Dubey, R., et al.: Big data and predictive analytics and manufacturing performance: integrating institutional theory, resource-based view and big data culture. Br. J. Manag. **30**(2), 341–361 (2019)
35. Salleh, K.A., Janczewski, L.: Technological, organizational and environmental security and privacy issues of big data: a literature review. Procedia Comput. Sci. **100**, 19–28 (2016)
36. Phillips-Wren, G., et al.: Business analytics in the context of big data: a roadmap for research. Commun. Assoc. Inf. Syst. **37**(1), 23 (2015)
37. Kelemen, B.K., Hohmann, B.: Is there anything new under the sun? A glance at the digital services act and the digital markets act from the perspective of digitalisation in the EU. Croatian Yearbook Eur. Law Policy **19**, 225–248 (2023)
38. Regulation (EU) 2022/2065 of the European Parliament and of the Council of 19 October 2022 on a Single Market For Digital Services and amending Directive 2000/31/EC (Digital Services Act) (Text with EEA relevance). Legislative Body: EP, CONSIL, October 2022. http://data.europa.eu/eli/reg/2022/2065/oj/eng. Visited 17 Feb 2025
39. Regulation (EU) 2024/1689 of the European Parliament and of the Council of 13 June 2024 laying down harmonised rules on artificial intelligence and amending Regulations (EC) No 300/2008, (EU) No 167/2013, (EU) No 168/2013, (EU) 2018/858, (EU) 2018/1139 and (EU) 2019/2144 and Directives 2014/90/EU, (EU) 2016/797 and (EU) 2020/1828 (Artificial Intelligence Act) (Text with EEA relevance). Legislative Body: CONSIL, EP, June 2024. http://data.europa.eu/eli/reg/2024/1689/oj/eng. Visited 17 Feb 2025
40. Kokoulina, O.: Challenges in digital compliance: risk assessment and fundamental rights under the GDPR and the EU AI Act (2024)
41. Thomaidou, A., Limniotis, K.: Navigating through human rights in AI: exploring the interplay between GDPR and fundamental rights impact assessment. J. Cybersecur. Priv. **5**(1), 7 (2025)
42. Pandit, H.J., Rintamäki, T.: Towards an automated AI Act FRIA tool that can reuse GDPR's DPIA (2024)

Open Access This chapter is licensed under the terms of the Creative Commons Attribution-NonCommercial-NoDerivatives 4.0 International License (http://creativecommons.org/licenses/by-nc-nd/4.0/), which permits any noncommercial use, sharing, distribution and reproduction in any medium or format, as long as you give appropriate credit to the original author(s) and the source, provide a link to the Creative Commons license and indicate if you modified the licensed material. You do not have permission under this license to share adapted material derived from this chapter or parts of it.

The images or other third party material in this chapter are included in the chapter's Creative Commons license, unless indicated otherwise in a credit line to the material. If material is not included in the chapter's Creative Commons license and your intended use is not permitted by statutory regulation or exceeds the permitted use, you will need to obtain permission directly from the copyright holder.

Information Inference Diagrams: Complementing Privacy and Security Analyses Beyond Data Flows

Sebastian Rehms[1](✉), Stefan Köpsell[1,2,3], Verena Klös[4], and Florian Tschorsch[1]

[1] Technische Universität Dresden, Dresden, Germany
{sebastian.rehms,stefan.koepsell,florian.tschorsch}@tu-dresden.de
[2] Centre for Tactile Internet with Human-in-the-Loop (CeTI), Dresden, Germany
[3] Barkhausen Institute, Dresden, Germany
stefan.koepsell@barkhauseninstitut.org
[4] Carl von Ossietzky Universität Oldenburg, Oldenburg, Germany
verena.kloes@uni-oldenburg.de

Abstract. This work introduces Information Inference Diagrams (I2Ds), a modeling framework aiming to complement existing approaches for privacy and security analysis of distributed systems. It is intended to support established threat modeling processes. Our approach is designed to be compatible with Data Flow Diagrams (DFDs), which form the basis of many established techniques and tools. Unlike DFDs, I2Ds represent information propagation, going beyond mere data flows to enable more formal reasoning in threat modeling while remaining practical. They define inference and sharing (flow) relations on information items to model how information moves through a system. To this end, we provide formal definitions for information items, entities, and flows. By introducing classes as a type system, our formal rules are both generic and allow conformance to existing vocabularies. We demonstrate the applicability of I2Ds through examples, that showcase their versatility in system analysis.

1 Introduction

Security and privacy analyses often begin with a description of the target system. These descriptions form the foundation for systematic analysis, enabling tasks such as identifying risks associated with system elements or verifying compliance with specific requirements. In particular, Data Flow Diagrams (DFDs) have gained widespread adoption for practical threat modelling [18]. Techniques such as STRIDE [14] and LINDUN [5] employ DFDs systematically and have been extended for specialised scenarios and contexts [11,23]. Furthermore, these methods have been integrated into tools for threat modelling [8,16,20].

While data-flow-centric approaches are productive for assessing privacy and security, they often fail to address deeper, fundamental aspects of security and

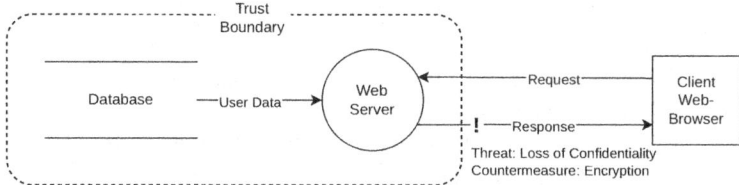

Fig. 1. Data Flow Diagram of a typical web application (request-response scenario).

privacy: protecting data is often the means to an end; safeguarding the information implicitly or explicitly derived from the data and its surrounding context. Information, in this context, refers to the interpretation of data, which can include unintended insights drawn from metadata, contextual factors, or background knowledge. Please note that this is a qualitative notion of information [15] and not quantitative like entropy.

DFDs, while effective for visualizing data flows, are not designed to explicitly represent the information level of a system. This limitation makes it difficult to analyse how information *propagates* through a system or to evaluate information access, especially in terms of contextual or background knowledge. Practical analyses using DFDs often address these gaps only implicitly through annotations or ad hoc interpretations. In Fig. 1, we provide a simple example illustrating some of the discussed problems. It depicts a DFD of a distributed application delivering data to a user via a web app, with an annotated threat and countermeasure: the response contains confidential user data at risk. This annotation relies on additional, implicit knowledge. It is implied that data is confidential, that data is included in the request (despite no explicit link between the database and response), transmitted over an untrusted channel, and mitigated by encryption. It is also unclear, how adding encryption affects the system, e.g., if new data flows are necessary to manage keys and identities, if new risks like identifiability arise (as the mitigation is only indicated as an annotation). Such knowledge is not visible because DFDs are not designed for structured reasoning. DFDs are popular partially because they abstract from these kinds of details. However, given higher demands on precision and granularity of a threat modelling process, it becomes necessary to facilitate such aspects within a data flow model. It is also possible that only smaller critical parts of a system need to be analysed in depth.

In this paper, we address these challenges by introducing *Information Inference Diagrams (I2Ds)*, a novel methodology for reasoning about privacy and security. I2Ds provide a structured representation of a system's information view, enabling a clearer understanding of how information propagates to facilitate the analysis of security and privacy properties. Our approach is designed to complement existing methodologies, such as DFD-based threat modelling, by bridging the gap between data-level and information-level analysis. I2Ds are intended to fill the space between formal information flow analysis [13] and classical threat modelling. They are intended to be used in DFD-based analysis to enable detailed inspection.

To this end, I2Ds provide a framework for modelling the existence of *information items* within a system, their propagation pathways, and the inferences that can be drawn from them. This enables I2Ds to capture and analyse the impact of successful attacks or architectural changes on the system. I2Ds are specifically designed to allow direct translation from DFDs, enabling integration with established system modelling practices. They follow a modular approach, allowing focused analysis on selected parts of a system while abstracting others. An important property of I2Ds is their support for incremental model construction, where additional information can be iteratively incorporated by the user. I2Ds can be either constructed manually or automatically generated from existing system descriptions. However, the automatic generation of I2Ds, which depends heavily on the specific characteristics of the input model, is beyond the scope of this paper.

The contributions of this paper can be summarised as follows. We introduce Information Inference Diagrams (I2Ds) by providing definitions for all elements and by explaining certain concepts making them versatile for complementing existing DFD-based analysis endeavours. Furthermore, we demonstrate the utility of I2Ds through illustrative examples, showcasing their effectiveness in identifying and mitigating security and privacy risks in various scenarios.

The remainder is structured as follows. In Sect. 2, we define I2Ds and their foundational concepts. In Sect. 3, we demonstrate their application through examples. In Sect. 4, we discuss key challenges and design decisions. In Sect. 5, we review related work and position I2Ds in context. Lastly, in Sect. 6, we conclude and propose directions for future research.

2 Information Inference Diagrams

In this section, we introduce the foundations of I2Ds and their construction principles. I2Ds are intended to complement DFD-based reasoning by switching to information level relations. Therefore they can build on existing DFDs.

Figure 2 shows an I2D for the scenario depicted in Fig. 1. Independent of their type, all nodes are represented as *entities* sharing information through *information flows*. The trust boundary is also an entity containing sub-entities. Each simple entity has an associated set of *information items*. *Inference rules* ($\mathbb{R}$) describe the inference relation over these items. Last, a *normative* requirement rule ($\mathbb{N}$) describes privacy and/or security requirements. In the following, we define all these elements and provide syntax rules. We will refer back to the example in the next section and also in Sect. 3, when all foundations have been laid out.

2.1 Elements

At its core, an I2D represents entities and the information that is available to them. Information can be available for an entity by definition. Information can become available to an entity by learning it from another entity (represented by flows) or by inference.

I2Ds contain descriptive and, optionally, normative declarations. Normative declarations ($\mathbb{N}$) express requirements that should hold. The descriptive part is composed of three aspects:

First, the information available to different entities. Second, the flow of information between entities. Third, inference rules (designated by $\mathbb{R}$) which may be automatically evaluated during the reasoning process.

Entities and Information Items. The core elements of an I2D are entities. Each entity e has an associated individual information item set $\mathcal{I}(e)$ (it "possesses" items). An information item is an object representing some fact. For example: given some message different information items can be defined, referring to aspects of the message itself, inferred properties of that message or context of the message. One may for example define information items for the content of a message or the length of the message. Regarding the security, one can define an item referring to the inferred state of the message's integrity. Similarly, one may define an item representing the time the message was received. An information item represents arbitrary knowledge or even capabilities for an entity and we make no restrictions on that, enabling to express a variety of security and privacy properties.

$\mathcal{I}(e)$ is a fuzzy set, allowing to express uncertainty on information items. Information items can be annotated with classes, meaning that they can be annotated with additional class symbols assigning them to classes (e.g., an item may be marked as "personal data" or "high clearance level"). We denote the set of all information item classes by $\mathfrak{C}^I$ and define an information item as a triple:

$$i = (n, p, C),$$

where n is a unique name (identifier), $p \in [0,1]$ is the degree of membership, and $C \subseteq \mathfrak{C}^I$ is a set of item classes the item is assigned to. As a shorthand notation, one can write $n_p^{c_0,\ldots,c_n}$ where $c_0,\ldots,c_n = C$. If $p = 1$, the subscript

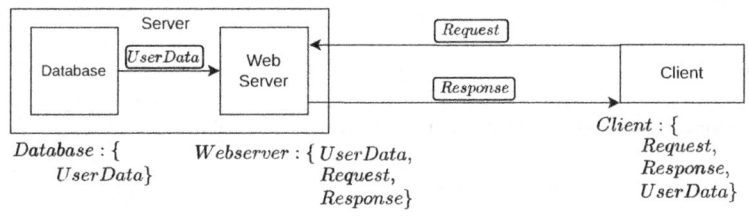

$\mathbb{R}$: $UserData, Request \vdash Response$;
$Response \vdash UserData$;

$\mathbb{N}$: $UserData \not\subseteq untrusted$

Fig. 2. A representation of the example system from the Introduction.

can be dropped yielding $n^{c_0,\ldots,c_n}$ in the shorthand notation. Classes work like annotations for elements, allowing to define group-based rules, which we introduce later. $C(i)$ denotes the projection of the classes of the item i. In Fig. 2 the information items for each entity are visible below the respective boxes representing the entities' item sets (e.g. $Database : \{UserData\}$) – probabilities and classes are not used.

$\mathcal{E}$ is the set of all entities. An entity can be simple or complex, where $\mathcal{E}^s$ is the set of all simple entities and $\mathcal{E}^c$ the set of all complex entities. A simple entity is again a triple:

$$e = (n, I, C),$$

where n is a name, I is a set of information items (thus, $\mathcal{I}(e) = I$), and $C \subseteq \mathfrak{C}^E$ is a set of entity classes ($\mathfrak{C}^E$ refers to the set of all possible classes for entities).

A complex entity consists of a name, classes it belongs to, and child entities:

$$ec = (n, C, E),$$

where (n, C, E) is a tuple representing a complex entity. n is a name, E is a non-empty set of sub-entities and C a set of entity classes. The sub-entities may be simple or complex, allowing nesting of entities. As $E \neq \varnothing$, the leaves of the resulting logical tree are always simple entities. $C(e)$ designates the class set of an entity e. The function $\mathcal{I}(ec)$ for a complex entity returns the set of all information items of it's children by recursively folding all information items from its child entities into the into the parent entity's information set, using fuzzy set standard union, selecting the highest probability. In essence, this creates the union of the information sets of all leaf nodes in the hierarchy.

In I2Ds, the notion of an entity is very general. It may represent physical components (e.g., a router), virtual components (e.g., an API endpoint), humans, or physical and virtual channels. In Fig. 2 the entities are represented as boxes (where the *Server* is a complex entity with two simple sub-entities). No classes are used.

Flows. $\mathcal{F}$ represents the set of all flows. A flow can be simple or complex. In Fig. 2 there are three simple flows without classes (the arrows). A simple flow consists of an origin, a target, associated information, a name, and classes:

$$f = (n, o, t, I, C)$$

The construction of complex flows is similar to entities:

$$fc = (n, o, t, C, F),$$

where n designates the name of a flow. $o, t \in \mathcal{E}^s$ and $o \neq t$ designate the origin and target of a flow which are always simple entities. $C \subseteq \mathfrak{C}^F$ designates classes for flows, where $\mathfrak{C}^F$ is the set of all flow classes. F is an ordered list of sub-flows. I is a set of information items associated with a flow.

Flow-associated items express that information available at the origin is shared with the target. Let i be any information item, a, b simple entities and f a simple flow from a to b with associated information items $\mathcal{I}(f)$, then:

$$i \in \mathcal{I}(a), i \in \mathcal{I}(f) \Rightarrow i \in \mathcal{I}(b).$$

Note, that a flow does not necessarily mean, that information is sent from one entity to another; a flow rather represents that *only if* some information is available at one entity this information is also available to the other. We allow the wildcard symbol $*$ as information item on a flow to express that the origin entity shares all its information with a target entity.

Complex flows allow to specify the structure of information exchange and can therefore be used to model protocol-like interactions (therefore the child-list is ordered). Complex flows contain a list of possibly complex children flows. As every flow has an origin and a target entity, complex flows logically also contain associated entities, denoted by $\mathcal{E}(F)$, where F is a complex flow. These entities can be "external" to the original flow, i.e., they are not required to be the origin or target. Helper entities therefore can be introduced to describe complex flows. In fact, complex flows can be seen like nested diagrams.

Rules. New information items have to be added to the information sets of entities if inference rules in $\mathbb{R}$ apply (cf. Fig. 2). In the simplest form, these rules follow the syntax

$$a_0, a_1, \ldots \vdash_p^C b_0, b_1, \ldots$$

Here, $p \in [0, 1]$ is a probability, $a_0, a_1, \ldots$ and $b_0, b_1, \ldots$ are finite lists of information items, and $C \subseteq \mathfrak{C}^E$ is a set of entity classes to which the rule is applicable. An omitted class annotation implies that the rule is applicable to all entities. If all information items $a_0, a_1, \ldots$ are present in an entity set the rule applies, triggering an addition of the items $b_0, b_1, \ldots$ with degree p to the respective entity set (if p is omitted, then $p = 1$). Class-based rules can be written according to this syntax:

$$c_0(x), c_1(y), \ldots \vdash^C b_0, b_1, \ldots \quad \text{or} \quad c_0(x), c_1(y), \ldots \vdash^C x^{d_0}, y^{d_1}, \ldots$$

where $c_0, c_1, \ldots, d_0, d_1, \ldots \in \mathfrak{C}^I$ are item classes and x, y are variables (must not be bound by an item name). The first rule schema conditionally adds items. The second rule schema serves the purpose to conditionally rewrite classified items, e.g. the rule $c0(x), c1(y) \vdash x^{d_0}, y^{d_1}$ would apply to the item set $\{a^{c_0}, b^{c_1}\}$ and generate the new items a^{d_0} and b^{d_1}.

It is important to prevent infinite recursion. This can be done by implicitly marking the outcome by the generating rules and prohibit re-application.

Classes in rules can be negated (effectively yielding the complement set): $c(x), \neg d(x) \vdash i$ applies if $c \in C(x) \land d \notin C(x)$.

For class rules, one can use the variable x in the outcome, which can be useful, e.g., to "rewrite classes". For instance, if c is a class, then the rule $c(x) \vdash x^{c,d}$ would add a new item with classes c, d to x.

A wildcard class $*()$ can make a single-class-rule to be applied to multi-classed items. For example, $c(x), *(x) \vdash j$ applies to an information item $i^{c,d}$, although d is not explicitly mentioned in the rule. Using a class variable, indicated by the wildcard $*$, allows to propagate the classes to the outcome: $c(x), *v(x) \vdash j^v$.

An arrow can be used to express replacement of items on all outgoing flows. If i and j are information items, c is class and x a variable, then the two rules

$$i \xrightarrow{m} j \quad \text{or} \quad c(x) \xrightarrow{m} j$$

express that all outgoing flows containing i or c-classified items instead contain j but only if j is available for the entity the rule is applied for (entities classified m). Such rules can be used, to automate the expression of transformations of items at intermediate stations (like pre-processing etc.). In Fig. 4 an example is given how such a rule in combination with other inference rules can be used to represent man-in-the-middle-like attacks.

Entity classification rules allow to automatically add items to information sets of entities, add new flows or child-entities based on classification. If c is an entity class symbol, i an information item, E is an entity and f is a simple flow, then one can use:

$$C(c) \vdash i \quad \text{or} \quad C(c) \vdash e \quad \text{or} \quad C(c) \vdash f$$

The first means that all entities of class c possess i. The second means, that if an entity is of class c, then it automatically has a child E, transforming the parent entity into a complex one if it is not already one (note that we allow E to be complex itself). The third means that a c-classified entity is part of a flow. For flows we force that the respective entity is either the origin or target of the flow. If the other entity does not exist, it is created. Note that the associated information items are not required to be in the entities' sets (cf. the definition of flows above). Similarly, rules allow the automatic addition of nested entities and flows.

One aspect to heed is, that automatic changes triggered by class rules may add items to complex entities. This is problematic because complex entities can be classified but do not possess their own information sets (only the leaf entities). Therefore in such cases the triggered rules need to be resolved to add the according elements to leaf elements.[1]

Normative Declarations. All aspects presented so far are purely descriptive, as they focus solely on enabling the representation of a system. By introducing

---

[1] The alternative would be to differentiate between specific classes for simple and complex entities. This, however, would also make a resolving step necessary, as the class of a simple entity needs to be transformed into the class of a complex entity when adding sub-entities. Our approach fits together with the concept of views introduced further down. One may simply introduce an abstract "virtual storage" leaf entity collecting items of higher levels.

normative requirements, it becomes possible to evaluate whether any issues exist within the current system model. This step is entirely optional.
Requirements follow the patterns:

$$a, b, \ldots \in E \quad \text{or} \quad a, b, \ldots \notin E,$$

where $a, b, \ldots$ are information items, and E is a simple or complex entity. One can use a wildcard $*$ to represent every entity and add exceptions using the usual set-exclusion operator "$\backslash$". For example $*\backslash F, G$ excludes entities F, G. Requirements state that an entity shall or shall not have access to specific information items. If E is a complex entity, this implies that the respective information item is/is not present at any/at least one sub-entity (cf. the definition of views). Instead of E, one can also use an entity class, effectively making it possible to declare policies for sets of entities.

2.2 Transformations

Recall that models are inherently incomplete, which is why we focus on the construction process of I2Ds. In this section, we describe how an I2D can be further refined and specified through transformations. In this context we highlight that a model is continuously built, while introducing changes to a model (e.g., starting out from a model in a different "language" like DFDs and then translated, effectively changing the model by adding additional details based on the modelling method).

Transformations refer to any change of the model during the modelling process. Many rules explained above can be understood as automatic transformations of the model. But during the modelling process, the user introduces also manual changes according to the possibilities of the modelling method. This can be understood as manual transformations, effectively creating new versions of the model by adding additional knowledge.

Simple transformations include the addition of information items, the introduction of simple entities and flows, the classification of existing elements, and the creation of rules.

More elaborate transformations involve refining entities by adding sub-entities or refining flows, both of which result in the creation of complex elements. When a simple entity is transformed into a complex entity through the addition of nested sub-entities, incoming flows directed at the parent entity must be rewritten to target specific child entities. This adjustment aligns with the definition of flows, which do not permit complex entities as origin or target.

For the creation of a complex flow, we specifically introduce the concept of a *bisection*. This manual transformation answers the question: *how is the information exchange mediated?* A bisection introduces a mediating entity in between two information sharing entities. This new entity represents the logical path enabling the sharing of information. Depending on the scenario, the mediating entity can be very general (e.g., an ISP) or very specific (e.g. a physical channel). A bisection implies that the information set of the mediating entity contains all

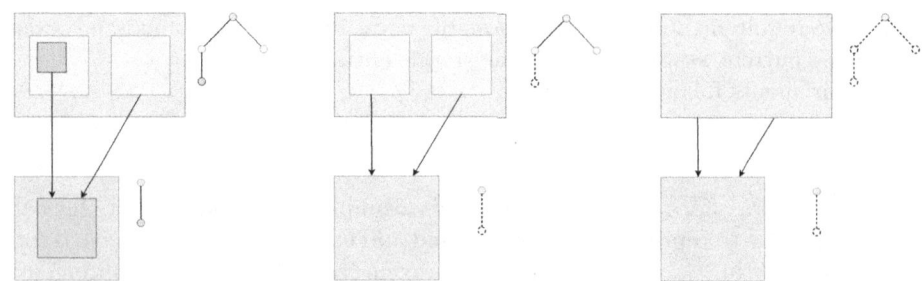

Fig. 3. Views on two entities (without information items). The tree representation next to each entity shows the abstracted sub-tree. Colours indicate different possible views, which may vary between entities.

information items belonging to the flows—otherwise it would not be mediating the information.

The result of a bisection is a complex flow which can be specified further, e.g., by adding other entities or flows. For example, the ISP entity might be composed of multiple routers; the physical channel might imply that other entities can eavesdrop on it and therefore a new flow can be added. A bisection is used as example in Fig. 4b.

Each transformation possibly triggers a cascade of changes and therefore an iterated re-evaluation of rules is necessary.

2.3 Views

A view of a complex entity represents its abstraction at a specific depth of the tree, reducing it to a simple entity. A complex entity aggregates the information of its children using $\mathcal{I}(e)$. Flows directed to the child entities are redirected to the newly instantiated simple entity. Figure 3 illustrates this process: Nested boxes represent entities and the colours represent possible views. Tree representations next to each complex entity show abstracted components. Left to right depicts three levels of abstraction, omitting specific information items.

Views serve two main purposes: First, they aim for complexity reduction by abstraction. Second, they can be interpreted as inverted specification: Abstracting a view hides the specification done for the respective element. Turning this around allows us to state: simple elements can be understood as not yet specified, emphasizing incompleteness of models.

Views of complex flows are not straightforward, as such flows may involve multiple entities and additional sub-flows. A complex flow can be represented as a simple flow by removing all sub-elements from the diagram's representation. Alternatively, each complex flow can be "deconstructed," as a complex flow can be interpreted as a named or classified section of the I2D.

2.4 Schemata

All elements can be predefined in form of a schema before starting the construction of an I2D. Such schemata can support the analysis by ensuring adherence to a specific vocabulary or by forcing the analysis to address particular requirements.

For instance, a schema may define protocol symbols and provide corresponding inference rules for those protocols. The class TCP could be predefined with inference rules such as $TCP \vdash fingerprinted\_operating\_system$, or the class $TLS \vdash authenticated$. Another example could involve the classification of information items and entities according to European GDPR properties (similar to [6]). I2Ds in this sense can be used as kind of a meta-language.

2.5 Patterns

One may define patterns, which describe structural parts of I2Ds reoccurring in modelling processes. They may refer to specific flow-entity-inference relations. For example, one may find the (comparably simple) pattern "state-free processing" in which an item i flows to an entity where a rule $i \vdash j$ is applied and j flows out. As another example, consider a complex flow pattern "intercepting", in which a mediating entity learns all information along the flow (cf. bisection) and shares it with another external entity. As a third example one can think of a pattern "authentication" in which an integrity-classified item is derived from a set including a secret.

A pattern can be understood as a partial predefined diagram where all elements, including inference rules, are represented by not-yet assigned variables (not necessarily the case of classes).

One additional aspect here is, that one can also search an existing I2D for patterns to look for certain properties in a system.

3 Application Examples

In this section, we provide application examples, illustrating how I2Ds can be used for analysing systems. The main purpose is to highlight the use of different properties and why they have been defined the way they are.

3.1 Example 1: Request/Response Scenario

Here, we refer back to the contrasting example from Fig. 1 and Fig. 2, showing a possible representation of the DFD-based system description as I2D. The original trust boundary is represented by a complex entity (e.g., a server running two services). Note that this is an interpretation of the underspecified situation in the original DFD. (We will address the topic of trust boundaries later in Sect. 4). The database shares the item *UserData* with the web server through a flow. As the item *UserData* is an element of the information set of the database, it is also an element of the information set of the web server.

Another flow represents the client request. In the original DFD, the "Request" expresses that some data flows across the trust boundary. Here, the item *Request* is an abstract item representing the information contained in the request that is initiated by the client. The *Request*-item is an element of the information set of the web server because of two facts: the flow, stating, that the information is shared if it is present at the origin and the fact that it is indeed present at the client (the client possesses the information of the *Request* by definition).

The same holds to the response flow: in the I2D, the server shares the *Response* item with the client only, if it is part of its information set. A rule allows the server to *infer* a response from both the *Request* item and the *UserData* item from the database. I2Ds prompt to make such connections between information items explicit. The flow applies and the *UserData* is available at the client.

The annotated threat in the DFD is represented through a normative rule in ℕ (in green). The rule states that *UserData* must not be an element of any entity classified as *untrusted*. This is the case so the rule is not violated. This rule is the equivalent of a *confidentiality requirement* on a concrete item. Any confidentiality requirement can be stated like that as it precisely encodes confidentiality: only authorised parties get access to some information. We will address the relation of protection goals and threats in I2Ds later in Sect. 4.

3.2 Example 2: Complex Analysis

The next example illustrates how our method can be used in different ways to analyse a system. The example is a generic version of the first one, representing a typical client-server relation (Fig. 4a, where the entity "Server" is providing content for a generic "Client" (see Fig. 4b)). One can think of the server as an abstracted view on the complex entity from the first example as we focus on the relation to the client. The server holds the information item c representing some content. Through the flow (for simplicity we omit names for flows in this example) the information item c is available for the client too.

Figure 4c presents a flow bisection in which the ISP is introduced as *mediating entity*. The complex parent flow is indicated by the dotted line. Mediating entities need to know the mediated information (therefore c is in the newly introduced information set of the ISP). Additionally, two class annotations are introduced: *sec* for the content c expressing that it is secret and u for the untrusted ISP-entity. Therefore, the normative requirement states that *sec*-classified items should not be available to u-classified entities.

Figure 4d represents a transformation introducing a simple encryption to prevent the rule violation. Multiple steps lead to the shown representation. First, an item kC_priv is added to the information set of the client, representing a private key. The first inference rule in ℝ applies to the client and adds a public key kC_pub to the information set of the client. A new flow is introduced, transferring a public key of the client (kC_pub).

Information Inference Diagrams   213

(a) Content provided from server to client:

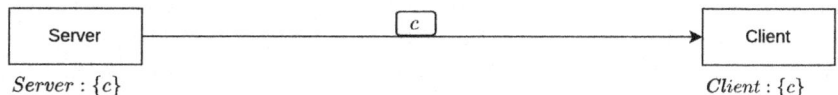

$Server : \{c\}$ \hspace{5cm} $Client : \{c\}$

(b) Bisected flow mediated by ISP:

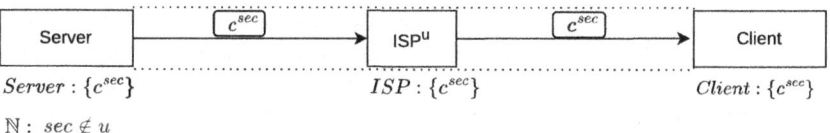

$Server : \{c^{sec}\}$ \hspace{3cm} $ISP : \{c^{sec}\}$ \hspace{2cm} $Client : \{c^{sec}\}$
$\mathbb{N} : sec \notin u$

(c) Simply encryption added to prevent content leak:

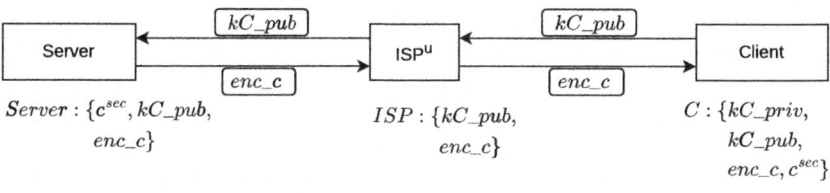

$Server : \{c^{sec}, kC\_pub,$ \hspace{2cm} $ISP : \{kC\_pub,$ \hspace{2cm} $C : \{kC\_priv,$
$enc\_c\}$ \hspace{4cm} $enc\_c\}$ \hspace{4cm} $kC\_pub,$
\hspace{10cm} $enc\_c, c^{sec}\}$

$\mathbb{R} : kC\_priv \vdash kC\_pub; \quad kC\_pub, c^{sec} \vdash enc\_c; \quad enc\_c, kC\_priv \vdash c^{sec} \quad \mathbb{N} : sec \notin u$

(d) Representation of a Man-in-the-Middle attack using class-based rules:

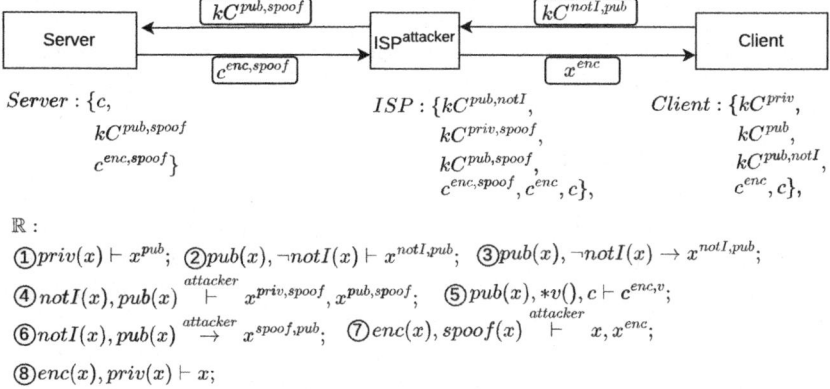

$Server : \{c,$ \hspace{3cm} $ISP : \{kC^{pub,notI},$ \hspace{2cm} $Client : \{kC^{priv},$
$kC^{pub,spoof},$ \hspace{3.5cm} $kC^{priv,spoof},$ \hspace{3cm} $kC^{pub},$
$c^{enc,spoof}\}$ \hspace{3.5cm} $kC^{pub,spoof},$ \hspace{3cm} $kC^{pub,notI},$
\hspace{6.5cm} $c^{enc,spoof}, c^{enc}, c\},$ \hspace{2cm} $c^{enc}, c\},$

$\mathbb{R} :$
① $priv(x) \vdash x^{pub};$ ② $pub(x), \neg notI(x) \vdash x^{notI,pub};$ ③ $pub(x), \neg notI(x) \rightarrow x^{notI,pub};$
④ $notI(x), pub(x) \overset{attacker}{\vdash} x^{priv,spoof}, x^{pub,spoof};$ ⑤ $pub(x), *v(), c \vdash c^{enc,v};$
⑥ $notI(x), pub(x) \overset{attacker}{\rightarrow} x^{spoof,pub};$ ⑦ $enc(x), spoof(x) \overset{attacker}{\vdash} x, x^{enc};$
⑧ $enc(x), priv(x) \vdash x;$

Fig. 4. Development of a Server-Client relation.

ISP learns kC_pub and another flow adds it to the information set of the server. The second rule applies, deriving the encrypted content, which is propagated to the client. The last rule allows the inference of the content. The normative requirement is not violated.

Figure 4 analyses how a man-in-the-middle attack can be represented. For didactic purposes, we switch here to class-based rules. *pub* and *priv* mean that the item is of class public and private key material, *enc* that something is encrypted and *notI* means that there is no integrity protection on the item. Other possibilities for representing integrity are possible, e.g. by introducing an integrity information atom which can be inferred from the private key. A *spoof*-class expresses that something has been altered by an *attacker*-classified entity. *kC*-items refer to client key material.

Rule ① generates the public key from the private one. ② generates a public key which is not integrity protected (the rule applies to kC^{pub}). ③ uses a rewrite arrow, ensuring that the not-integrity-protected key is sent. Rule ④ generates a spoofed public and private key – note that rule ① would not apply, as it does not explicitly state *notI* as target class. ⑤ exemplifies the wildcard syntax: an encrypted variant of any information atom with name c can be inferred, independent of its classes; the only additional requirement is that some other *pub*-classified item is present. The rule applies at the ISP as well as the server, in both cases generating $c^{enc,spoof}$ and only for the ISP c^{enc}. ⑥ is a rewrite rule, ensuring that an attacker entity (here the ISP) is indeed trying to replace unprotected public keys with a spoofed version. ⑦ enables the attacker to generate the client-decryptable version of the content. Lastly, ⑧ enables the client to regularly decrypt by using its private key.

The whole attack could be represented in many other different and simpler forms. We mainly want to show how class-based reasoning may operate.

4 Discussion

In this section, we discuss several design decisions as well as advantages and limitations of our approach.

Translating DFDs to I2Ds. DFDs contain several specific aspects which are not directly encoded in I2Ds. The different elements in a DFD can be interpreted as encoding different states of data: for instance a database implies data at rest while a process implies data in use. In our model, classes of entities and classes of items can be used to represent such aspects. Additionally, data in transit can also be modelled through the rewrite operator.

Trust boundaries are a specific aspect in DFDs of which several interpretation are possible. From the point of a security analysis the significance lies in a hint for the analyst to be especially careful with data flows crossing a trust boundary as they originate from a lower trust environment, e.g. making an I/O validation appropriate to prevent injection attacks. As seen in Fig. 2, a trust boundary can simply be modelled as a complex entity; again, if necessary, one may use specific classes for such special collections of entities. In I2Ds, one can also add according normative requirements to ensure a check for specific validation inferences on items from untrusted entities, e.g. a normative rule may be added that requires an I/O validation or escape item to be present.

Reasoning During the Security Analysis Process. As stated above, we want to provide a method which can be used, given a DFD, to enable structured reasoning. This can be especially viable, when mitigations are to be added to a system, which often implies actually adding additional information to a system—for example when adding cryptography, keys need to be managed. In particular from a privacy perspective, it may be appropriate to reason exactly what effects the additional information can have; e.g. if there are new privacy relevant inference relations possible.

Additionally, our modelling method can be used to express specific circumstances of a system, e.g. in Fig. 4 a MitM attack. This is why we state that our tool allows structured reasoning in the greater context of security analysis: the elements of I2Ds allows to show exact information flow and inference conditions, which lead to the realization of a threat, and hence to analyse the effects of counter measures. The main features we consider relevant in this context are explicit information binding to entities, including the information propagation and the inference relation to understand where which information actually originated from.

As models are inherently incomplete, their core benefit lies in abstracting unessential parts for a specific interest and accentuating important ones. The challenge therefore lies in finding the *relevant* aspects. And while a system model can theoretically be taken as a fixed structure, it is always created in a process – and can hence also be understood as structured reasoning about system model parts (a change implies the statement that the change is actually adding something relevant to the model). Given this perspective, we included specific ways to transform I2Ds to support the search for aspects especially relevant to privacy and security: the nesting of entities and flows and the bisection operation as special complex flow constructor. These actions are intended to hint for privacy and security specific questions like: How is it possible that an information item is available at another entity? What are the components of a data-processing entity and do they imply additional information and inference possibilities? Are there more relevant subcomponents implying new flows?

Relation to Threat Modelling. One important facet is the relation of threats and I2Ds. A requirement is not necessarily connected to a threat (depending on the notion)—but every threat implies a requirement. Our modelling approach intends to clearly differentiate between normative and descriptive aspects; this forces the user to make the requirements behind threats explicit. In I2Ds, every requirement has to be represented through *element relations* on items and entities (cf. the definition of normative declarations in Sect. 2). Most protection goals can be represented like this if one understands an information item as a *capability* of inference or the absence of possible inferences. For example, integrity can be understood as the possibility to infer the state of integrity of something (e.g. with a rule $privKey, message \vdash i\_m$).

Threat modelling approaches address the incompleteness problem by providing threat categories which could possibly apply. They are often very generic and still require a lot of additional knowledge. To solve the issue in practice, LIND-DUN, for example, provides threat trees for privacy threat categories [5,19]. Such threat trees can be understood as extending the catalogue of threats by specific sub-catalogues of possible realizations. This helps during the modelling process to look for specific kinds of problems, supporting (but not ensuring) completeness. Such catalogues can also be used in our modelling method, sometimes this might actually be recommendable. I2Ds are intended not to replace established approaches in threat modelling but to complement the process. In I2Ds the user is required to be more specific about the exact condition, how a threat may manifest itself in relation to a requirement.

For instance, in LINDDUN, the threat of detection can be realized through the sub-threat of observed communications. In our model it has to be clear which entity might observe the traffic (which may be introduced through a bisection). One can also add a possible information item "communication patterns", an appropriate inference rule and a requirement prohibiting this item at the mediating entity.

Scalability. The modelling effort of I2Ds is higher in comparison to alternative methods like DFDs. In the following section, we address two aspects in this regard. Firstly, the additional modelling load is partially optional. Secondly, the framework is designed to enable a streamlining of the modelling process, thus reducing the overall load.

Concerning the first aspect: One can simply omit certain parts of an I2D (obviously reducing the reasoning capabilities). For example, considering Fig. 2, the inference relations could be removed, yielding a I2D that is closer to the original DFD, but also lacks, e.g., the semantics capturing the relation between the flows. Information encoded by a DFD (like the state of data in a process or data store) can be removed or annotated through classes. Therefore, I2Ds actually allow some trade-off between adding context knowledge for the reasoning process and according omission. In particular, the abstract nature of information items and entities allows to generalize largely in parts of the model or to model specific parts in more detail. In practice, it may be helpful to introduce stubs for parts of a system to collect general unattributed information.

The second aspect assumes an ecosystem of semi-automated modelling tools with a comprehensive database of schemata and patterns, providing pre-defined components and inference relations, similar to existing threat modelling tools. For example, regarding attacks, one can have predefined attack patterns for certain types of entities or flows (analogous to the MitM-example provided here).

Limitations. We want to shortly address some limitations of our modelling approach. All requirements have to be expressed in a specific way, which can be challenging in some situations. For example, the problem of unawareness is not straight forward. One solution may be to include it as a lack of integrity in the mental model of the user. Availability is another problematic aspect, as it requires some kind of time-dependency on information items, making it necessary to define all information items with logical time indices (one variable for each logical time step).

This shows that I2Ds are not a silver bullet but help analysing specific problems. Every solution needs to strike a balance between generalization (at which DFDs are very good) and specificity, making them applicable for more general or specific situations (the latter is the case of I2Ds).

One notable design decision is that there is no deletion of information items, making it hard to analyse a system in the sense of a data life cycle (as is required e.g. in [17]. The rationale here is twofold. First, we want to avoid a system process model or state machine to simplify modelling. Second, our approach intends to address hard security and privacy properties in which the loss of control over information is irreversible. As stated, our approach is not intended to be a universal tool for privacy analysis but a complementing one. Still, it is possible to express data deletion, if necessary, through classifying inference rules, which is, however not intuitive.

5 Related Work

Several works propose automation-focused approaches to threat modelling [9,21], including knowledge base requirements [26]. These works focus on the general threat elicitation.

In particular DFDs have been the subject of several works, addressing drawbacks like formal foundations [10], lacking specific representation [22], and automation [4]. Other works propose DFD extensions for special use cases like privacy policy representation [2,11,23]. Specific DFD-enrichment for security in applications through taint-tracking like techniques and accompanying code-model compliance also has been proposed [24,25], mainly operating at code level and therefore implying problems to generalize it to distributed systems. Refinement and transformation similar to our ideas have been presented in [1].

From our view, the research evolution of DFDs suggests three shifts: 1. a more information-centric focus, 2. formal foundation enabling automation and logic checking, and 3. enrichment with additional information to enable the representation of specific contexts. Our proposal supports these developments. It underlines the relations and dependencies of information and possible inferences, which is helpful for specific analysis tasks.

Other works focus on reasoning about security using security model languages, e.g., [7,12]). These approaches lack flexibility, as they require strict adherence to predefined vocabularies. In contrast, our approach allows freely specifiable schemata and can in this sense be understood as a kind of meta-language. Our work tries to bridge the gap between threat modelling and more formal analyses.

A similar idea to ours has been proposed by [3], which models data propagation in a system incorporating entity-bound information and probabilities. It also differentiates between descriptive and normative declarations. A key difference is that their approach uses entity-specific inference, requiring propagation, whereas our inference rules are, at least without further classes, global by default. This is an intentional design decision to underline a security insight: no security by obscurity – which means that any entity can infer if it has the respective information. Additionally, their work uses states to allow an order of events, which we do not do for conformance and simplicity purposes.

6 Conclusion

In this work, we introduced the theoretical foundations of Information Inference Diagrams (I2Ds). This framework enables modelling systems from an information-level perspective, focusing on security and privacy analysis. Unlike many established approaches centering on data, I2Ds provide a complementary tool for practical threat analysis. By abstracting to the information level, our approach enables to formally express security requirements as part of the model through *inference*. We provided formal definitions and demonstrated the application of I2Ds through illustrative examples.

For future work, we plan to implement an automatic reasoning engine, develop subject-specific schemata, explore the potential of patterns (especially for scalability) and integrate I2Ds into existing threat modelling tools, like OWASP Threat Dragon.

Acknowledgments. Parts of this work have been supported by the following projects and funding bodies: German Research Foundation (DFG) as part of Germany's Excellence Strategy (EXC 2050/1, Project 390696704, CeTI); TU Dresden's Disruptions and Societal Change research framework (TUDiSC); Federal Ministry of Research, Technology and Space (BMFTR), Project 16KISA038 (GANGES).

References

1. Alshareef, H., Stucki, S., Schneider, G.: Refining Privacy-Aware Data Flow Diagrams. In: Calinescu, R., Păsăreanu, C.S. (eds.) SEFM 2021. LNCS, vol. 13085, pp. 121–140. Springer, Cham (2021). https://doi.org/10.1007/978-3-030-92124-8_8
2. Alshareef, H., Tuma, K., Stucki, S., Schneider, G., Scandariato, R.: Precise analysis of purpose limitation in data flow diagrams. In: Proceedings of the 17th International Conference on Availability, Reliability and Security, pp. 1–11. ACM, Vienna Austria, August 2022. https://doi.org/10.1145/3538969.3539010, https://dl.acm.org/doi/10.1145/3538969.3539010
3. Bavendiek, K., Adams, R., Schupp, S.: Privacy-preserving architectures with probabilistic guarantees. In: 2018 16th Annual Conference on Privacy, Security and Trust (PST), pp. 1–10, August 2018
4. Berger, B.J., Sohr, K., Koschke, R.: Automatically extracting threats from extended data flow diagrams. In: Caballero, J., Bodden, E., Athanasopoulos, E. (eds.) ESSoS 2016. LNCS, vol. 9639, pp. 56–71. Springer, Cham (2016). https://doi.org/10.1007/978-3-319-30806-7_4
5. Deng, M., Wuyts, K., Scandariato, R., Preneel, B., Joosen, W.: A privacy threat analysis framework: supporting the elicitation and fulfilment of privacy requirements. Requirements Eng. **16**(1), 3–32 (2011)

6. Grünewald, E., Pallas, F.: TILT: a GDPR-aligned transparency information language and toolkit for practical privacy engineering. In: Proceedings of the 2021 ACM Conference on Fairness, Accountability, and Transparency, pp. 636–646. ACM, Virtual Event Canada, March 2021
7. Holm, H., Shahzad, K., Buschle, M., Ekstedt, M.: P^2 CySeMoL: predictive, probabilistic cyber security modeling language. IEEE Trans. Dependable Secur. Comput. **12**(6), 626–639 (2015), conference Name: IEEE Transactions on Dependable and Secure Computing
8. IriusRisk: IriusRisk Automated Threat Modeling Tool For Secure Software. https://www.iriusrisk.com/
9. van Landuyt, D., Pasquale, L., Sion, L., Joosen, W.: Threat modeling at run time: the case for reflective and adaptive threat management (NIER track). In: 2021 International Symposium on Software Engineering for Adaptive and Self-Managing Systems (SEAMS), pp. 203–209, May 2021, issn: 2157-2321
10. Larsen, P.G., Plat, N., Toetenel, H.: A formal semantics of data flow diagrams. Formal Aspects Comput. **6**(6), 586–606 (1994)
11. Leicht, J., Wagner, M., Heisel, M.: Creating privacy policies from data-flow diagrams. In: Computer Security. ESORICS 2023 International Workshops: CyberICS, DPM, CBT, and SECPRE, The Hague, The Netherlands, September 25–29, 2023, Revised Selected Papers, Part I, pp. 433–453. Springer, Heidelberg, March 2024
12. Lodderstedt, T., Basin, D., Doser, J.: SecureUML: a UML-based modeling language for model-driven security. In: Jézéquel, J.-M., Hussmann, H., Cook, S. (eds.) UML 2002. LNCS, vol. 2460, pp. 426–441. Springer, Heidelberg (2002). https://doi.org/10.1007/3-540-45800-X_33
13. Mantel, H.: Information Flow and Noninterference. In: van Tilborg, H.C.A., Jajodia, S. (eds.) Encyclopedia of Cryptography and Security, pp. 605–607. Springer, US, Boston, MA (2011)
14. Mircosoft: The STRIDE Threat Model, November 2009. https://learn.microsoft.com/en-us/previous-versions/commerce-server/ee823878(v=cs.20)
15. Oliver, D.I.: Privacy Engineering: A Dataflow and Ontological Approach, 1st edn. CreateSpace Independent Publishing Platform, North Charleston (2014)
16. OWASP: OWASP Threat Dragon | OWASP Foundation. https://owasp.org/www-project-threat-dragon/
17. Rost, M.: Das Standard-Datenschutzmodell (SDM). 2. Auflage. Springer (2024)
18. Shostack, A.: Threat Modeling: Designing for Security. John Wiley & Sons (Feb 2014), google-Books-ID: YiHcAgAAQBAJ
19. Sion, L., Van Landuyt, D., Wuyts, K., Joosen, W.: Robust and reusable LINDDUN privacy threat knowledge. Comput. Secur. **154**, 104419 (2025). https://doi.org/10.1016/j.cose.2025.104419, https://www.sciencedirect.com/science/article/pii/S0167404825001087
20. Sion, L., Van Landuyt, D., Yskout, K., Joosen, W.: SPARTA: security & privacy architecture through risk-driven threat assessment. In: 2018 IEEE International Conference on Software Architecture Companion (ICSA-C), pp. 89–92, April 2018.https://doi.org/10.1109/ICSA-C.2018.00032, https://ieeexplore.ieee.org/abstract/document/8432187
21. Sion, L., Van Landuyt, D., Yskout, K., Verreydt, S., Joosen, W.: Automated threat analysis and management in a continuous integration pipeline. In: 2021 IEEE Secure Development Conference (SecDev), pp. 30–37, October 2021
22. Sion, L., Wuyts, K., Yskout, K., Van Landuyt, D., Joosen, W.: Interaction-based privacy threat elicitation. In: 2018 IEEE European Symposium on Security and Privacy Workshops (EuroS&PW), pp. 79–86. IEEE, London (Apr 2018)

23. Sion, L., Yskout, K., Van Landuyt, D., Joosen, W.: Solution-aware data flow diagrams for security threat modeling. In: Proceedings of the 33rd Annual ACM Symposium on Applied Computing, SAC '18, pp. 1425–1432. Association for Computing Machinery, New York, April 2018
24. Tuma, K., Peldszus, S., Strüber, D., Scandariato, R., Jürjens, J.: Checking security compliance between models and code. Softw. Syst. Modeling **22**(1), 273–296 (2023). https://doi.org/10.1007/s10270-022-00991-5, http://arxiv.org/abs/2108.08579, arXiv:2108.08579 [cs]
25. Tuma, K., Scandariato, R., Balliu, M.: Flaws in flows: unveiling design flaws via information flow analysis. In: 2019 IEEE International Conference on Software Architecture (ICSA), pp. 191–200 (2019). https://doi.org/10.1109/ICSA.2019.00028, https://ieeexplore.ieee.org/document/8703905
26. Wuyts, K., Sion, L., Van Landuyt, D., Joosen, W.: Knowledge is power: systematic reuse of privacy knowledge for threat elicitation. In: 2019 IEEE Security and Privacy Workshops (SPW), pp. 80–83, May 2019

Open Access This chapter is licensed under the terms of the Creative Commons Attribution-NonCommercial-NoDerivatives 4.0 International License (http://creativecommons.org/licenses/by-nc-nd/4.0/), which permits any noncommercial use, sharing, distribution and reproduction in any medium or format, as long as you give appropriate credit to the original author(s) and the source, provide a link to the Creative Commons license and indicate if you modified the licensed material. You do not have permission under this license to share adapted material derived from this chapter or parts of it.

The images or other third party material in this chapter are included in the chapter's Creative Commons license, unless indicated otherwise in a credit line to the material. If material is not included in the chapter's Creative Commons license and your intended use is not permitted by statutory regulation or exceeds the permitted use, you will need to obtain permission directly from the copyright holder.

Author Index

B
Beltrán, Marta 77
Biczók, Gergely 102
Biega, Asia 153

F
Ferwerda, Bruce 29

G
Gerken, Jorina Freya 29
Gruschka, Nils 178

H
Hansen, Malte 178

J
Jensen, Meiko 178

K
Karegar, Farzaneh 3
Kitkowska, Agnieszka 29
Klös, Verena 202
Köpsell, Stefan 202
Kyi, Lin 153

L
Lestyán, Szilvia 102
Letrone, William 102

M
Morel, Victor 3

P
Pandit, Harshvardhan J. 127

R
Rehms, Sebastian 202
Reinhardt, Delphine 49
Robustelli, Ludovica 102
Roesner, Franziska 153
Runge, Greta 178

S
Santos, Cristiana 3, 153
Schillinger, Sebastian Jakob 49
Shams, Shirin 49
Shivakumar, Sushil Ammanaghatta 153

T
Tschorsch, Florian 202

W
Wang, Zhaoying 29